Rywka's Diary

Rywka's Diary

The Writings of a Jewish Girl from the Lodz Ghetto, Found at Auschwitz in 1945 and Published Seventy Years Later

Rywka Lipszyc

Edited by Anita Friedman and Originally Published by Jewish Family and Children's Services of San Francisco

Translated from the Polish by Malgorzata Markoff with Annotations by Ewa Wiatr

HARPER

An Imprint of HarperCollinsPublishers

HarperCollins books may be purchased for educational, business, or sales promotional use. For information, please e-mail the Special Markets Department at spsales@harper collins.com.

Originally published as *The Diary of Rywka Lipszyc* in 2014 by the Jewish Family and Children's Services Holocaust Center in partnership with Lehrhaus Judaica.

FIRST EDITION

Designed by Renato Stanisic

Library of Congress Cataloging-in-Publication Data has been applied for.

ISBN: 978-0-06-238968-8

15 16 17 18 19   OV/RRD   10 9 8 7 6 5 4 3 2 1

Rywka Lipszyc was one of hundreds of thousands of Jewish teenagers living in Nazi-occupied Europe who never had the chance to experience the typical pleasures and pains of adolescence. Like her, every one of them had hopes and dreams, fears and sorrows, joys and loves.

Too few survived, and of those who were killed, only a handful left behind a record of their lives. We dedicate this book to those young men and women whose words are forever lost and to their families.

Anita Friedman,
Editor

Contents

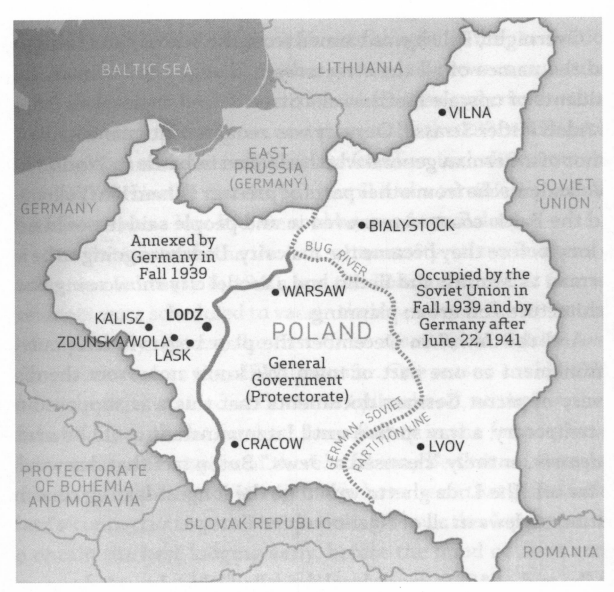

Poland after the Nazi conquest, September 1939

Preface

THE DIARY'S JOURNEY FROM AUSCHWITZ TO AMERICA

JUDY JANEC

In the spring of 1945, a doctor with the liberating Red Army plucked a diary from the ruins of the crematoria at Auschwitz-Birkenau. The physician, Zinaida Berezovskaya, a fierce Soviet patriot and committed Communist, had left her home to fight the great battle against the invading Nazi army and had accompanied the Soviet troops to Auschwitz.

Zinaida took the diary with her when she returned to her home in Omsk, in southwestern Siberia, where she and the diary remained until her death in 1983. Her effects were sent to her son, Ghen Shangin-Berezovsky, who lived in Moscow. Upon his death in 1992, Ghen's belongings went to his wife, Lilavati Ramayya. It was at her mother's house in Moscow that Ghen's daughter, Anastasia Shangina-Berezovskaya (granddaughter of Zinaida), first encountered the diary on a visit in 1995. Immediately sensing its value, she brought it back to San Francisco, where she had emigrated in 1991.

Over the ensuing years, Anastasia made several attempts to find an appropriate institution to collaborate with—one that could identify the diary's value and perhaps translate and publish it. In June 2008, she contacted Leslie Kane, executive director of what was then the Holocaust Center of Northern California. Leslie passed on her e-mail to me as the center's archivist and librarian, and within days, Anastasia brought the diary to our library.

It was a breathtaking artifact—an unknown diary written in the Lodz ghetto—and a rare opportunity to add to the historical record. Handwritten in Polish, in a school notebook, the diary was in relatively good condition. The first two pages were detached from the rest; part of the writing was obscured; and there were some water stains and rust. But considering its age and its provenance—the ruins of the crematoria at Auschwitz—it was remarkably well preserved.

One hundred twelve pages long, the diary was accompanied by a note (see page 217) and two newspapers from the time. The diary's first entry was dated October 3, 1943, Litzmannstadt [Lodz] ghetto. It concluded in the ghetto on April 12, 1944. Clearly, this was a remarkable document. How remarkable neither Anastasia nor others could determine without assistance. We decided to digitally reproduce a few pages so that we could share them with experts in the field. Carefully, we scanned several pages, and in this way began the process of bringing this diary, which had slumbered in darkness for over sixty years, to light.

On the recommendation of Zachary Baker, the curator of Judaica at Stanford University and a member of the board of directors of the Holocaust Center, with whom we first shared the scans, we approached Professor Robert Moses Shapiro of Brooklyn College, an eminent scholar and expert on the Lodz ghetto and its diaries, as well as a fluent reader and speaker of Polish, Hebrew, and Yiddish. Dr. Shapiro quickly recognized the special value of the diary. After viewing the sampling of pages that we had scanned, he felt sure of its authenticity. Over the course of the next months, several steps were made to ensure that this extraordinary diary would be shared with the world.

The first step was to make a high-resolution digital reproduction of the diary. In this way its intellectual content would be preserved forever. Even if something were to happen to the actual artifact, the words of the diarist would be saved. The scans of the diary were viewed by Marek Web, former archivist at YIVO Institute for Jewish Research in New York City, who also confirmed its authenticity.

The next step was to have it transcribed. At the recommendation of Dr. Shapiro, we turned to Ewa Wiatr of the Center for Jewish Research at the University of Lodz. She agreed to transcribe and provide annotations to the diary. It was Ewa who discovered the identity of the writer and confirmed it through a check of the Lodz ghetto records. The diarist helped with this identification by naming herself in the diary. Thus we began our acquaintanceship with Rywka Lipszyc.

In December 2010, the Holocaust Center of Northern California was dissolved, and it donated its collection of books and artifacts to Jewish Family and Children's Services (JFCS) of San Francisco, the Peninsula, Marin, and Sonoma Counties, headed by Dr. Anita Friedman. JFCS developed a new Holocaust education program and worked in partnership with Lehrhaus Judaica, a nondenominational Bay Area center for adult Jewish education, founded by Fred Rosenbaum, to publish the diary. In a fortunate coincidence, Rosenbaum had just coauthored a book about a young woman's experiences in the Lodz ghetto and Auschwitz—*Out on a Ledge* (River Forest, IL: Wicker Park Press Ltd., 2010)—with its subject, Eva Libitzky.

We now had to translate the diary into English, including the annotations that Ewa Wiatr had prepared. Working with two translators, Malgorzata Szajbel-Kleck and Malgorzata Markoff, we soon had an English translation available. Alexandra Zapruder, the editor of *Salvaged Pages: Young Writers' Diaries of the Holocaust* and the winner of the 2002 National Jewish Book Award for Holocaust literature, agreed to join our project as editor of the diary and to offer an introduction to and perspective on an adolescent's emerging identity in the face of extraordinary circumstances. Historian Fred Rosenbaum provided an essay on the Lodz ghetto, and Hadassa Halamish, the daughter of one of Rywka's cousins, contributed her mother Mina's and aunt Esther's recollections of their time with Rywka in the ghetto and in the camps. Esther also provided a postscript.

So, with the assistance of archivists, historians, Holocaust survivors, translators, and editors—as well as the support of philanthropists, agency directors, and so many others around the world committed to Holocaust education—our goal has been achieved. Rywka Lipszyc will not remain a nameless victim of the Holocaust. Her words will survive her.

Part I

BACKGROUND

Papers left in the street after deportation. *(Courtesy of Yad Vashem Photo Archive, Archival Signature 4062/76)*

A Polish Girl Comes of Age in a Jewish Ghetto

ALEXANDRA ZAPRUDER

Rywka Lipszyc began the sole surviving volume of her Lodz ghetto diary shortly after her fourteenth birthday. She filled more than 100 handwritten pages over six months from October 1943 to April 1944, and then suddenly stopped. A year later, a Soviet doctor, accompanying the Red Army's liberating forces, found it near the ruins of the crematoria in Auschwitz-Birkenau. If the diary's journey suggests the path Rywka took toward almost certain death, its pages tell a far deeper story, for in it Rywka struggled to understand and express herself, capturing both the physical hardships of life in the ghetto and the emotional turmoil of coming of age during the Holocaust.

Born on September 15, 1929, Rywka was the eldest of Yankel and Miriam Sarah Lipszyc's four children. A son, Abram, called Abramek, was born in 1932, followed quickly by a daughter, Cypora, known as Cipka, in 1933. The baby of the family, Estera, nicknamed Tamarcia, came along in 1937. Rywka's parents were both natives of Lodz, Poland. Yankel—the fifth son of eight children born to Avraham Dov and Esther Lipszyc—lived with his family in close proximity to his siblings and extended relatives in Lodz. Through his older brother Yochanan's wife, Hadassah, the family was distantly connected to Moshe Menachem Segal, the famous "last rabbi" of the Lodz ghetto. He was terrorized and tortured after the Germans invaded Lodz and was murdered in 1942 near Kielce.[*]

As Orthodox Jews, the family was devoutly observant. In the diary, Rywka reveals her strong attachment to the rituals of the Jewish Sabbath and holiday calendar and her unwavering faith in God. "I love God so much!" she wrote on February 2, 1944:

> **I can always and everywhere rely on God, but I have to help a little since nothing is going to happen by itself! But I do know that God will take care of me! Oh, it's good that I'm a Jewish girl, that I was taught to love God . . . I'm grateful for all this! Thank you, God.**

By the time Rywka began her diary, she had lived in the Lodz ghetto for more than three years, and she had already lost both of her parents. The Germans had ruthlessly beaten her father on the street one day, causing severe and lasting injuries, from which he never fully recovered. He died on June 2, 1941, as a result of lung disease and his other ailments. This is a memory that Rywka vividly recalled toward the end of the diary.

Her mother cared for her four children in the ghetto alone for a year before she died on July 8, 1942. The exact details of her death are not known, but she likely succumbed, like tens of thousands in the ghetto, to illnesses related to malnutrition and exhaustion. Rywka's father was buried in the Jewish cemetery in Marysin at the northeastern periphery of the ghetto; the final resting place of her mother's body remains unknown. Even so, Rywka was from time to time possessed with an urgent desire to visit their graves.

---

[*] http://kehilalinks.jewishgen.org/lodz/rabbi.htm, accessed March 12, 2012.

"For a few days something has been drawing me to the cemetery," she wrote on February 4, ". . . apparently some unconscious force. I'd like so much to go there! To Mommy, to Daddy. I'm so drawn to it!"

Entrance to the Lodz ghetto. *(Courtesy of Yad Vashem Photo Archive, Archival Signature 4062/200)*

The surviving family adopted the orphaned Lipszyc children. An uncle took in Abramek and Tamarcia while Yochanan and Hadassah Lipszyc opened their home to Rywka and Cipka. A scant two months later, Rywka and her siblings endured one of the most traumatic events in the ghetto's history, the infamous *szpera* (Polish for "curfew") of September 1942. The German authorities demanded that the ghetto surrender for deportation 15,000 Jews under the age of ten and over sixty-five, in addition to the sick and infirm.

Mordechai Chaim Rumkowski, the so-called Eldest of the Jews, conveyed this appalling order to the ghetto population. In his speech, he exhorted parents to do the unthinkable in order to avoid a still worse fate for the entire ghetto population. He implored an assembled crowd of thousands of wailing and weeping parents:

> **A grievous blow has struck the ghetto. I never imagined I would be forced to deliver this sacrifice to the altar with my own hands. In my old age I must stretch out my hands and beg: Brothers and sisters, hand them over to me! Fathers and mothers, give me your children!** [*]

During the *szpera*, Yochanan and a desperately ill Hadassah tried to save not only themselves and their three daughters (Estusia, Chanusia, and Minia) but also Rywka, Cipka, and another cousin named Esther, who was only three. Somehow, the German authorities only seized Yochanan, leaving Hadassah with six girls at home. By the time the weeklong roundup ended, however, Abramek and Tamarcia had also been wrenched away from their adopted uncle. Only Rywka and Cipka survived from a family that less than a year before had numbered six. The *szpera* remained an open wound

---

[*] Chaim Rumkowski, "Give Me Your Children!" in *Lodz Ghetto: Inside a Community Under Siege*, ed. Alan Adelson and Robert Lapides (New York: Viking, 1989), 328–31.

Opposite:
Rywka Lipszyc's
Lodz ghetto
registration card.
*(Courtesy of Archiwum
Państwowe w Łodzi)*

Left: Poster
announcing the
infamous *szpera*
(curfew) on
September 5, 1942.
*(Courtesy of Yad Vashem
Photo Archive, Archival
Signature 4062/189)*

for Rywka and indeed for the entire ghetto population from that point forward. In January 1944, at a friend's apartment, the conversation turned to this painful memory:

> **We talked about the *szpera*. Ewa talked to her heart's content and it seems that she got it off her chest. I kept silent, what was I supposed to say? . . . That conversation, the whole thing upset me . . . I don't feel well . . . Oh, I have no strength . . . my heart has become a heavy stone . . . I'm choking, choking . . .**
>
> **(JANUARY 15, 1944)**

While the exact fate of the unfortunates was not known at the time, the ghetto population feared the worst. Rywka repeatedly expressed her dread—her gnawing suspicion, in fact—that she would never see her siblings again. It was not until after the war that the truth became known. The German authorities trucked the deportees to the killing center at Chelmno— the destination for 70,000 Lodz Jews prior to the final liquidation in August 1944. Here they were stripped of their clothing and valuables, loaded into rudimentary "gas-vans," and asphyxiated by carbon monoxide poisoning. The SS murdered over 152,000 Jews from Lodz and neighboring areas in Chelmno between 1941 and 1944.[*]

Hadassah, still gravely ill and now widowed, continued to care for all six girls until she, too, died of illness on July 11, 1943. At that point, Estusia, the eldest at age twenty, took on the extraordinary responsibility of caring for her two siblings and the Lipszyc daughters—all of whom were minors. (Another aunt adopted the youngest cousin, Esther.) They shared an apartment at 38 Wolborska Street, under circumstances of tremendous hardship and tension.

---

[*] Estimates for those killed at Chelmno vary widely. We have cited the minimum number, used by the United States Holocaust Memorial Museum, while others have assessed it as anywhere from 172,230 to as many as 350,000.

The Juvenile Protection Committee, which had been established to care for orphans in the ghetto, provided a small
measure of aid for Rywka and Cipka. This entity offered such
services as tickets to see a dentist, coupons for warm clothing, and
other basic necessities. In addition, the girls received an extra food ration,
a so-called *bajrat*, or B ration, which supplemented their otherwise meager
portion. In spite of these forms of aid, it is clear from the diary that Rywka
and her cousins lived—like most of the ghetto inhabitants—under the ever-
tightening vise of extreme hunger and deprivation that characterized life in
this harshest and longest-lasting of German ghettos.

Rywka was one of several young diarists whose notebooks have come
down to us from the Lodz ghetto. Dawid Sierakowiak, a brilliant young

**Children about to be deported,
parting with their relatives.**
*(Courtesy of Yad Vashem Photo Archive,
Archival Signature 4062/410)*

9

Pupils dancing during a break at the Franciszkańska secondary school in Lodz. *(Courtesy of Yad Vashem Photo Archive, Archival Signature 4062/53)*

student, wrote the longest and best-known of the Lodz ghetto diaries. His five volumes—with gaps due to lost note-books—span the period from June 1939 to April 1943. In them, Dawid recounted his agonizing decline from an intellectually curious, shrewdly observant, and often wickedly funny young man to a mere shadow of himself—bereft of his parents, unable to work or study, barely enduring his daily agony of starvation and hopelessness. His diary ended a few months before he himself succumbed to tuberculosis in August 1943. An anonymous girl wrote a fragmentary diary over the months of February and March 1942. In her diary, she describes the ruthless grip of starvation on herself and her family, capturing its brutally reductive nature and the personal, social, spiritual, mental, and moral costs attendant to it.

Finally, an anonymous young man, writing in four languages (Polish, Yiddish, Hebrew, and English) in the margins and end pages of a French novel entitled *Les Vrais Riches*, recorded the final moments of the ghetto's existence in the summer of 1944, when the few remaining survivors—Rywka among them—waited helplessly and urgently for the arrival of the Red Army and deliverance. His diary is filled with the desperation of that moment and the despair that arose with news of the final liquidation of the ghetto in August 1944.

Rywka wrote from October 1943 to April 1944, filling a gap in time not covered by any of these diarists and thereby providing a young writer's perspective on the major events of the ghetto that transpired in that period. It is not only the timeframe but also Rywka's perspective as an Orthodox Jewish girl that set her writing apart from the other young writers' diaries from Lodz. While each diarist grappled in some way with existential questions, most writers asked and answered their questions within a secular framework. By contrast, Rywka viewed the world through a religious lens: she believed fervently in God's benevolence and she strived to live according to Jewish law and ethical teaching. At the same time, Rywka was a modern young person, intellectually ambitious, curious about the world and her place in it, and blessed (or cursed) with a strong personality that did not allow her to quietly absorb indignity. Rather, she would stand her ground, protest, and fight for herself when needed.

Rywka's diary is characterized by an ebb and flow between her internal and external worlds. She described the practical matters of her life: the mechanics of survival in the ghetto, unremitting work and the momentary reprieves provided by school and other activities, and the outside events that affected the ghetto at large and her in particular. Within this structure, however, Rywka dwelled primarily in her interior world—focusing on her efforts to write; her emerging identity; her friendships, especially her deep attachment to her mentor Surcia; her philosophy of life (that is, her attempts to make meaning of the world through the lens of her experience); her grief for her family; her effort, under constant assault from exhaustion, despair, hunger, and fear, to hold on to her strength; and her faith. Rywka's entries are an intermingled, sometimes even jumbled, combination of reports, reflections, feelings, news, sensations, and ideas. When untangled, her diary not only provides a fresh perspective on daily life and survival in the Lodz ghetto, but—perhaps more importantly—reflects the impossible struggle to come of age within this crucible of imprisonment, deprivation, and oppression. Above all, Rywka sought comfort and salvation in writing her diary. Its survival testifies to the anguish of her doomed struggle.

"It is after the first holiday," Rywka writes in her first entry on October 3, 1943, beginning, fittingly, with Rosh Hashanah, the Jewish New Year. At that time, Rywka moved from a job in the Central Accounting Office to a position in the Clothing and Linen Workshop, managed by Leon Glazer. Headquartered at 14 Dworska Street, the workshop had begun production of undergarments and dresses in early 1941 with 157 workers at seventy-seven machines. One year later, the pool of workers had grown nearly ten times in size, and the factory began producing men's clothing and linens as well, much of which went toward the German war effort. Several hundred children worked there, protected in some measure from deportation by learning a useful trade. Since Rywka was friendly with a person she calls only "Zemlówna" (Ms. Zemel)—who was related to Mr. Zemel, one of the managers—she secured for herself a spot in this rather extraordinary ghetto institution, reporting to the workshop located at 13/15 Franciszkańska Street.

From the beginning of the diary, then, the structural foundation of Rywka's daily life was work and the schooling that came with it. Much of this education was practical—learning how to use a sewing machine, to measure for a skirt, to make an "honest stitch"—under the tutelage of her

teacher, Mrs. Kaufman. In addition, the children had some traditional lessons in subjects such as Hebrew, Yiddish, and mathematics. Rywka appreciated the value of the skills she acquired in the workshop. Dreaming of life after the war, she wrote:

Sign on the Kleider und Wäsche-Abteilung workshop where Rywka worked. *(Courtesy of Archiwum Państwowe w Łodzi, Archival Signature 1108: 28-853-7)*

I can see: an evening, a modest room with lights, all my family sitting at the table. It's so nice . . . so warm, cozy . . . Oh, it's so good! Later, when they all go to bed, I sit at the sewing machine and I'm sewing . . . sewing . . . it's so sweet, so good . . . so delightful! Because everything I make with my own hands is our livelihood. It pays for bread, education, clothes . . . almost everything. The work I do with my own hands . . . I'm very grateful to Mrs. Kaufman for this . . .

(FEBRUARY 28, 1944)

Jewish girls in a sewing workshop in the Lodz ghetto. *(Courtesy of Archiwum Państwowe w Łodzi, Archival Signature 1108: 8-210-2)*

At the same time, work could be drudgery, and Rywka mainly depended on it to get a portion of soup at lunchtime. She describes long days of boredom and moments of frustration and conflict with the girls in her class. Rywka most hated the occasional compulsory attendance at the workshop on Saturday, the Jewish day of rest. For religious Jews, the Sabbath—which marks the cessation of God's labors in creating the world—is a sacred day to study, to pray, and to be with family and friends. It is meant to foreshadow the harmony and peace that will fill the world when the Messiah comes and the Jewish people are redeemed once and for all from suffering. For Rywka, working on the Sabbath was not only a violation of this deepest-held element of Jewish ritual observance; it robbed her of one of her few sources of pleasure in an otherwise bleak existence. On February 20, 1944, she wrote,

Oh, God! I'll never forget this feeling, I felt so bad, I was suffocating, I felt like crying! Crying . . . crying . . . I watched people going to the workshops as usual. This day, this holy, sacred day, is for them an ordinary and normal weekday.

[. . .] For me, going to the workshop on Saturday was a terrible agony. I thought involuntarily: If I have to do it again (I wish I wouldn't), will it become commonplace for me, will I get used to it? Oh, God, do something so I wouldn't have to go to the workshop on Saturday! I felt so bad! I wanted to cry!

Rywka filled her diary with details about her daily life, reporting on the chores that dominated her days—doing the laundry, peeling the potatoes, running errands, cooking, picking up briquettes of coal, and making the bed. She also described the

Jewish girls studying together in the Lodz ghetto. *(Courtesy of Archiwum Państwowe w Łodzi, Archival Signature 1109: 71-2369-3)*

myriad small and large problems that befell her, such as a headache or a bad tooth, the disintegration of her shoes, ongoing hunger, and bouts of miserable weather. In January, she reported on a flu epidemic that swept through the ghetto, reducing the workforce by nearly half and depleting the already insufficient medical supplies on hand:

> Flu pervades the ghetto, wherever you go, flu is everywhere . . . in the workshops and offices there is nobody . . . a lot of sick leaves. (Mr. Zemel joked that he would place the sick leaves at the machines so they could continue production.) . . . Chajusia* has the flu, Surcia's mother, too . . . I'll run out of pages to write down who is sick . . . Maryla Łucka and her father are sick, too. In Mrs. Lebenstein's family everybody is sick except her; Samuelson is sick; Jankielewicz has replaced Berg because Berg is sick. Rundberg, half-sick, came in the afternoon . . .
>
> (JANUARY 14, 1944)

Against the backdrop of work, drudgery, and the struggle to survive that dominated the lives of the entire ghetto population, Rywka confided in her diary the problems that were specific to her own circumstances. In particular, she struggled to get along with her older cousins. She recorded the small and large fights that erupted over chores, sharing food, and the effects of living in tight quarters. In one typical example on March 4, 1944, she wrote:

> Chanusia is rushing me to bed, she says I can finish tomorrow. Oh, does she even know what writing is? She apparently has no idea. Time? Estusia received a coupon and

---

* Not to be confused with Rywka's cousin Chanusia.

**told me to pick it up tomorrow and to take the bed linen to
the laundry and this and that and this generous Chanusia
tells me to go to bed and finish tomorrow.**

While Chanusia may well have had good reasons for rushing her to
finish—staying up to write after dark meant burning a candle or using
limited electricity, since they would have had only one 15-watt bulb—Rywka
felt misunderstood.

It is utterly impossible to tell from the diary what the real circumstances
were, and, in any case, this is not the diary's role. Instead, we enter and
inhabit Rywka's perspective: her loneliness, her feeling of being put upon,
criticized, and judged. She was, after all, an adolescent grappling with the
problems of identity and selfhood that come with this developmental phase
in life. However, without the stability of a normal life and, above all, without
the unconditional love of parents to teach and guide her, she was utterly at
sea, lost in a world with no bearings and only her imperfect sense of right
and wrong to guide her. In one dramatic fight, Estusia, only twenty herself,
lost patience with Rywka, struck her, and threatened to kick Rywka out. "Oh,
God, I am so lonely!" Rywka wrote on February 15, 1944:

> **I don't know if she will do what she promised . . . She keeps
> saying that she is pleased with me, but now? Right now,
> would she say that she doesn't want me anymore? It seems so
> unbelievable . . . Not only are the times horrible and tragic,
> but I don't even have a shelter called "home."**

As she battled in turn with Estusia, Chanusia, and Minia, each fresh
argument served only to underscore the impossible tensions of life in the
ghetto and her terrible sense of isolation and alienation. Within this context,
Rywka's relationship with her younger sister, Cipka, was an unalloyed source

A food distribution line in the Lodz ghetto. *(Courtesy of Yad Vashem Photo Archive, Archival Signature 4062/461)*

of joy. It is clear that she not only loved her but felt a great responsibility for her, expressing concern over her well-being, both physical ("Nowadays I'm hungrier when Cipka doesn't eat and fuller when she does") and emotional ("Chajusia told me to get closer to Cipka, to talk to her, to ask her what she thinks about this or that. I'll try, after all it's my duty, I have to replace her mother for her as much as I can"). She reported often on caring for her younger sister, seeing to it that she got her fair share of food, making her a dress, setting up the bed for her, or doing an errand on her behalf. At the same time, Rywka took great pride in her younger sister's accomplishments in school, her generosity and thoughtfulness with friends, and her developing personality. "I have noticed that I love Cipka more and more," she reflected on December 13, 1943, "when she does something good, gets good grades (she is the best student), when she understands what happens at the assemblies. It fills me with pride and I feel happy . . ."

As in other ghetto diaries, and in particular in Lodz, Rywka returned again and again to the problem of food and hunger.

> Hunger has always had a very bad impact on me, today is the same.
> For Cipka and me last year it was, so to say, a challenge to fight
> hunger. Oh, it's so exhausting! It's a terrible feeling to be hungry.
> I don't like to stay at home. I prefer to be in class . . . or I don't
> know where, but not at home, it's almost dangerous at home.
>
> (FEBRUARY 10, 1944)

The lack of food led to further breakdowns in relationships between people. At home, Rywka often confided to her diary her sense of disgust at what she felt was her cousins' apparent reluctance to share supplies equally and their view of her as lacking self-control in the consumption of her rations. In response, she resolved to stop accepting food that they offered to her:

I have decided, as I mentioned before, not to use what is exclusively theirs. Cipka can't overcome it, she's just a kid, but I succeed and it pleases me. Sure, if they buy something, for example, onions, garlic, things like that, then I take it, even if they didn't want me to, because it is shared—mine and theirs—but the ration . . . but the ration . . . it's a different story.

(DECEMBER 31, 1943)

In fact, at a certain point, the problem of sharing food became so acute that a social worker (and an important mentor for Rywka) named Miss Zelicka was called in to mediate. By March 22, 1944, the hunger had taken a physical toll on Rywka. She told her diary, "I'm so weak that sometimes I don't feel any hunger. It's awful (hunger used to have a bad effect on me). A skirt that was made for me at the beginning of the course (a few months ago) is hanging loose on me. I don't exaggerate."

As in many other contemporaneous accounts, Rywka witnessed the way extreme hunger broke down the social order and caused otherwise decent people to betray their moral code. She reported with horror in her diary about the instances in which friends and family members stole from each other, describing her friend Dorka Zand's brother as a "swindler" for "borrowing" potatoes and rutabaga from Dorka and another friend without telling anyone. Later, she reports on the collective efforts of a group of children at school to collect potatoes and the distressing news that one of the adults, a Mrs. Perlowa, had eaten some of them. "Mrs. Perlowa!" she wrote on January 25, 1944, ". . . I'd never believe it . . . who else is going to disappoint me? Oh, it's terrible . . . hypocrisy, hypocrisy . . . It really hurts!"

In February, Rywka and the cousins found themselves confronted with this problem in their own home. It is one of the few times that they seemed to bind together in the face of a common problem. The first sign of trouble came when Cipka noticed some missing marmalade; she later

People looking for edible roots near the Lodz ghetto.
(Courtesy of Yad Vashem Photo Archive, Archival Signature 4062/370)

pretended to be asleep and heard the person (unnamed in the diary) "munching" on some sugar. Later, Minia reported sugar missing and other food strewn around, and the following day, some of Cipka's bread went missing. At first, everyone blamed someone else—Estusia thought it was Cipka and Rywka; Rywka thought it was Minia. Rywka seemed to know who the culprit was, but she refrained from writing it explicitly, referring only to "that person" or using similarly oblique terms. It is almost as if the shame of such a transgression was so overwhelming that she could not bring herself to put it down in black and white. "I can't get it out of my head," she wrote in despair on February 16. "Oh, God! If you can't trust people like that, then whom can you trust? Whom? Oh, trust! It's so ugly! God! Oh, such rotten tricks! It's disgusting! It's unbearable! It's what the ghetto did!"

In spite of her daily hardship—amply documented in the diary—Rywka also reported on the various "extracurricular" activities in which she was involved outside of work and school. Rywka visited friends, took walks, shared her diary and read those of her friends, and studied psalms or other Jewish texts together with them. In her entry of March 4, 1944, she described her reading:

> **I have a good book entitled *Les Misérables*, which I'm sharing with Chanusia. This book has fallen apart. Some chapters have more pages and we have to wait for each other. Right now, I'm waiting for Chanusia. That's what reading in the ghetto is like . . .**

As in other ghettos, the young people in Lodz engaged in structured cultural and educational efforts of all forms as well, seeking a reprieve from the grinding reality of their days. Rywka helped to organize a library, donating two volumes of *War and Peace* to the collective effort, and joined several literature clubs. In these organizations—not easily distinguishable from one another in the diary—the girls read stories, wrote newspapers, discussed short stories, and the like. As Rywka described it on January 3, 1944, "Once a week we'll study only literature or something else, and on Sundays we'll also have one hour of fun (so we won't turn into old bags)." From the diary, it appears that there was considerable teenage-style drama in these groups, with various parties being elected, then ousted, hurt feelings, misunderstandings, rival groups being formed, and so on. Rywka also faced the sticky point of boys being included. As an Orthodox Jewish girl, she was extremely conservative in matters of mixing with the opposite sex. "Yesterday I wasn't pleased and I didn't even talk about it," she wrote in the same entry. "But now I'm happier because, first, they have their opinions and if I don't like them, I can tell them, and second, I'll be with Lusia, Hela, and Edzia and I'll get to know them better."

Of all her activities, however, Rywka remained most attached to the activities of the Beys Yaacov, an organization that had been formed in 1917 by Sarah Schenirer in Krakow, Poland, as a response to the lack of religious schooling provided for religious Jewish girls. While boys traditionally attended religious schools such as cheder, Talmud Torah, and yeshiva, girls—if they received any education at all—were typically sent to free, generally public, secular schools, where they received minimal religious instruction. Seeing in this an explanation for the high rate of assimilation among religious girls, Schenirer created a school-based Jewish education especially for young and adolescent Jewish girls. While the foundations of the curriculum were religious and conservative, it was by definition a progressive step within the Orthodox community. Her school eventually blossomed into a network of similar schools across Europe.

Fajga Zelicka, a young teacher from the Beys Yaacov school in Krakow, began leading informal gatherings (which Rywka and others called "assemblies") for young girls in the Lodz ghetto, reading and studying the Bible, Psalms, and ethical Jewish texts such as *Pirkei Avot* (Wisdom of the Fathers) and *Hovot ha-Levavot* (Duties of the Heart). At the time that she began her diary, Rywka had been attending Miss Zelicka's sessions under the influence of Estusia's schoolmate and friend Surcia Selver. In fact, it was Estusia who had asked Surcia to reach out and help Rywka because they were both writers, and Estusia hoped that Surcia might mentor and guide her young cousin. Although Rywka never acknowledged it in the diary, this is an example of Estusia's efforts to help Rywka find her way in a confusing

and painful world. Indeed, Surcia, above all, together with another friend named Chajusia and Miss Zelicka, became deeply important figures in Rywka's life.

Rywka found comfort, social engagement, ways to better herself, and even some fun in these assemblies. She mentioned in the diary a Hanukkah celebration and time spent in the company of friends, learning, studying, and, in many cases, wrestling with questions of personality and character. In Surcia's postwar memoir, she painted a picture of Miss Zelicka and the effect she had on the young women in her circle:

She was young, not much older than most of us, her eager listeners. But she opened a whole new vista before our eyes . . . Throughout [her] lectures, I felt as though she was speaking solely to me, as though she was answering the questions that bewildered me and gave me no respite . . . She infused us with a love of the Bible, she uncovered its treasures to us, she interpreted everything as if it had been written especially for us . . . She imparted to us the spiritual tenets of Judaism, its numerous ethical values and humanistic spirit.*

Rywka's growing attachment to Surcia is a thread that runs throughout the diary. It was Surcia, Rywka told her diary, who inspired her to begin writing and who encouraged her to continue. Time and again, Rywka

---

* Sara Selver-Urbach, *Through the Window of My Home,* 3rd ed. (Jerusalem: Yad Vashem, 1986), 64–65.

wrote that her diary could be called "Surcia"—her confidante in living form and on paper fusing into one entity. At the same time, she often expressed concern that the intensity of her feelings and her sadness would "scare" Surcia or upset her. It is clear that inasmuch as she intended to share everything with Surcia, she recognized a certain limit in her older friend's willingness to hear her grief. "Oh . . . Last night I was feeling so bad, so weak! What has happened to me? I've changed so much! I decided not to give my diary to Surcia tomorrow, because she'd be upset by all this," she wrote on March 23, 1944.

In addition to writing her diary with Surcia in mind and sharing it with her from time to time, Rywka wrote a series of passionate letters in which she poured out her heart—her struggles, her ideas about life, and most of all her need for love, acceptance, and friendship. Sometimes, Rywka sounds like a love-struck teenager infatuated with Surcia:

> **At this moment, I'm thinking about the passionate emotions. And I'm thinking about Surcia. I feel I love her more and more. Oh, I feel true affection for her. Oh, power of love! Oh, it's a real power. [. . .] I want to write more, and maybe I'll express myself. I do feel affection for Surcia. Maybe not for her, but for her soul, which means for her, after all. Oh, Surcia. I take delight in the sound of her name. (It's good that we are of the same sex.) Otherwise, what would it look like, such writing?**
>
> **(DECEMBER 24, 1943)**

Though her love for Surcia was certainly romantic—she singled her out, depended deeply on her, and admired her without reserve—it was not erotic; instead, it seemed to stem from her deep loneliness, her sense of being misunderstood, and her need to find acceptance, affection, and love in a world filled with rejection, loss, hardship, and alienation.

It is clear that, at some point, Rywka's letters and writings caught Surcia's attention. She spoke to Miss Zelicka about Rywka, who in turn, requested a private meeting with her. With some excitement, Rywka writes, "She showed Miss Zelicka my letter in which I wrote about life. That's why Miss Zelicka sent me a notice through Surcia that she'd like to talk about it on Tuesday at eleven a.m. It's so unexpected . . . I'm thinking about it a great deal . . ." As it turned out, however, the first meeting between them was a bitter disappointment. Miss Zelicka had apparently spoken with Estusia, too, and endeavored to encourage Rywka to model herself a bit more after her cousin. For Rywka, it was a devastating blow.

> Cipka knew that I had seen Miss Zelicka so I reluctantly asked
> her if she knew what was the subject of the conversation
> between Miss Zelicka and Estusia. Thanks to Cipka I found out.
> Estusia said I was stubborn, that before I came to live with them
> I wasn't obedient and in the beginning I was being hysterical. In
> other words, she presented me in a dazzlingly negative light. At
> that point I understood. [. . .] I can't find a place for myself.
> I don't share anything with anybody, only with my diary and
> Surcia, my beloved Surcia. I don't know anything, oh, I don't
> know anything, I'm helpless . . . What's going to happen?
>
> (DECEMBER 22, 1943)

In time, Rywka recovered from this disappointment and eventually developed a relationship of her own with Miss Zelicka, visiting her apartment when she was ill, bringing her a pound cake, and relying upon her as so many other girls in the ghetto did. Indeed, Miss Zelicka stands with educators and mentors such as Mrs. Kaufman, Mrs. Milioner, and a handful of other adults who attempted to regulate and guide these lost adolescents fending for themselves in the ghetto.

Over time, Rywka decided that she wanted to attend the assemblies of the older girls, so as to participate in discussions where she felt she would better fit in. In fact, Rywka's confidence in herself and her ambition remained strong in spite of her circumstances and what she perceived as constant criticism by her cousins. She was plucky, determined, and confident—qualities that led her to be accused of being conceited by some of her friends. And though she confided to her diary her doubts about her knowledge and abilities, she persisted in striving for more. After Rywka gained attendance to the older girls' assembly, Surcia warned her that she could attend only one time. Rywka's response is surprising, given how she worshipped and depended upon the older girl:

> When on Friday Surcia and I went to the assembly . . . Surcia told me that the other girls might be jealous that I was going but they were not going. And she added, "This time only" . . . I was a little worried, because it's beneficial for me, but I couldn't argue with Surcia. When the assembly started I came to the conclusion that I simply had to come again. [. . .] Too bad . . . I was a little upset because I didn't want to defy Surcia, but in this case I decided to do it anyway . . .
>
> (FEBRUARY 7, 1944)

She followed this entry with a passionate letter to Surcia explaining why she must attend the sessions and pleading her case, though it is clear that she had already made up her mind to attend. Rywka may have been young, orphaned, a witness to boundless cruelty, lacking a complete education, and living amid relatives who she felt did not understand her, but she was a strong-willed, deeply feeling young girl whose spirit for self-improvement, learning, and personal growth remained unshakable in the face of everything she experienced.

Inasmuch as the diary contains great details about aspects of life in the Lodz ghetto at this particular historical moment, it does not seem that it was Rywka's main purpose to record these external aspects of her life. In fact, in her entry of January 7, 1944, she laments their encroachment on her writing: "Oh, really, I describe 'external' life so much that I won't have time to write about my 'inner' life." Instead, Rywka clearly saw her diary as a place for her to pour out her heart and her feelings, to confide her troubles, and to safeguard her memories.

At the same time, Rywka's internal voice in the diary—her struggle to know herself, to define her beliefs, and to maintain hope in the face of daunting despair—was inevitably shaped by external circumstances. If adolescence is a time of establishing the essentials of the self (Who am I relative to my parents, my siblings, my friends, my religion, my culture, my nationality? Where do I choose to place myself in the world?), then stability, a dependable framework against which to push, is an essential element in the process. For Rywka—and countless teenagers like her—coming of age in the ghetto meant grappling with the developmental challenges of adolescence against a backdrop of extreme trauma, loss, instability, and mortal fear.

At age fourteen, she had been uprooted from the life she knew before the war (her childhood home, school, friends, extended family, and social network) and rudely thrust into the hostile environment of the ghetto and a crowded apartment shared with relatives who, she felt, neither understood nor appreciated her. She found herself deeply isolated, missing parental shelter, understanding, and love, alone with the last of her three siblings. She had strong faith, to be sure, but this central element of her identity—being a Jew—also constituted, by definition, a mortal threat, as it did for all Jews living under the Nazi regime. This was an intractable existential problem, difficult enough for an adult to contend with, let alone a teenager. In virtually every significant way, Rywka was cut adrift from the stable base that she needed to thrive and left to find her way amid shifting, uncertain terrain.

Against this backdrop, Rywka's struggle for self-betterment and the development of her character was a heroic one. She tried to refrain from *lashon hara*, the sin of gossip or slander, and she often chastised herself for failures of character, as when Miss Zelicka granted her permission to attend Friday-evening meetings and she felt disappointed ("Oh, what kind of person am I? When they let me do one thing, I want more") or when her pride was wounded because a schoolmate was asked to read a poem she wrote at a public assembly:

> (I was told to write it, to make some effort, etc., and after all
> that I'm disposable? If I were a bad speaker and Juta a good
> one, then it would be understandable, but it's not like that . . .
> anyway, why should I write about it? I have to get rid of this
> thought and not be so selfish!)
>
> (MARCH 17, 1944)

In her struggle to develop into the person she wanted to be, she leaned heavily on Surcia and the circle of girls in the Beys Yaacov, including Miss Zelicka and Chajusia, whom she saw as her only positive role models. She tried repeatedly in the diary and in her letters to find comfort in these relationships, to find stability and solace, and to learn from Surcia, in particular, how to live. In one typical letter, dated December 11, 1943, she wrote:

> Oh, Surcia, I'd love so much to talk to you, to see you. I miss
> you. You are a big plus in my life. Oh, I can't imagine not
> knowing the group of you and you in particular . . . Please
> reply. It will be a lesson for me. Your Rywcia is asking you.

At the same time, and later in the diary, Rywka tried to reach out to Surcia and Chajusia, to offer them help and comfort when they needed it.

She was aware of her youth and inexperience and at the same time desperate to show that she had something to contribute, that she had some wisdom and advice that might help even the older girls she so fervently admired. After reading a series of letters between Surcia and her deceased friend Miriam, Rywka wrote an emotional response to Surcia:

> Now I know how much Miriam meant to you and I feel your pain; . . . And . . . I shyly suggest that you confide in me a little. I see how much you need it . . . Oh. Surcia, I wish you the best. I love you so much, Surcia, let me replace Miriam a little bit . . . Surcia, now when I write you that I love you, it will seem as if I'm trying to equal Miriam, that I'm fond of you and that's why I want to have you, but keep this in mind: I love you profoundly . . .
>
> (JANUARY 31, 1944)

Rywka often used her diary—and the letters she wrote to Surcia—to reflect her developing ideas about bigger questions on the meaning of life, the nature of humanity, and the world as she saw it. It is true that she was prone to sophomoric analogies ("life is like a dark road" or "people are like teeth"), but who can blame her? She was only fourteen. The gesture—the effort to think deeply about the world as she saw it and to draw metaphors to understand it more fully—is an admirable one, limited as it may have been by her age, her inexperience, and her lack of education. She also struggled with the desire to do something meaningful in the ghetto—surely an outgrowth of the fundamental Jewish concept of *tikkun olam*, which requires of each person a lifelong effort to help repair our broken world. For Rywka, this mostly meant guiding people toward better behavior. It may sound presumptuous to contemporary readers, but her sentiments might be read more compassionately as a youthful urge to have a positive influence on her peers and to make a difference in the world, On March 29, 1944, she wrote:

> At this moment I'd like to do so much for the world. I see
> many, many defects and I feel so sorry that I can't find a
> place for myself. And when I realize that I don't matter
> in the world, that I'm just a speck of dust, that I can't do
> anything, at this moment, I feel much worse, I'm suffocating
> and I'm helpless . . . In order to screw up my courage I tell
> myself, "After all, I'm still young, very young. What else
> can happen?" But time is passing by. It's the fifth year of
> the war. [. . .] The only thing that's encouraging me (as
> I've mentioned before) is the hope that it won't always be
> like this and that I'm still young. Maybe I'll grow up to be
> somebody and then I'll be able to do something.

In fact, Rywka was all too painfully aware of her limitations—both in her character and in her education—and their effect on her ability to express herself. Surely as a result of her truncated education (her formal schooling would have come to an end in 1939, when she was only ten), she struggled to express herself in Polish. She did not write fluidly, and she made many mistakes in grammar and mechanics. Her punctuation was idiosyncratic at best. She herself recognized time and again how difficult it was to express herself, the way in which her lack of education—not to mention the effects of hunger, cold, and fear—hindered her ability to organize her thoughts, sustain a particular line of thinking, and find the words she needed to convey the nuances and subtlety of her ideas. "Yesterday I wanted to write," she confessed on January 5, 1944, "i.e., I felt I had something to write, but even if I had time, I wouldn't know what to write, I simply forgot. I have become such a scatterbrain . . . I can't find a place for myself."

Still, she persisted. For many young people who kept diaries during the Holocaust, the written word was a necessary tool to document their experiences, record their feelings, and testify to their existence on earth in the face of total annihilation. Only a handful—such as Anne Frank, Yitskhok Rudashevski, Petr Ginz, the anonymous boy from Lodz—expressed a passion for writing for its own sake, a desire that went beyond the specific circumstances of the war and connected to a deeper sense of what they wanted to do in the world. In spite of the limits of her education, Rywka was one such writer, expressing time and again how much her writing meant to her, her gratitude for it, and its centrality in her life. Her ambitions as a writer went beyond her diary; she took seriously the letters she wrote to Surcia, her philosophical reflections, and a number of poems that she included in the diary, even as she recognized their limits. In an entry written on February 22, 1944, she wrote:

> I was sitting with my head down and reading. I don't want to waste a moment. I decided to read more. And I have a problem. I don't write anything special besides the diary, sometimes a poem, but what about prose? Oh, I can't write prose at all. Have I become incompetent? Oh, I thought I had nothing to write, but in the course of writing . . . everything in the course of writing. I've written an essay for the class and thanks to Surcia I have something special . . . maybe I've written it a bit clumsily, but truthfully!

As in many other diaries—those of the anonymous girl in Lodz, Petr Ginz in Terezin, Ilya Gerber in the Kovno ghetto, and others—Rywka mentioned her friends' diaries as well. It appears that Surcia kept one, and that Rywka encouraged her friends Ewa, Fela, Dorka, and Mania to begin as well. She gave a notebook to Fela, who began by reading a published diary to find inspiration. Rywka dismissed this approach, writing, "in my opinion you don't need any models to write a diary. It's true that it's hard in the beginning. I'm the best example of that, but later one gets more experienced"* (February 12, 1944).

Another aspect of Rywka's inner life, as she captured it in her diary, centered on her memories of her family and her struggle to absorb and come to terms—if such a thing were possible—with the staggering losses she had endured. Over the course of the diary, she panned, almost like a camera lens, across the landscape of her family, stopping now and then to focus her gaze on each departed member. On January 26, 1944, recalling the deaths of her parents, she described her father:

> **Daddy! He appeared in front of me as if he were alive. [. . .]**
> **I can see his eyes, his wise and expressive eyes, and I**
> **suddenly remembered his handshake. I still feel it. It**
> **was when they let us into the hospital on Yom Kippur (on**
> **Łagiewnicka Street) and Daddy squeezed my hand while**
> **saying good-bye. Oh, how much that handshake meant to me,**
> **how much fatherly love it had. Oh, God, I will never forget**
> **it! My daddy, alive, my loving daddy, the dearest of all the**
> **dearest creatures in the world.**

In the same entry, she remembered growing closer to her mother in the wake of her father's death:

> **Only then . . . then I noticed that my mom understood me.**
> **Mommy . . . I did feel it. At that moment we got closer and**
> **we were living not like mother and daughter, but like best**

---

* As in the case of diaries mentioned by other writers, none of the diaries that Rywka's friends wrote seems to have survived.

friends . . . The age difference was unimportant (I was twelve then). Oh, God! And then Mom was dead and what she hadn't told me remained a secret forever.

For Rywka, the deaths of her parents left her in the position—at age twelve—of essentially becoming a mother to her three younger siblings. As she recalled it, "Abramek appointed me as mother. 'You are our mother,' he used to say." And, like any mother, she suffered crippling pain and remorse in the wake of their deportation from the ghetto in the *szpera* of September 1942. Her guilt and anguish over not having been able to protect them from deportation took many forms—in one entry she laments how Abramek, "such a good kid," gave her his bread and, as a result, "looked bad," which led to his being taken away. It was, unfortunately, a calculation born of experience; people were often judged on their appearance and what it conveyed about their ability to work and be productive. "Looking bad"—that is, showing signs of malnutrition (swelling or water retention), illness, or bearing the early hallmarks of general decline—could result in deportation and death.

In another entry, written on January 19, 1944, she wrote about her baby sister:

Through the fog of my tears, I saw Tamarcia's frightened eyes (that's how she looked in the picture) . . . Oh, I'm afraid to write about it . . . She looked like she was calling me, like she was crying for help . . . I did nothing . . . Oh, Tamarcia, where are you? I want to help you . . . I'm tossing and turning, well, I'm tied down . . . Oh, how many tragedies are contained in these words!? I'm scared, I miss her, I'm drenched with cold and hot sweat.

Time and again, Rywka revisited her grief over the loss of her brother and sister and, however unwarranted it might have been, she suffered terrible guilt on their behalf. At the same time, she did not lose sight of those who bore the ultimate responsibility, writing on January 15, 1944, "Abramek, where are you? Tamarcia! . . . Oh, go to hell, you plunderers and murderers . . . I'll never forgive you, never. But in the face of 'them' I'm helpless."

There is a familiar strain that appears in many writings of the period in Rywka's diary. In one sense, she suspected and even knew that her siblings were gone. On the other hand, her mind would not allow her to fully accept it; the unresolved nature of the loss, namely, deportation to an uncertain fate, always left open the tantalizing thought that they might, somehow, have survived. In general, a particular confluence of elements—the lack of definite information, deliberate obfuscation by the German authorities, the tacit acknowledgment by the Jewish community, the incapacity to fully comprehend and believe, the emotional refusal to know what the mind does not want to know, the remote possibility of an alternate fate—combined to torture the survivors when contemplating the fates of their loved ones. Rywka writes on numerous occasions about her dreams—waking and sleeping—in which this excruciating hope takes vivid form. On February 7, 1944, she wrote:

> On Saturday morning I had a dream . . . Suddenly the door opened and Abramek came in (at first I thought it was only Abramek), then Tamara and Mommy. I pounced on them. I caught Tamara's hand. I noticed that Tamara was a little taller but she looked the same, the same way we saw her last time. Abramek was decently dressed and he was taller, too . . . Tamara told me that where they had been they were forced to misbehave and if somebody was behaving properly he was punished . . . and . . . I woke up . . .

Dreams notwithstanding, the chilling reality crept into Rywka's consciousness, as her mind gradually taught itself to accept the increasingly

Deportation from the Lodz ghetto, 1942. *(Courtesy of Yad Vashem Photo Archive, Archival Signature 4062/109)*

inescapable reality. In one entry, dreaming of her future after the war, she wrote, "I could see a modest apartment which I share with my sister—earlier I thought it was Tamarcia, but today it's more probable that it's Cipka" (February 28, 1944).

In Rywka's constellation of "inner thoughts," there is one last theme that bears examination—her struggle to maintain strength in the face of mounting despair. It is a theme that exists in nearly every diary of the period—regardless of the writer's age, education, status, or circumstance. It is impossible to understand this vacillation between hope and despair without considering the nature of time itself during the Holocaust. As the war dragged on and information of mass killings made its way into the collective consciousness, Jewish victims of the Nazi regime came to realize that survival depended entirely on holding out longer than the Germans. Certainly by 1943–1944, when Rywka was writing, the trickle of information through clandestine radios and other sources made the population, even in the sealed Lodz ghetto, aware that it was only a matter of time until the Germans were defeated. But time was everything. The question remained whether those in the ghetto could hold on until the end or whether their lives would be claimed first by illness, by malnutrition, by accident, by random violence, or by deportation. Rywka put it succinctly on January 28, 1944: "I'm waiting for the war to end. Oh, this waiting is tragic, too!"

Inasmuch as survival depended on luck, it also hinged on one's ability to maintain hope—to have the strength to fight and stay alive—and not succumb to despair, to indifference, to the apathy that led inevitably to death. Rywka was acutely aware of this dynamic. She exhorts herself (and, in other entries, her friends) to fight, to hold on:

> My longing is growing . . . there is more and more longing . . . the only thing that could stop it is so far away . . . and it's receding . . . What shall I do? Blow myself into pieces? No! I can't do that! Wait patiently? Oh, it's too much! It's nerveracking. Oh, I'm afraid I can't take it anymore! I cry with all my might, "Hold on!" Because it's most important! And most difficult! God! What a struggle! What a terrible struggle! . . . I can't give up! But who's thinking of giving up? . . . Oh, I feel that I'm sinking more and more into a swamp and mud . . . and . . . I can't get out . . . No! I won't let it happen! I'll do my best! But again I'm overwhelmed by exhaustion! Oh, how can I stop it? Who can help me? This ghetto is a terrible hell.
>
> (FEBRUARY 23, 1944)

In fact, Rywka had little reason to hope; she was essentially defenseless against forces that outstripped her in every way. In another dream, on March 2, 1944, Rywka's subconscious laid out the perils that lay in every direction:

> Oh, what was my dream?! It was dark . . . Chajusia came and said that she reported for a deportation out of honesty. Not only she . . . others did the same thing. I remembered Miss Zelicka and Surcia . . . I was choking. I wasn't able to utter a word. I fought an internal struggle whether I should report, too, or stay . . . I had to be with Cipka, but I couldn't part with Surcia. Oh, what a horrible feeling! [. . .] Oh, nerves . . . nerves . . . I'm exhausted. It's horrible . . .

Rywka's struggle to hold on intensified over the course of the diary, reaching a sort of fever pitch as winter dragged on. In February and March, a new deportation order shut down life in the ghetto, and hunger became nearly intolerable. In this context, Rywka's faith was a bulwark—sometimes the only one she had—against total despair:

> How many people have wondered: why, what for, and slowly, step-by-step, they lose their faith and have been discouraged with life. Oh, it's so terrible! . . . That's why I'm grateful to God three times over, even four, for giving me the opportunity to believe. If it weren't for my faith, I, like other people, would lose my will to live. [. . .] [H]ave patience, with God's help everything will be all right.
>
> (FEBRUARY 12, 1944)

Early on February 8, 1944, the ghetto was faced with a new crisis. The German authorities demanded 1,500 men for labor outside the ghetto. The deportees were to be drawn only from the ghetto administration, not from the workshops or the transportation or coal departments.* Rywka reported the news for the first time five days after the initial order was issued. By this time, the ghetto administration had not been able to gather the necessary transport of men. In response to too many years of experience, those whose names appeared on lists went into hiding and refused to report. As a result, the affected men found their ration cards blocked in an attempt to force them out of hiding upon pain of starvation, and relatives of those called up were held as hostages. Rywka wrote on February 12:

> Oh, God, what's happening in the ghetto? Resettlements again! There are many children, even five years old, at Czarnieckiego Street. They are held hostage for those who received the summonses . . . I found out that Mania was at Czarnieckiego Street as a hostage for her father . . . God! It hit me like a bolt from the blue. Mania at Czarnieckiego Street! No, it isn't possible!

Rywka recounted a speech given by Mr. Zemel in the workshop in which he conveyed Rumkowski's warnings against aiding those in hiding. She witnessed a group of deportees and reported the scene in her diary:

> Oh, today we were at Edzia's and we saw a batch of men (one). They were going to Czarnieckiego Street—we could hear them

---

* Lucjan Dobroszycki, ed., *The Chronicle of the Łódź Ghetto, 1941–1944* (New Haven, CT: Yale University Press, 1984).

crying. Oh, it's heartbreaking! It is! We are all in shreds . . .
we are in shreds! God, unite us! Blend us into one big and
inseparable whole! Oh, when will it happen? When will Geula
[Redemption] come?

(FEBRUARY 15, 1944)

On February 20, the ghetto administration imposed a curfew on the entire ghetto and the Jewish Order Police carried out searches from apartment to apartment. It was enough to trigger the traumatic memories of the *szpera* of September 1942. Rywka scribbled in her diary:

The *szpera*! How many tragic memories, how much pain and
longing, how much anxiety (I can't even enumerate all of them)
are contained in this single word? Oh, God, how much horror?
Just a single memory . . . and what if there's a *szpera* again? Is
it a *szpera*? Fortunately it's not, thank God, like the other time.

(FEBRUARY 20, 1944)

In fact, although there was no reason for the ghetto dwellers to believe it, this deportation order was different from the others. Those who were called up for labor were to be sent to Czestochowa to work, not to the killing site of Chelmno, as so many before them had been. Still, years of terror and mistrust in the ghetto could not be assuaged by promises or guarantees. People refused to report, and the ghetto administration faced a crisis that dragged on through March. At a certain point, unable to gather the required number of men, the administration began snatching women and holding them at the Central Prison. Rywka reported that even some of the girls from Bnos—meaning friends from the Orthodox Jewish community—were taken as well. On February 24, 1944, Rywka confided her despair, her sense of being pulled under by the weight of the existential crisis in the ghetto:

We are in darkness . . . somebody is pushing us . . . and pushing . . . we can't resist . . . and we're sinking . . . and we're getting stuck . . . God, help us get out!!! Unfortunately, help isn't coming yet. Who knows if it's going to come in time? Oh, everything is in God's hands! What can we do? It's dark and empty around us! It's terribly dark and foggy! And this fog is getting into my heart . . . I can hardly breathe. Oh, impossible . . . we'll suffocate. Oh, more fresh air. Oh, we miss it so much . . . God! God! It's so tragic, hopeless, bad.

Children who were rounded up during a *szpera* march toward a deportation assembly point. *(Instytut Pamieci Narodowej, courtesy of United States Holocaust Memorial Museum, Photograph 50334)*

Even though Rywka was herself not at risk of deportation, she commented in the diary on the effect of the deportation on those around her. In a letter to Chajusia, she attempted to bolster her friend's courage, writing:

"[Y]ou must come to your senses! Don't stay at home all day! Take a walk! Maybe you'll feel better! . . . Oh, Chajusia, you may think that I can't understand it, but believe me! . . . The trick is to control yourself and not to let the evil control you . . ."

(FEBRUARY 14, 1944)

Still, those who witnessed events at the Central Prison—Surcia, Estusia, Mania Bardes, and others—reported chilling, horrific scenes. The entire ghetto was affected as it became, essentially, a labor camp in which all existence depended on the continued ability to supply the Germans with goods for the war effort. Rywka wrote plaintively in her diary on February 17, 1944:

[I]n our school (not school anymore, because its name was changed to *Fach Kurse*) we won't have any Hebrew classes or math, only five hours of productive sewing and one hour of technical drawing. Neither books nor notebooks are allowed at work. It's all secret, they (the workshops) must cover up for us, us—the children—because studying is forbidden. It hurts so much (for them we are not humans, just machines).

The deportees left the ghetto in transports of 500 to 750, beginning in early March. By the end of the month, news reached the ghetto from the deportees who, it was said, were working in an appliance factory under fairly good conditions and with enough food to eat. The mood in the ghetto calmed down, and life—such as it was—resumed a normal pitch. Hunger continued unabated. "Recently there has been nothing, nothing," Rywka wrote on March 13. "We're busy analyzing our stomachs (I don't like it), we've simply become animals . . . we're more like animals than humans. How horrible it is."

Toward the end of the diary, as winter gave way to spring, Rywka's tone suddenly brightened. It is true that hardships continued to assail her—she was deeply grieved during Passover, remembering the past, writing several long entries recalling her father and his illness, and suffering over his absence at the Seder—but eventually the warm weather and the sunny days improved her mood. As for so many writers, the arrival of spring brought with it a renewed sense of hope. On April 11, 1944, she wrote:

> Thank you, God, for the spring! Thank you for this mood! I don't want to write much about it, because I don't want to mess it up, but I'll write one very significant word: hope! [. . .] I'm so happy. Maybe it'll be better, maybe finally it'll be all right? Oh, as soon as possible! Oh, this excitement. It seems to be overcoming everyone. In a way it's because of this wonderful change in the weather. Yes, no doubt about it. [. . .] Only the Lord knows what we need and . . . Oh, God, give us what we need! Give it to us! (Oh, summer rain is falling!)

The diary ends abruptly in the next entry, in the middle of a cryptic paragraph about eligibility for longer work shifts that would bring supplemental food rations. Those who wished to register, according to Rywka, had to procure a certificate stating that they were born in 1926–27, meaning that they would be seventeen or eighteen years of age in 1944. Rywka, who was born in 1929, fell short of the age restriction. Oddly, in the last line of the diary, she wrote that she was born in 1927. It is unclear if she simply wrote the wrong date in her diary or if she was thinking about trying to register. In any case, the diary ends there, the last words, "but actually . . ." appearing

Group portrait of teenage girls and teachers wearing Stars of David in a sewing workshop in the Lodz ghetto *(United States Holocaust Memorial Museum, Photograph 21400, courtesy of Ruth Eldar)*

in the middle of the page. The rest of the last page in the copybook is blank. This suggests that Rywka did, in fact, stop in the middle of this entry, not that the rest of the pages of the diary were lost.

Why did she so suddenly and unexpectedly stop writing? What could possibly have happened to make her cease in the middle of an entry, never to return to the diary that meant so much to her? There are no answers to this question. What we do know is that within one month of ending her diary, the ghetto was again gripped by a terrifying series of deportations that took place in May and June. Following a brief period of respite in July, the German authorities called for the final liquidation of the ghetto in August.

Rywka, Cipka, Estusia, Chanusia, and Minia remained together in the ghetto until they were all deported to Auschwitz, together with almost all of the remaining inhabitants of the ghetto. Rywka carried her diary with her on the train from the Lodz ghetto to Auschwitz, where it was found after the liberation in the spring of 1945. In her last entry, dated April 12, 1944, Rywka expressed all of the contradictions and struggles of her young life: the beauty and joy of the world and the misery of her existence; the crushing weight of despair and the effort to maintain hope and, above all, a desire to live that remained strong in her in spite of everything she endured.

> At moments like this I want to live so much. There is less sadness, but we're more aware of our miserable circumstances, our souls are sad, and . . . really one needs a lot of strength in order not to give up. We look at this wonderful world, this beautiful spring, and at the same time we see ourselves in the ghetto deprived of everything, we're deprived of everything, we don't have the smallest joy, because, unfortunately, we're machines with well-developed animal instincts. They're visible everywhere (mostly during the meals). [. . .] Why shall I even write about it? I want it, I want it so much. When I realize that we're deprived of everything, that we're slaves, I try to put off this thought in order not to spoil this joyful little moment. How hard it is! Oh, God, how much longer? I think that only when we are liberated we will enjoy a real spring. Oh, I miss this dear spring . . .

Lodz

A History of the City and the Ghetto

FRED ROSENBAUM

Rywka Lipszyc's hometown of Lodz was the site of the most isolated and oppressed ghetto in all of Nazi-occupied Europe. Yet before World War II, and even more so during the half century before World War I, the metropolis had a well-deserved reputation for cultural pluralism and economic dynamism. From 1865 to 1914, four ethnic groups coexisted side by side and the population grew an astounding seventeen-fold.

During this golden age, the Jewish community constituted a major thread in Lodz's rich multicultural tapestry. The city had been part of the Czarist Empire since 1815, but Jews finally won basic political rights in Russian Poland in 1862, and commercial opportunity quickly followed. Jewish industrialists like Izrael Poznanski, a pioneer in replacing handlooms with steam-powered machines, were essential in making Lodz one of Europe's major textile hubs, a saga narrated in detail by the great Yiddish novelist I. J. Singer in his sweeping *Brothers Ashkenazi*.[*] Other Jews, like the Rosenblatts,

---

[*] I. J. Singer, *The Brothers Ashkenazi* (New York: Alfred A. Knopf, 1936). Another social panorama of Lodz during the industrial revolution is that of Nobel Prize winner Władysław Remont in *The Promised Land* (New York: Alfred A. Knopf, 1927), based on three main characters—a German, a Jew, and a Pole.

Ginsbergs, Konstadts, and Jarocinskis, were also major cloth manufacturers, while still others were leaders in banking, real estate, utilities, and shipping.

By 1900, Jews constituted nearly a third of the population and half of the businessmen in Lodz. They interacted with the Poles, of course, but also with the two other large minority groups: ethnic Germans, known as *Volksdeutsche*, and Russians. Interethnic relations were relatively good for East Central Europe, for no single group had majority status. The Poles were the largest group, but the Jews, Germans, and Russians collectively outnumbered them.* The communities usually did not mix socially, but tolerance generally prevailed and four languages—Polish, Yiddish, German, and Russian—were heard on the streets and in the stores.

After World War I, Lodz became part of the new Polish Republic. With the flight of the Russians and the emigration of many *Volksdeutsche*, the demographic balance shifted in favor of the Poles. After 1918, they were unquestionably the majority and—after more than a century of foreign rule—finally the masters in their own house. Still, Lodz's diverse Jewish population of more than a quarter of a million souls continued to comprise almost a third of the city. With its Hasidim and Orthodox, Bundists and Folkists, every manner of Zionist, and assimilationists, Lodz was home to the second-largest Jewish community in the new Poland and smaller in size only than Warsaw.

Especially after the death in 1935 of Poland's chief of state, Jozef Pilsudski, who during a nine-year rule had sought to protect the national minorities, anti-Semitism intensified in Lodz, as in the rest of Poland. It emanated from the government, the Church, and chauvinistic pressure groups. But Rywka Lipszyc, born in 1929, and enrolled in a traditional Jewish day school for

---

* Religion coincided closely, although not precisely, with ethnicity, because there were small minorities of German Catholics and Polish Protestants. See Julian K. Janczak, "The National Structure of the Population in Lodz in the Years 1820–1939," in *Polin: Studies in Polish Jewry*, ed. Antony Polonsky, 6 (Cambridge, MA: Blackwell Publishers for the Institute for Polish-Jewish Studies, Oxford, 1991), 25.

The synagogue on
Wolborska Street in
Lodz *(Courtesy of Yad
Vashem Photo Archive,
Archival Signature 37B07)*

girls, was no doubt buffered from most of the hatred and discrimination. Her childhood revolved around her respected rabbinic family, her friends, and her studies. She likely felt fairly secure.

Yet with Hitler's invasion of Poland on September 1, 1939, the world as Rywka knew it came to an end. In the first week of World War II, the *Wehrmacht* overran Lodz, less than 100 miles from the German border. Poles and *Volksdeutsche* immediately took advantage of the New Order by beating and otherwise humiliating Jews in the streets. Within a day or two of the German occupation, Jewish homes and businesses were looted as well. Religious Jews in particular came in for abuse, and hooligans often delighted in cutting the beards of Orthodox men, such as Rywka's distinguished uncle Yochanan Lipszyc, head of Lodz's rabbinical court, and his eminent father-in-law, Rabbi Moshe Menachem Segal.*

Others endured much worse. Rywka's father, Yankel, was badly beaten by Germans. It remains unclear if these were soldiers or *Volksdeutsche*, but the injuries he sustained contributed to his death a year and a half later.

The jubilant *Volksdeutsche*, perhaps 10 percent of Lodz's population in 1939, proved their loyalty to the Reich by giving the Nazi salute and displaying the swastika on banners and flags throughout the city. They received special privileges, while Jews were quickly stripped of their rights. The occupiers froze Jewish bank accounts and seized Jewish factories and stores. They closed all the synagogues and banned Jews from parks, theaters, and public transportation. Jews weren't even allowed to walk on Piotrkowska Street, Lodz's most fashionable boulevard, where before the war a good number of businesses had been Jewish-owned. Of course, the Germans required Jews to wear the infamous yellow Stars of David, front and back, which helped the new rulers enforce the strict curfew. Any Jew on the streets from five p.m. to eight a.m. was arrested.

---

* "Lodz," in *Encyclopedia of Jewish Communities in Poland I*, www.jewishgen.org/yizkor/pinkas_poland/pol1-00004.html.

In the wartime state of emergency, food distribution centers were hurriedly set up throughout the city, and residents were forced to wait in long lines for the most basic provisions. Here, too, prejudice and malice prevailed: even after waiting for hours, Jews were often kicked out of the queues by Poles or *Volksdeutsche* and frequently roughed up as well.

Facing such enmity from their fellow citizens, as well as the peril posed by the Nazi invaders, tens of thousands of Lodz Jews fled east. Many hoped to reach eastern Poland, invaded by the Red Army on September 17 and annexed by the USSR as the result of a secret protocol in the Molotov-Ribbentrop Pact, a nonaggression treaty signed by the two totalitarian powers the month before. With public transportation disrupted, the Jewish fugitives packed their belongings on horse-drawn carts or left by foot, their bundles on their backs. Some did make it to the USSR, only to be caught in the Nazi net in the summer of 1941.

The majority of Lodz Jews, including Rywka's family, stayed in their homes, but the situation deteriorated even further. While most of the rest of German-occupied Poland was designated a protectorate, ruled by military force but nevertheless a "home for Poles," Lodz's fate would be different. Because of its strategic significance, the large presence of ethnic Germans, and the fact that it had once been part of the kingdom of Prussia, Lodz and most of the area to its west were annexed by the Reich and incorporated into Germany proper.

A key part of the plan, which was hardly kept secret, was to alter the demographic balance, for the second time in a generation, by moving in *Volksdeutsche* from other parts of prewar Poland, with the goal of creating a German majority.* Four new German provinces were carved out of western Poland, and Lodz was awarded to one of them, Wartheland, named for the

---

* Gordon J. Horwitz, *Ghettostadt: Lodz and the Making of a Nazi City* (Cambridge, MA: Belknap Press of Harvard University, 2008), 36.

Piotrkowska Street becomes Adolf-Hitler-Strasse after Lodz is occupied by Nazi Germany.
(Courtesy of Gérard Silvain, Fonds Gérard and Olivier Silvain)

Warthe River. The new rulers banned Polish from the schools and theaters and also changed the names of all of the streets from Polish to German. Upscale Piotrkowska Street now became Adolf-Hitler-Strasse. The name of the city itself was changed, to Litzmannstadt, in honor of Karl Litzmann, the German general who had captured Lodz from the Russians during World War I. Even Jews quickly adopted the new name, and Rywka begins each entry of her diary with Litzmannstadt followed by the date.

Formal annexation meant that Lodz would be subjugated not only by the SS, but also by the Gestapo and the *Kripo*, the internal criminal police. The headquarters of the latter, in a brick parish house, was benignly dubbed the Little Red House, but was in fact infamous among Lodz Jews as a site of torture and murder.

Yet the tight control did not usually come directly from the German authorities. For almost half a decade, Lodz Jews would be accountable to a *Jewish* dictator, a kind of "King of the Jews," as a historical novel about him is entitled.* Chaim Rumkowski, the former head of a Jewish orphanage who was in his mid-sixties, with a mane of white hair, often appeared like a fatherly figure, but in reality he was power-hungry and egotistical. He was chauffeured around in a fancy, black-lacquered droshky (carriage) and received glowing tributes from groups ranging from schoolchildren to factory workers. His portrait hung in almost every public building.

As early as October 13, 1939, Rumkowski had been appointed chairman (technically his title was *Aelteste*, meaning senior in rank) of a thirty-man *Judenrat*, similar to the Jewish governing councils the Germans would set up to carry out their decrees across all of East Central Europe. But in Lodz, as virtually nowhere else, all the other *Judenrat* members—representing the very broad spectrum of the Jewish community's political and religious life—were soon purged, deported, or shot. Rumkowski alone remained in charge. He oversaw an enormous ghetto bureaucracy, employing over 10,000 people at its peak. He ordered the printing of currency—known as rumkis and worthless anywhere else—and postage stamps with his image. He supervised the fire department, court system, prison, and even a Jewish police department of more than 1,000 men, armed with rubber clubs.† Later, he would compile the lists of the deportees, thus holding the power of life and death over every Jew in Lodz.

---

* Leslie Epstein, *King of the Jews* (New York: Coward, McCann & Geoghegan, 1979).

† Dobroszycki, ed., *The Chronicle of the Łódź Ghetto*, xlviii.

Jewish Council Chairman
Mordechai Chaim Rumkowski
(white hair) attends a
ceremony in the Lodz ghetto.
*(Courtesy of United States Holocaust
Memorial Museum, Photograph 63014B,
courtesy of Gila Flam)*

But if the Jews were all answerable to Rumkowski, of course he was answerable to the Germans. No doubt he tried to ease the plight of the Jews—he believed he had great leadership qualities that were desperately needed in this crisis—but the savagery of the Nazis took him by surprise again and again. In mid-November 1939, barely two months after the beginning of the New Order, Lodz's two most beautiful synagogues, one Reform and one Orthodox, were burned to the ground. But before setting fire to the latter, the Germans forced Rabbi Segal, a distant relation of Rywka, to don a tallis and tefillin and desecrate the Torah scrolls.* A host of smaller synagogues, chapels, and study

---

* "Lodz," in *Encyclopedia of Jewish Communities in Poland I*, www.jewishgen.org/yizkor/pinkas_poland/poll-00004.html.

halls were set aflame as well. The horrendous destruction of the holy sites occurred just after the one-year anniversary of *Kristallnacht*, when hundreds of synagogues were put to the torch in Germany in a single night. For Lodz Jews, these events were an excruciating indication of what it meant to be living in the Reich, and they learned something, too, about their chairman's ultimate weakness in the face of the Germans.

In the following month, a far greater shock came in the decree that created ghettoization and affected every Jew in Lodz. Posters announced that within two months, on February 8, 1940, all the Jews—they still numbered 175,000 even though many had already fled—would be required to live in an area of barely one and a half square miles. The segregation was even worse than the confinement imposed on European Jews half a millennium earlier. The medieval and Renaissance ghettos were closed at night but open during the

Ruins of the synagogue on Wolborska Street *(Courtesy of Yad Vashem Photo Archive, Archival Signature 4062/365)*

day for business and other contacts between Jew and non-Jew. The Nazi ghettos would be sealed at all times.

Lodz was one of the very first of the 200 ghettos set up by the invaders, and it would be the longest-lasting. As the only major one "on German 'soil,'"* it would also be the most impenetrable. The Germans demolished all of the houses around the boundary, creating a kind of no-man's-land between the barbed-wire fence and the Aryan side. A special German police guard, the *Schutzpolizei*, known as the *Schupo*, patrolled the perimeter with orders to shoot any Jew for merely approaching the fence. As a result, hundreds were killed whether they were trying to escape or not.

The ghetto in Warsaw, established the following year, would be better known, largely because of its heroic uprising in May 1943. But in the Lodz ghetto, which lacked even a sewer system, it was almost impossible to smuggle in weapons or food, or for anyone to escape. Sealed on April 30, 1940, the Lodz ghetto received no mail, newspapers, or packages from the outside world. There was neither telephone nor telegraph contact, and from the beginning, the possession of a radio was a capital crime.

But the Lodz ghetto was not only completely isolated. It was physically revolting. The Germans had chosen to concentrate the Jews in one of Europe's worst slums. Baluty, a neighborhood on the northern edge of the city that had only recently been incorporated, lacked even streetlights. Flimsy tenements sat alongside warehouses and factories on crooked, unpaved alleys with no concern for sanitation, ventilation, or fire hazard. The quarter was filled with vermin, disease, and crime; it was a nest of drug dealers, prostitutes, and thieves. Before the war, the term "being from Baluty" was synonymous with being a degenerate.

Early on, Rumkowski concluded that the sole chance of survival—that is, avoiding slow starvation or deportation to the east—was for the Jewish

---

* "Anonymous Girl: Lodz Ghetto," in *Salvaged Pages: Young Writers' Diaries of the Holocaust*, ed. Alexandra Zapruder (New Haven, CT: Yale University Press, 2002), 227.

population to make itself useful to the Germans. "Our only path is work," he declared repeatedly. He would take advantage of the extensive industrial infrastructure in Baluty and Lodz's many skilled Jewish artisans to make the ghetto an essential manufacturing center for Germany. In a sense, he succeeded: in more than 100

The fence surrounding the Lodz ghetto and a warning sign in German stating: "Living Area of the Jews. Entrance Forbidden." *(Courtesy of Yad Vashem Photo Archive, Archival Signature 4062/311)*

factories, Lodz Jews produced needed goods that in turn allowed the ghetto to survive well after the liquidation of most of its counterparts, including the ghettos of Warsaw and Krakow. The chairman worked under the chief German ghetto administrator, Hans Biebow, a callous, corrupt businessman in his late thirties. He shipped the finished products at cut-rate prices to the *Wehrmacht* and private German companies, making an illicit profit for himself and his cronies in the process. If Rumkowski raised any objections to Biebow's demands, he was beaten by the much younger man.

Rywka originally worked in an accounting office for the ghetto administration. But soon after beginning her diary in October 1943, she writes of using her personal connections (known by the Hebrew word *protectzia* and often invaluable in the ghetto) to transfer to a large clothing and linen workshop on Franciszkańska Street. It was under the direction of a benevolent employer, Leon Glazer. At least a bit of good fortune had finally come the way of the orphan girl who had been so traumatized in the past two years.

Most schools were closed in the Lodz ghetto after 1941, but Glazer's workshop offered an alternative. As Alexandra Zapruder indicates earlier in this volume, the hundreds of child laborers, among a total workforce of about 1,500, were provided vocational education in the use of sewing machines and the manufacture of clothing. At first, the young workers were also offered classes in Hebrew and mathematics. There were school assemblies and plays, and students set up a lending library. The teenagers even produced a remarkable album entitled *The Legend of the Prince*. It's a long poem, lavishly illustrated in color, in which the oppressiveness of daily life in the Lodz ghetto is masked in the form of a child's fable.*

But in this regard Rywka's experience was an anomaly. Few of the exploited workers in Lodz were able to be so creative, much less receive any educational training. Overall, the laborers were exhausted, malnourished, and often sick. Working conditions were generally atrocious, and the Lodz ghetto may be thought of as an urban slave-labor camp. Rywka was grateful to be learning a trade at Glazer's workshop, but even she complained that the academic subjects were no longer being taught by February 1944. The fourteen-year-old was unhappy, too, about the endless tedium of turning out garments, and she especially chafed at being made to labor on the Sabbath.

---

* Irena Kohn, "The Book of Laughter and Unforgetting: Countersigning the Sperre of 1942 in *The Legend* of the Lodz Ghetto Children," *Partial Answers: Journal of Literature and the History of Ideas* 4, no. 1 (January 2006): 41–78.

Rywka greatly benefited from the midday soup, served in Glazer's workshop as in most factories, but food was a paramount problem from the outset. In 1941 alone, over 2,000 Lodz Jews died of starvation.* Nevertheless, the ghetto actually had more mouths to feed by the fall of 1941 due to the influx of tens of thousands more Jews: well-educated professionals from big cities like Berlin, Vienna, and Prague whom the Reich removed to Lodz. Because they often carried jewelry or other valuables, the arrival of the western Jews sharply drove up the price of food on the black market. Ration coupons were distributed to workers, but the average caloric intake in the ghetto was only two thirds of what was needed for a human being to function, let alone perform manual labor.† In 1942, the rate of starvation more than doubled from the year before, and, except for heart disease, was the ghetto's leading cause of death.‡

The food was of the lowest quality, but the shortage of edibles of any kind created a new social hierarchy. Supplemental rations were awarded for overtime and night work and to those with special skills or occupying the top posts. Sometimes extra coupons went to those from leading families, like Rywka's, whose uncles were prominent rabbis and whose great-grandfather, Rabbi Eliyahu Chaim Meisel, had been chief rabbi of Lodz in the nineteenth century. But with or without extra coupons, malnourishment was prevalent and often pitted family members against one another. The tension in this regard between Rywka and her cousins was all too common.§

Disease, too, was widespread. Tuberculosis, to which Rywka alludes,

* Isaiah Trunk, *Łódź Ghetto: A History* (Bloomington: Indiana University Press, 2006), 208.

† Walter Laqueur and Judith Tydor Baumel, eds., *The Holocaust Encyclopedia* (New Haven, CT: Yale University Press, 2001), 260.

‡ Trunk, *Łódź Ghetto*, 208.

§ Among many examples, see Eva Libitzky and Fred Rosenbaum, *Out on a Ledge: Enduring the Lodz Ghetto, Auschwitz, and Beyond* (River Forest, IL: Wicker Park Press Ltd., 2010), 81–82. A twenty-year-old ghetto worker steals a slice of bread from her ailing mother but is soon filled with remorse.

was rife, but dysentery, typhus, and pneumonia plagued the ghetto as well. Needless to say, medication for any illness was very difficult to obtain, and Lodz Jews often put their faith in remedies ranging from potato peels to a synthetic vitamin known as Vigantol, both thought to have wondrous healing powers. Yet during the life of the ghetto, almost a quarter of its residents died from hunger or disease.[*]

The greatest danger was deportation. In the winter of 1942, tens of thousands of Jews deemed unfit for labor by Rumkowski's administration were issued summonses—"wedding invitations" in ghetto slang—to report to the authorities. No one knew what the deportees were facing, but most assumed it was something even worse than the ghetto, such as hard labor in the mines. Others harbored fears that it meant execution, and death was in fact the fate of the large majority of those expelled by Rumkowski and the Jewish police. Most of them were murdered in Chelmno, less than forty miles from Lodz and a prototype of the more elaborate death camps to come. They were asphyxiated in large, paneled trucks with carbon monoxide pumped through a tube from the exhaust pipe.

In September 1942 came the cruelest deportation, when many thousands more Jews, including the elderly, were taken from their homes, the sick dragged from their hospital beds, and, most appalling of all, children under ten sometimes ripped from their mothers' arms. As Alexandra Zapruder writes, this *szpera*, or general curfew (*shpere* in Yiddish; *Gehsperre* in German), devastated Rywka for the rest of her life, because two of her three siblings, her younger brother, Abramek, aged ten, and sister Tamarcia, five years old, were among those seized. As the oldest child in the family, Rywka had been a surrogate mother to them. Not yet thirteen years old herself, she was helpless in preventing their deportation. Her diary, begun more than a year after the *szpera*, repeatedly evokes feelings of guilt, loss, and anger

---

[*] Raul Hilberg, *The Destruction of the European Jews* (New York: Holmes & Meier, 1985), 96.

about her profound loss. Her sister Cipka, nine years old, somehow avoided capture; she would become all the more precious to Rywka, who shared a tiny dwelling with her and their three older cousins on Wolborska Street, near the ghetto's southern border.

At the outset of the *szpera*, Rumkowski, himself a widower and childless, delivered a speech to more than 1,000 ghetto residents in a central public square, famously imploring them to "Give me your children!" Even in extremis, he felt his course was correct: "I must cut off limbs to save the body itself. Give into my hands the victims so that we can avoid further victims." The typically arrogant chairman, now openly weeping, declared himself a "broken Jew," recalled that he had headed an orphanage, and admitted that he didn't know how he'd survive or where he'd "find the strength."* But when a man in the crowd shouted that each family ought to be left with at least one child, Rumkowski was unmoved. "Brothers and sisters, hand them over to me," he demanded.[†]

Some parents tried to hide their children while others sought to bribe the authorities. But those who simply refused to part with their offspring were shot on the spot. The roundup was carried out by the Jewish police but needed to be supplemented by other ghetto public service workers, all Jews. Their children and parents received exemptions from the deportation. According to the authoritative historian Isaiah Trunk, the weeklong "orgy of murder," which commenced on September 5, 1942, resulted in 15,859 deportations to the Chelmno killing center as well as a minimum of 600 shot to death in the ghetto.[‡] At the conclusion of the operation, about 90,000 Jews remained in Lodz. Nearly every one of them had a child or parent among the victims of the *szpera*.

---

* Chaim Rumkowski, "Give Me Your Children!" in *Łódź Ghetto: Inside a Community Under Siege*, ed. Alan Adelson and Robert Lapides (New York: Viking, 1989), 328–31.

† Ibid., 331.

‡ Trunk, *Łódź Ghetto*, 247.

Women and children on either side of a chain-link fence in the Lodz ghetto. *(Courtesy of Yad Vashem Photo Archive, Archival Signature 4062/459)*

Jews being deported
from the Lodz ghetto.
(Courtesy of Yad Vashem Photo
Archive, Archival Signature
4062/160)

While gloom and deprivation pervaded the ghetto, it remained a major manufacturing center for the Germans for almost two more years. But by the spring of 1944, with the Red Army only ninety miles away on the east bank of the Vistula, Berlin made the decision to liquidate Lodz Jewry while it still had the opportunity. From mid-June through mid-July, over 7,000 more Jews were sent by train to Chelmno and gassed to death there. But the full-scale annihilation of the remainder of the community took place in the month of August. Over 67,000 Jews, including Rumkowski himself, were put on the trains to Auschwitz, where most were killed within hours of their arrival. In Lodz, many Jews at first went into hiding, carefully venturing out at night to scavenge for food, but the Jewish police, augmented by the fire department, was assigned the task of apprehending them.*

The authorities were overwhelmingly successful, and by the end of August, only 1,500 Jews remained in the ghetto.† Some labored in a tailor workshop that was still functioning, but most of them worked directly under the Germans to sort the possessions that the deportees had left behind. Over a five-year period, a community of nearly a quarter million had been almost entirely eradicated. The Soviets finally entered Lodz in January 1945, almost half a year too late. They could identify only 877 survivors.‡

Rywka, her sister, and three cousins left Lodz together in early August 1944 in a cattle car bound for Auschwitz. Each deportee was allowed to take items weighing a total of twenty kilograms, the equivalent of forty-four pounds. Among Rywka's belongings was her diary.

* Libitzky and Rosenbaum, *Out on a Ledge*, 96.

† Trunk, *Łódź Ghetto*, 267.

‡ "Anonymous Boy: Lodz Ghetto," in *Salvaged Pages: Young Writers' Diaries of the Holocaust*, ed. Alexandra Zapruder (New Haven, CT: Yale University Press, 2002), 368.

Part II

THE DIARY OF RYWKA LIPSZYC

TRANSLATED FROM THE POLISH BY
MALGORZATA MARKOFF, WITH ANNOTATIONS
BY EWA WIATR

SUNDAY, OCTOBER 3, 1943

It is after the first holiday (Rosh Hashanah).* It wasn't bad for me personally. Yesterday was Saturday. We had an assembly. Surcia was reading a newsletter. Oh, it was wonderful and so moving! . . . Later we had an assembly with the elders. Mr. Berliner delivered a speech . . . And yesterday after the assembly I noticed that compared to my friends, I am at a higher level and that is why they admire me. In their opinion I know a lot and have many skills . . . Oh, they are so wrong, so mistaken . . . I confided to Ewa about it. She confirmed that I could offer them something, although not all that much, but I could. And I feel that I know so little . . . That I have few skills . . . I have to write a letter to Surcia.

WEDNESDAY, OCTOBER 6, 1943

Just a moment ago Łucki told me to come to the office on Friday (today is Wednesday). Yom Kippur† is on Saturday. I was in the middle of writing a letter to Surcia. Then he said (out of the goodness of his heart) that it would be better

---

* The Jewish New Year.

† Yom Kippur—the Jewish Day of Atonement—is the most sacred day in the Jewish calendar. It is a day of fasting and prayer to atone for the sins of the past year.

for me to work in the workshop so I could learn something.* He asked who my guardian was. I told him that it was Estusia and that she was twenty years old. He wanted her to come tomorrow. He needs to talk to her. Interesting . . .

FRIDAY, OCTOBER 8, 1943

There is a big commotion in the office. It is because tomorrow is Yom Kippur—Judgment Day (or Day of Atonement). But it doesn't matter much to me. Yesterday after work I went to see Zemlówna.† I talked to her about joining the workshop. If she can, she will arrange it. Her brother is some kind of a manager in Glazer's workshop.‡

SUNDAY, OCTOBER 10, 1943

It is after the fast—it wasn't so bad—but I was and still am very weak. I spent almost the entire day in the company of Fela, Sala, Ewa, and Ryfka (Mandelzis). We went down to the street, but not too far. We weren't strong enough. In the evening, after dinner, Cipka, Sala, and I went down again because it isn't very healthy to go to sleep right after eating. We discussed some things, which I should write about, but unfortunately I can't. Maybe I will in the future (it's about my cousins). [. . .]

---

* Rywka uses the Polish word *resort* for factory, workshop, or division, which early on became part of the ghetto's language. Gradually, all of the ghetto's institutions and worksites came to be called *resorty*. Ghetto inhabitants toiled in factories to produce goods for German clients, principally state authorities, such as the military, police, and paramilitary organizations.

† Rywka frequently refers in the diary to Zemlówna, who was the sister of Mr. Zemel, a manager in the Clothing and Linen Workshop and, eventually, Rywka's boss. While it would be customary to render the name as Ms. Zemel, it is not clear how old this person was and whether she was a contemporary of Rywka. Since her identity is not clear, we have left the name as Rywka wrote it throughout the diary.

‡ Leon Glazer ran the Clothing and Linen Workshop at 14 Dworska Street, where workers produced undergarments, dresses, and other clothing inside the ghetto. Several hundred children were employed there and also attended school within the workshop.

TUESDAY, OCTOBER 12, 1943

Today is my last day in the office. I even have a release form from the office and a required document from the workshop. Everything will be arranged today at one p.m., probably. Yesterday I was at Chajusia's (I had to return a book to her), and we talked about the cousins. Later I felt a little strange. My heart is breaking. At the moment, I have no idea why. Yesterday in the office I was reading a novel that I returned to Chajusia later. I was reading A *Sonata of Suffering*. Ah, it is written so well that I really admire the author. There is much in the novel I identify with, but there are also things I oppose. Let's take, for example, faith. I am a religious person. He wanted to believe but he couldn't find solace in faith. It's simply brilliant. But I agree with his internal struggle. Ah, it really got into me. Perhaps that's why my heart broke. As I have mentioned before, at such moments I'd like to be on my own or alone with a person who would understand me. I was visiting Fela Działowska. I tòld her about it but neither I nor she had any more time. Time, this awful lack of time . . . It takes its toll on me (not only on me but on everybody). Ah, I feel now that my heart is breaking . . . God! God! What's going to happen? The world is too small for me. I can't find my own place, but I am sitting on the chair quietly and I am not showing my emotions. If somebody started telling jokes now, I'd burst into laughter. And later I'd say to myself, "This is foolish." What can I do? Yesterday I was lost in my thoughts for a while. I was thinking that a fourteen-year-old girl can be regarded as a child, if we take age into consideration. My friends are the best evidence. But to tell you the truth, the ghetto affects them (it affects me, too) and clearly it doesn't do us any good. Unfortunately, people only take age into consideration, and not brains. They consider me, a fourteen-year-old, to be a child (I am lucky to be nicely developed physically), but they are wrong. I am going to waste. But nobody knows it. I can only feel that if I were older, people would understand me better. Well, I can't move a step forward. Let's suppose that I think a lot, but what's it good for? I am helpless . . .

SUNDAY, OCTOBER 17, 1943

Today is Sukkot and after a long time, this is finally a free Sunday for me.* On Wednesday I was assigned to the school (at 10 Żydowska Street) but I am on a waiting list right now because there is no place for me. I am very glad and, anyway, I get the soup. But I didn't want to write about this. On Friday there was a big mess. After lighting the [Sabbath] candles, Estusia and Minia went to Lola's (they had to bring her something). Something was not right there. The light was on in Lola's apartment but nobody answered the door. It was getting dark. Minia called but there was no answer. They took a walk in the street and when they came back the window was covered. No doubt somebody was in the apartment. Estusia went upstairs and knocked at the door. Suddenly she heard Majer's voice. He spoke very softly, "Go away, I will join you soon." They had no choice, so they came back home. When we found out, we didn't know what to think. Nacia, Bronka, and Pola Dajcz were with us.† [. . .] We had to wait. Minutes seemed like hours. Finally, Lola and Majer showed up. And what happened? The secret police were looking for a neighbor who was hiding in their

---

* Sukkot recalls the wandering of the Israelites after the Exodus from Egypt, during which they lived in fragile huts or booths.

† Rywka is referring (using familiar nicknames) to members of the Dajcz family, who lived in a neighboring apartment (38 Wolborska Street, apartment 15). According to the official registration cards, they included twins Nucha-Brana and Perla-Rajza (born on November 19, 1925), Chejwit-Rywka (born December 5, 1926), and Sura (born November 10, 1928).

place.* That's why they couldn't open the door. But the whole thing wasn't so terrible in the end.

[. . .] Today we are going to the bathhouse. I'm worried again because I can't study . . . Last night I had a dream that I bought a book about nature . . .

TUESDAY, OCTOBER 19, 1943

Tomorrow I am starting work at eight a.m. (Franciszkańska Street 13/15).† What is more, on Thursday we have a third assembly and we will probably organize a show . . . May it be a success! [. . .]

SATURDAY, OCTOBER 23, 1943

The holidays are over. Oh, I have so much to write that I don't know where to start. I know I can't write everything today. On Wednesday I went to school—I liked it very much . . . We were learning how to take measurements for a skirt. Actually, the course is starting on Monday. I'm glad because I haven't been there since [last] Thursday due to the holidays. [. . .] I am still hesitating over whether I should keep writing . . . I have neither patience nor time. Well, no, I will stop . . . [. . .]

---

* This is an allusion to the Special Section (*Sonderabteilung, Sonderkommando*) that was a unit of the ghetto's Order Service or Jewish police. They confiscated goods and carried out roundups on orders from the Germans. Because of their role in plundering personal possessions and seizing people for work or deportation, their presence evoked terror among the ghetto population.

† This address, at the corner of Smugowa Street, originally housed a school, and, after October 1941, served as the temporary quarters of Prague Jews deported to the ghetto. By the time Rywka began writing her diary, the building was used for Glazer's undergarment and clothing factory.

TUESDAY, OCTOBER 26, 1943

I am feeling better but Sunday evening I had a high fever . . . On Sunday we had a lot of work: laundry (not finished yet), windows, bedsheets, some errands in town. Estusia was not feeling well; she had a slight fever and went to bed. I was feeling bad, too, and had a terrible headache. When I came back from town (at the Juvenile Protection Committee I got a ticket to see a dentist),* I was feverish. My temperature kept going up until the evening. Minia changed my bedsheets and made the bed. She was saying all the time that she was such a good cousin, etc. She wanted me to put it in writing.

FRIDAY, OCTOBER 29, 1943

I have very little time. Minia is working in the bank and tomorrow is the day Chanusia will start her trial period and maybe she will work there, too.† Estusia has replaced Minia in the *Treiberiemen-Reparatur.*‡ I was at school today. I am very glad.

I am very anxious but I don't have time to write about it . . . Simply, as

---

* The Juvenile Protection Committee (*Komisja Opieki nad Młodocianymi*), formed on September 22, 1942, placed orphans with foster families on the basis of adoption decrees introduced by Rumkowski. The need for extending special protection over children was apparent after the deportations of September 1942 (the so-called *szpera*), when, despite the Germans' order that all Jewish children be deported as "unproductive elements," many parents were sent away instead, having hidden their children and thus left them without guardians. Rumkowski appealed to families to take in the orphaned children, offering supplemental food rations as incentive, and the Juvenile Protection Committee facilitated and supervised adoption and provided linens, clothing, shoes, and other forms of financial support. Rywka and Cypora Lipszyc, who were orphaned by 1942, were adopted by their older cousins and aided by the JPC.

† The Eldest of the Jews Bank (Bank Przełożonego Starszeństwa Żydów), established on June 26, 1940, was located at 71 Marysińska Street and later moved to 7 Ciesielska Street. Its branch was created on July 8, 1940, at 56 Limanowskiego Street. Among its principal tasks was supervision over the issuance of the ghetto's money, colloquially known as "rumkis" after Rumkowski.

‡ The *Treiberiemen-Reparatur* (transmission-belt repair workshop) was established in August 1942 at the initiative of the *Komisja Fachowa* (Craft Commission) and was located at 4 Plac Kościelny.

Surcia says, I am a restless spirit . . . I need to write, but unfortunately there is no ink in the school, so I leave out many things. Oh . . .

SUNDAY, OCTOBER 31, 1943

Today is Sunday. Estusia and Minia are working. Chanusia is not working at the bank. It is very cold. I am very upset. This morning it came back to me that Abramek and Tamara were deported and that Mama was dead . . . I became so sad, so overcome by pain. And I thought: I laugh, I am cheerful, though I think a lot about them, I also think about other things but I am always full of remorse that I did something one way instead of another. Could I ever imagine that we would be separated? It never crossed my mind. When before the war and at its beginning I was reading some sad books, I'd get very emotional, but once I finished reading I thought, "Yes, it's so beautiful, but it's only a novel. Could it happen in reality?" I couldn't even imagine that I would be left without parents. And today? . . . Today I have gone through it myself. I learn the hard way . . .

WEDNESDAY, NOVEMBER 3, 1943

Recently, in the ghetto, provisions have been scarce and probably our *bajrat*° will be taken away. Oh, I am tired of this . . . Last year they took away our *bajrat*. Minia went to Gertler and thanks to our connections we got it back (along with some other families).† But now nothing will help. Who knows? It's up to God's grace. I am ill at ease . . . [. . .]

° *Bajrat* or B Allotment (Przydział "B") belonged to privileged persons in the ghetto. The Polish term *bajrat* refers to the German *Beirat*, another name for the Council of Elders.

† Dawid Gertler was a person with particularly broad connections in the ghetto. It is possible that Rywka's and her cousins' "connections" had to do with the fact that they were granddaughters of the famous last rabbi of Lodz, Moshe Menachem Segal.

As far as the school is concerned, it isn't bad, I am very pleased. I'll be able to see a dentist for free and get a custom-made coat (thanks to Juvenile Protection).

Oh, my diary, if I could only write what I feel, if I had more time! Oh, I have a heavy heart . . . [. . .]

THURSDAY, NOVEMBER 4, 1943

Today we were using a sewing machine. We were supposed to have other classes, too, but during our first "machine" class not all the girls could sew because there were not enough machines. That's why we had [another] class of machine sewing. I had time to make an "honest stitch."

Besides, I'm very sad (I don't show it but sadness is tearing my heart apart), I yearn for something better, and I miss Abramek and Tamarcia. In the past I used to sing "Kinder yorn" to them . . . I felt so good!*

About two weeks ago Surcia whispered into my ear that when she had been walking with Chajusia she met Estusia and Minia. They told her that I had changed for the better. I was racking my brains over what they meant by that. I can only explain it by the fact that I do more [around the house] than I say. More? Almost everything! So it isn't surprising. But maybe there is something else that I'm not seeing? Maybe Surcia told me that just to make me happy? Oh, my diary, what is going to happen? God only knows!

FRIDAY, NOVEMBER 5, 1943

Today I was late for work. Not only I, but a lot of girls were late. They weren't willing to let us in and they didn't. I went home. Although Cipka

---

* This is likely a reference to a popular Yiddish song, "Kinder yorn" (Childhood), by Mordechai Gebirtig.

arrived late with me, they let her in. I had to bring her breakfast and a soup pot, so the guard allowed me to see her. Just in case, I gave her my *Arbeitskarte** and told her to ask Dorka Zand to get some soup for me. Maybe she will manage to do it . . .

Yesterday I witnessed (I don't know how to call it) a little scene: our house is simply a "madhouse." Last night I wanted to gather some wool for today and I was really about to finish the job. In the meantime all of them lay down and as soon as Chanusia went to bed, she said she couldn't fall asleep and had to turn off the light. I said I would turn it off when I was done. Chanusia didn't wait and turned off the light herself. What was I supposed to do? I turned the light [back] on. I didn't even get to the table when Chanusia turned it off again. [. . .] I felt like crying. I sat down and wept quietly. I was the one who was right . . . [. . .] But I couldn't leave everything right where it had been tossed on the table. For the sake of order and for my own satisfaction, I said loudly, "All day I am busy at home. I don't have a spare moment and when I want to finish something, you don't let me!" [. . .]

MONDAY, NOVEMBER 8, 1943

This morning I was a little anxious before going to school. I hadn't been there for two days and I was afraid that I wouldn't be able to catch up. My fears grew when I saw other girls showing some new skirts (paper designs) to one another. I didn't have any but fortunately I wasn't the only one from a lower grade. A few new girls joined us, so the class was repeated. We had to survive among them; then we had a Hebrew class. The teacher was talking about Sholem Aleichem . . .

Yesterday (Sunday) there was soup for everybody. Perhaps it will be like that every Sunday. Last night I saw Surcia, but both of us had very little

---

* Work identification card.

time. Before we parted Surcia said that she had something to tell me, but she couldn't do it in haste, as we say, and she also wanted to hear my response . . . I'm racking my brains over what it could be . . . I have no time . . .

SUNDAY, NOVEMBER 14, 1943

Tomorrow Estusia is going to be twenty. Chanusia (through Lola) was to buy her a present but they won't manage to do it for tomorrow. Cipka was the most thoughtful and bought her a card. I have no patience . . . I have a cold, I'm coughing . . .

WEDNESDAY, NOVEMBER 17, 1943

Yesterday we had the first snow. We were to pick up some clothes and shoes but we didn't show up on time and so had to do it today. I couldn't go to school, and neither could Cipka, and my nose was running terribly. [. . .] Oh, I wrote a letter to Surcia. I love her more and more. What a pity we don't see each other much . . .

Ewa and Fela told me that as of a little while ago I had changed both for the better and for the worse, that I had become conceited. I reply that it may be because I'm friends with Surcia, etc. . . . Ewa told me that she thought I was gossiping with Surcia about the girls, including about her. Oh, they are so wrong. Maybe they are simply jealous, well, maybe not . . . There is a heavy weight on my heart . . .

WEDNESDAY, NOVEMBER 24, 1943

(I don't have any time to write a diary) . . . I'm sick of my entire life . . . These never-ending grudges of my cousins etc. etc. (besides there is no *bajrat* anymore). [. . .] Oh, dear God, when is it going to end? I don't want to live at all. I have just thought, "What a pity that Jews are not allowed to kill themselves."* It seems that you mustn't even think about it. I can't stand it anymore. I'm writing these words standing at the small table. That's why I'm scribbling so much. It seems to me that I'm not showing my feelings. Maybe a little. Oh, when will there be liberation? Because I really will go crazy . . . I don't have time . . . (Nobody is at home right now.)

SATURDAY, DECEMBER 4, 1943

Unfinished . . . detached, perhaps, and abstract . . . Something is happening in me and I don't know what. Today after the assembly Chajusia said what she thought about each girl. She told me that I knew something, that I felt something, but that I couldn't express it and present it in the proper way. I know this is so. I asked her to tell me more but she didn't. Maybe some other time? . . .

Dorka Zand's mother came back from the "K"† with a broken arm. She went to the hospital. Maybe she will stay there. Dorka looks awful . . .

> Sometimes when I think at night
> Looking at what's "far away"
> I feel like my heart was being squeezed
> And I feel so sorry . . .
> I think about Tamarcia, Abramek,
> Where the cruel fate took them,
> I want to have them back so much,
> Like a flower covered with fresh dew.

---

* Jewish religious law, Halacha, rejects suicide and any measures intended to shorten human life.

† The German Criminal Police (*Kripo*) were located at 6/8 Plac Kościelny in the prewar parish building, known as the Little Red House. This is where the *Kripo* carried out interrogations, often torturing the detained. As a result, this building evoked universal fear among the ghetto's inhabitants.

Then I have dreams, sweet dreams,
I see everybody next to me,
I send them sweet smiles,
I plan their future . . .
But when suddenly a thread
Of the sweet silent dreams is broken,
Then I feel so sorry,
My heart hurts, full of feeling . . .

SATURDAY, DECEMBER 11, 1943

Surcia read my diary. She said that I should write more so I could develop a clear style and that while writing I must control myself. She asked me for a long letter in which I would tell her about my thoughts and feelings and what I thought about human life. She asked me to pay no heed to my level of knowledge. Before I started to write I was very nervous, but it seems that during writing all the nervousness goes away. I only seem to see positive features in Surcia. When I have a problem, I think about her all the time. Oh, there is no shortage of problems. I have to finish, dinner is waiting . . .

Dear Surcia!
Sometimes I think that life is a dark road. On this
road among the thorns there are other, more delicate
flowers. These flowers have no life, they suffer because
of the thorns. Sometimes the thorns are jealous of the
flowers' beauty and hurt them more. The flowers either
become thorns themselves or suffer in silence and walk
through the thorns. They don't always succeed but if
they persevere, something good will come of it. I think it

happens quite rarely but in my opinion every true Jew who is pursuing a goal suffers and keeps silent. Besides, I think life is beautiful and difficult, and I think one has to know how to live. I envy people who have suffered a lot and have lived a difficult life, and yet have won the battle with life. You know, Surcia, such people (when I read or hear about them) cheer me up. I then realize that I am not the only one or the first one, that I can have hope. But I'm not writing about myself.

You know, when I'm very upset I admire life. Then I wonder. Why at the same time are some people crying, while others are laughing or suffering? At the same time some are being born, others die or get sick. Those who are born grow up. They mature in order to live and suffer. And yet all of them want to live, desperately want to live. A living person always has hope (sometimes unconsciously). Although life is difficult, it is also beautiful. Life has its strange charm. (I will tell you the truth: I don't feel like living, it's too much for me, I will go to sleep soon and I don't want to get up.) Oh, Surcia, if I really couldn't get up! Very little will be missing and this paper will be totally wet . . . Surcia. When I give you this letter, it will be over and I will still be alive. But I have no idea if I will be able to cope with this difficult life . . . I doubt it.

Oh, Surcia, I'd love so much to talk to you, to see you. I miss you. You are a big plus in my life. Oh, I can't imagine not knowing the group of you and you in particular. I'd break. But even you won't listen to such a litany of sorrows . . . Oh, you wanted to know what I have been working on recently. Well, I want to make sure that I express the right opinion about this and that, not about things but mainly actions and thoughts, for example whether I make wrong judgments. Please reply. It will be a lesson for me. Your Rywcia is asking you.

Regards!

(Surcia is not well.)

MONDAY, DECEMBER 13, 1943

[. . .] [W]e have found out something ugly about Mania. She was copying poems from books, pretending they were hers. It's very ugly! I'm going to write her a letter to arrange a meeting with her. I want to talk to her! I can see that the girls aren't doing anything and mostly count on me. This annoys me a great deal. [. . .]

Yesterday Miss Zelicka* left me a note to show up at her place tomorrow at noon about some personal matter. I'm very curious . . .

What's more, there is a new order by Biebow that those who will work fifty-five hours a week will receive a coupon (a half kilo [about 1 pound] of bread, 2 dkg [about ¾ ounce] of fat, 10 dkg [about 3.5 ounces] of sausage).† Passes are not being issued and people are speeding up production. This coupon will take away more than it will bring.

I miss Surcia . . . I miss Abramek, Tamarcia. I love them. I have noticed that I love Cipka more and more, when she does something

---

* Fajga Zelicka was a young teacher who had taught in the Beys Yaacov school in Krakow. The school was founded by Sarah Schenirer in 1917 and provided, for the first time, systematic religious instruction for Orthodox girls. Miss Zelicka led meetings and assemblies for religious girls in the ghetto on Jewish subjects and matters of personal development.

† Hans Biebow (1902–1947) was the chief manager of the German Ghetto Administration (*Gettover-waltung*). In this capacity, he held a very powerful and independent position that had a decisive influence on the character of the Lodz ghetto as essentially a forced-labor camp. The ghetto's production brought huge profits for the economy of the Third Reich and for Nazi dignitaries as well. Workers assigned to extended work shifts received special allotments ("L"—*Langarbeiter* or *Lang*).

good, gets good grades (she is the best student), when she understands what happens at the assemblies. It fills me with pride and I feel happy, though not for too long . . .

I'd like so much for everything to be well! Oh! Oh, yes, we are collecting provisions for Dorka Zand. She is not well. [The family] is giving almost everything to their mother who is in the hospital. Probably she will need an operation . . . We'll make sure that she gets her ration through the workshop.

WEDNESDAY, DECEMBER 15, 1943

Dear Surcia!
Yesterday you were very excited (during the assembly we talked about how to organize Hanukkah because all the elders will come) and so was I. You asked me to keep writing, so here we are. Once, when I was at the dentist's, I was thinking: the world is like a mouth, people resemble teeth and like teeth they are sick or healthy. As long as they are healthy, they are useful, everybody defends them; in other words, they are needed. When they get sick, they are either treated and get a little better, or they are abandoned, they get even more sick, their treatment is impossible and then they are removed. They are removed because they are unfit, they can't give anything to the world . . . Surcia, isn't it like that? When I think about human life, I'm surrounded by so many thoughts, oh, we can only talk about it! And now, Surcia, I'd like to get a letter (a reply) from you! And more, and more!

Now, I will tell you something different! There are some incidents at home when I don't know what to do.

Once I prayed for somebody to appear in my dream to advise me . . . And I have noticed, let's say in a book, that if somebody who is older (never mind how old he is) has done something wrong, a younger person admonishes him in a very effective way. To my mind, this is just the author's fantasy. Such things rarely happen in real life. I am the best proof of it . . .

Besides, Estusia claims that I don't have a bit of good taste. I, obviously, never respond, but I want to know if it is true. When I, for example, do something and fail, but can correct it easily (we learn from our mistakes), she talks so much that not only doesn't she encourage me to correct it, [. . .] [but] she puts me off. [. . .] Or, when somebody else has done something wrong, she then uses categories, [calling them] Rywcia No. 2 and that sort of thing. What is she thinking? And one more thing, she isn't bashful in front of people, and that's the worst. Every day is like that . . .

Oh, Surcia, I'm so miserable, no wonder I don't feel like doing anything. And I repeat again, if it weren't for you, I don't know . . . Write to me, Surcia!

Yours,

Rywcia. Regards.

I don't have any time.

I'm adding: Surcia paid us a visit. [. . .] She brought me a reply to my previous letter in which she wrote she hadn't known that we were kindred spirits. And plainly she had wanted to see such a letter. We made a date for Friday.

SATURDAY, DECEMBER 18, 1943

Oh, I have so much to write about . . . Yesterday (Friday) I went to see Surcia. She let me read some fragments from her diary and while I was reading I noticed that I had so much to write myself . . . She showed Miss Zelicka my letter in which I wrote about life. That's why Miss Zelicka sent me a notice through Surcia that she'd like to talk about it on Tuesday at eleven a.m. It's so unexpected . . . [. . .] She told me to prepare myself . . . I'm thinking about it a great deal . . .

Today during the assembly we discussed staging a little comedy for Hanukkah. I'll play the interior minister. Later I talked to Chajusia. She told me that I should try to write a lot in my diary. And that I should study a lot . . . generally everything . . . Oh, I'd love to. I do have a desire to study . . . My inner life is so complicated . . . Both Chajusia and Surcia keep saying "chin up," but my chin is dropping . . . and it's difficult to lift it . . . Difficulties, difficulties . . . difficulties go hand in hand with sadness . . . Oh, now I realize how much I have thought and wondered about life.

[. . .] Whenever I say the word "life" I feel I'm standing before some power, some enormity. But what are human words worth? They express so little. I have just written an entire page but I haven't even described my feelings. It isn't easy and when one manages to succeed, it is beautiful. Oh, difficulties and beauty . . . Do they fit together? Perhaps yes. It seems to me that I'm lost in nonsense. I have no time. Estusia is telling me to do something. She could do very well without it. I'm losing my concentration . . . Oh, I can't stop writing. I feel I have so much to write. Dorka Zand is sick, the glands on her lungs are enlarged . . .* Her mother is getting better . . .

---

* Tuberculosis (TB)—colloquially called "Koch" in the ghetto (from the name of Robert Koch, who discovered the bacilli that cause the disease)—was a major cause of death in Lodz. The death rate rose from 8.9 percent of all deaths in 1940 to fully 39 percent during the final period of the ghetto's existence. Some 7,269 people lost their lives due to TB in the Lodz ghetto. See Leksykon [in:] *Kronika getta łódzkiego* . . . , vol. 5, s. 303.

MONDAY, DECEMBER 20, 1943

Today we celebrated the twenty-sixth wedding anniversary of Mrs. Kaufman. Our class bought her a mess kit—the FF type.* We didn't have a lesson, we were singing. Miss Sabcia is a lot of fun . . . It was really entertaining, but I felt that the atmosphere was artificial. Minia told me that on joyful occasions like this she has a heavy heart. I noticed a tear dropping from her eye. I don't have any time for writing . . . Maybe later.

WEDNESDAY, DECEMBER 22, 1943

I took some ink to school because I have so much to write . . . Yesterday I talked to Miss Zelicka . . . She told me that Surcia had talked about me a lot and that she—Miss Zelicka—was not only a social worker or a guardian from Juvenile Protection, but a member of Surcia's group, so our relationship is not just a formal one. What's more, she told me that she had talked to Estusia (she asked me to be totally sincere; well, how can I be sincere? . . . After all, am I here to complain?). Certainly, I had no idea what they talked about. She told me that I should learn from Estusia's vigor because it may come in handy. Because a person who is strong in spirit but has no vigor is somehow sluggish. And a person who is both energetic and resourceful is superior to a sluggish one. I should learn from Estusia about this energy, this resourcefulness in life. [. . .]

Sure, I understood what she was telling me, I understood it well. But I couldn't understand one thing at all, namely, what the reason was that she had called me. It was a mystery to me. Finally, Miss Zelicka said that I was

---

* This refers to one of several different kinds of mess tins used in the Polish, German, and American military. It would have been a metal container that held food, soup, or the like and that could be hung from a belt.

an exception in our group and I could always come to see her. She would always find time for me. She told me to think about it . . .

Sure thing, I thought about it. But I was more curious why she had called me at all . . . [. . .] Cipka knew that I had seen Miss Zelicka so I reluctantly asked her if she knew what was the subject of the conversation between Miss Zelicka and Estusia. Thanks to Cipka I found out. Estusia said I was stubborn, that before I came to live with them I wasn't obedient and in the beginning I was being hysterical. In other words, she presented me in a dazzlingly negative light. At that point I understood. I didn't and I don't know what to do. First, I have to talk to Surcia. I'm boiling inside . . . I feel that my eyes are covered. I can't see, but I have to see. I can't find a place for myself. I don't share anything with anybody, only with my diary and Surcia, my beloved Surcia. I don't know anything, oh, I don't know anything, I'm helpless . . . What's going to happen? What shall I do? Whom shall I ask, who's going to help me? Oh, there are so many questions and no answers. [. . .]

THURSDAY, DECEMBER 23, 1943

I was elected to the literature club . . . Today at seven I'm going to the tailor's. I will have seal fur on the collar and lapels, as well as a winter cap. [. . .]
At night I had an argument with Minia. Really, I don't recall about what (something about a chair). I only know that I was very upset and when I went to bed I felt like crying. Fortunately, I could cry, but very little. Honestly, I wanted to die. I tried to regain some balance, but I'm tired of life. I thought: I know that now when I want to die, I won't die. I'll die when I want to live, when I have a purpose in life. Who needs such a life? Isn't it better to die when there is no purpose, and not when you want to live? Those questions were left unanswered. Suddenly, I had an urge to talk to Surcia, to tell her that I don't know anything, can't do anything, don't understand anything . . .

Now, I don't feel that I know very little. I know nothing. I tried to catch up with my friends, but, well, they are so different . . . I need a school, I need to study . . . I repeat myself . . . I feel I'm tied up, I can't move. What's going to happen? [. . .]

Oh, I'm so far from being happy . . . But why am I writing all this? Can I do without it? Oh, I'm fed up . . . Last night I thought: happy is a person who is unaware, totally unaware, like a child. Unhappy is a person who is aware of his unawareness . . . I belong to the latter category. I'm miserable. What's worse, I can't find any solution. I don't know what to do . . . it's the same over and over again . . . I have only one answer to everything: Surcia. Oh, Surcia . . .

FRIDAY, DECEMBER 24, 1943

Oh, to write! . . . To be able to write, to make pen move on paper! I need to write. [. . .] At this moment, I'm thinking about the passionate emotions. And I'm thinking about Surcia. I feel I love her more and more. Oh, I feel true affection for her. Oh, power of love! Oh, it's a real power. [. . .] I want to write more, and maybe I'll express myself. I do feel affection for Surcia. Maybe not for her, but for her soul, which means for her, after all. Oh, Surcia. I take delight in the sound of her name. (It's good that we are of the same sex.) Otherwise, what would it look like, such writing? I'm completely honest with my diary. But I shouldn't digress from the subject! She is the only one allowed to read my diary and I'm not embarrassed at all.

Oh, I love so few people . . . So, when I do love somebody, the affection is stronger than in other cases. She and my siblings . . . Oh, I wish I could have them all with me!!! Every letter, every word she utters is almost sacred. I feel an even stronger bond with her. [. . .]

(It was a good idea to bring my diary, a pen, and ink to school. Otherwise, nothing would be written.) Oh, words are so empty, they express so little. In my opinion, with words one can only discuss ordinary, common things. Between people who love each other words desecrate everything. Those people can communicate without words. Their souls and eyes can speak, their emotions speak, they can feel . . . But why I am writing all this? Again, a question without an answer . . . Sometimes I wonder what would happen if I didn't know Surcia at all? . . . I don't know. I can't imagine it. I can appreciate my good luck. Emotions . . . I can't express myself with words, it's much easier for me to express myself with emotions . . . But enough. Today I will meet Surcia, may there be no obstacles!!!

SUNDAY, DECEMBER 27, 1943

[. . .] Those who had *bajrat* now get it only for one person. I wanted to get it yesterday but we were removed from the list. Maybe Estusia will arrange it . . . As for my cousins, I'd rather ignore them because it may all turn into *lashon hara** but I will write one thing: if we get a ration for five people, that's fine, but if only for three or one, I have to be strong enough to refuse it, even if they offer me something. I have nothing against them but I don't want anything, that's it.

Yesterday Chanusia collected the ration that was given by the chairman†—meat and sausage. She put a slice of sausage on Cipka's bread and it happened that she had to leave. Before Cipka ate it, Estusia showed up and when she saw Cipka eating she asked, "Is it the old sausage?"

"No, today Chanusia got a fresh one."

"She gave it to you?" asked Estusia.

She said it so casually but I heard it well. I promised myself that I'd never, never take anything from them. I can be that ambitious. When they

---

* Literally "tongue of evil" in Hebrew/Yiddish, meaning gossip or speaking the truth for bad purposes, which is specifically prohibited in Jewish law.

† The Jewish leader of the ghetto was Mordechai Chaim Rumkowski, known by the Polish title *prezes* (chairman) and in German as *Judenältester* (Eldest of the Jews).

(but not Chanusia) offer something that is theirs, they do it as if it were just an obligation, as if they had to. No, thanks . . . But enough of this. I didn't even want to write about it.

On Friday I met Surcia. She told me that Miss Zelicka was surprised (in a positive way) that I could judge (I can't find a better word) my situation like an adult . . . Somehow my writing is heavy going. [. . .]

THURSDAY, DECEMBER 30, 1943

I have so much to write. I'm excited. But I must start from the beginning. The evening was generally a success. Watching the comedy, the audience was laughing. Playing their roles, Dorka and Ruta Maroko were laughing, too. We had to wait for a long time before the top people showed up. When Bala Działowska came, she suggested that two girls should go to Miss Zelicka to find out what was going on. Dorka Borensztajn and I were chosen. Oh, what a walk we had! I'm not going to write much about it but I compared it to life. It went quite well. We fell only once. The courtyard between Żydowska Street and Brzezińska Street was long and dark. The path through was slippery and wet. I walked more boldly than Dorka, with my head up. Oh, if I could only walk through life with my head up!!!

Miss Zelicka had a cold and was in bed. She told us that Mrs. Milioner and others had just left and that she had sent a letter to us through them. She added that her spirit and her thoughts were with us and that she was delighted with our joy. When we came back, it had just started. Surcia was reading a paper. I won't describe it because I can't . . .

When it ended, Surcia and Chajusia handed out Hanukkah gelt and small notebooks among our girls.* In the notebooks there were comments

---

* *Gelt* (literally, money) was the traditional gift of coins to Jewish children during Hanukkah, the eight-day holiday in December that commemorates the Maccabees' heroic victory over Syrian Greek rulers, who had desecrated the Temple in Jerusalem, and its rededication.

written about each of them. When it was over I felt very sad and my heart was heavy. [. . .] Dear God, in order to save myself from such emotions, I shouldn't have a good time at all, nothing, nothing . . . no fun? . . . God, it's so hard! [. . .] Now I'm at the school in the classroom, but I can't write more because the break is over . . .

WEDNESDAY, DECEMBER 31, 1943

Today I can continue writing . . . So, in our class . . . I wrote about the literature club. I was elected to it, but later the girls were arguing. Some were against me. [. . .] Edzia told me all about it later. They wanted me to be in the club because I could be useful by writing, for example, articles for the school newspaper. Although I felt insulted, I couldn't now refuse (it would look like Edzia was turning me against them), but I did want to withdraw . . . The girls gathered in the evening, but who came? Very few older girls, mostly kids. The chairmen were not there. Oh, nonsense . . . just a headache, nothing else . . .

Yesterday Lusia said that they (Edzia, Hela, Jadzia, and Marysia Łucka) (again Marysia Łucka) and somebody else have a club, read literature, and publish a school newspaper. They want me to join them. Literature! Oh, I want to read it! [. . .]

I brought Miss Zelicka some pound cake and went to the tailor's to try on my cap. On the way back I stopped by at Chajusia's. She asked me to express my feelings and impressions about the "soirée." Somehow I can't . . . my heart is heavy. [. . .] Oh, my heart . . . I don't know if I could find some comfort in writing. Oh, if I could only write as much as I want! But I can't. As for my cousins (yesterday they received a B ration, for one person—probably there will be new categories "L," "S," and "N").* I have decided,

---

* "B" ration was short for *bajrat*, or "special food coupon." An "L" ration was for workers putting in long shifts (*Langarbeiter*), "S" was for those doing hard physical labor (*Schwerarbeiter*), and "N" was for those working at night (*Nachtarbeiter*). These special rations were introduced by Hans Biebow toward the end of 1943.

as I mentioned before, not to use what is exclusively theirs. Cipka can't overcome it, she's just a kid, but I succeed and it pleases me. Sure, if they buy something, for example, onions, garlic, things like that, then I take it, even if they didn't want me to, because it is shared—mine and theirs—but the ration . . . but the ration . . . it's a different story. I admire myself for how easy it is for me. I'm curious how it will develop, because so far the cousins haven't noticed anything. I'm curious how they will react . . .

Oh, I have so much to write and to think about, but it's difficult. Oh, the bell is ringing . . .

MONDAY, JANUARY 3, 1944

[. . .] Yesterday we had a meeting [of the other literature club] at Marysia Łucka. (From now on I'll have to name every assembly.) We read [Bolesław] Prus's short story "From the Legends of Ancient Egypt." Generally, I like everything, and most important, I can reap benefits from it. Later we made plans for the future. Once a week we'll study only literature or something else, and on Sundays we'll also have one hour of fun (so we won't turn into old bags). Boys will be allowed to join us. Yesterday I wasn't pleased and I didn't even talk about it. But now I'm happier because, first, they have their opinions and if I don't like them, I can tell them, and, second, I'll be with Lusia, Hela, and Edzia and I'll get to know them better.

That assembly made me think. Toward the end we touched on the subject of Communism, Bundism, etc. Lusia said she was a Zionist, so did Hela and Maryla Łucka. Jadzia didn't have any opinion. Finally, Lusia said that I was a Zionist for sure. I didn't respond, but I decided to talk to Lusia because she was wrong. I was thinking all the time: I, a Zionist; Maryla Łucka also a Zionist; Jadzia, too, they are all Zionists, so is she? It didn't make any sense. When we were going home, I asked Lusia what she meant by saying that we were Zionists. She started talking about the Zionist idea (the worst thing is that I can't express myself), but somehow we came to an agreement. What is ours, our idea is called Zionist by Lusia. Truly Jewish, ours. And Maryla and Jadzia have nothing to do with it. They just liked the idea, they took on its name, but there is nothing deep in it. I was relieved. [. . .]

WEDNESDAY, JANUARY 5, 1944

Yesterday during the assembly Chajusia was registering girls for the courses. (Surcia couldn't do it because she fell and hurt her arm terribly.) She was to divide the group but it was getting very late. I'm glad that the group will be divided, but I'm worried that Surcia and Chajusia will be separated. Everybody wants Surcia; I do, too, but Chajusia? . . . Chajusia told me that she and Surcia would prefer an older group, which is understandable . . .

Many girls from our class show up (Dorka Zand announced that I wanted to convert [!] the entire class). Oh, I wish I could do it! I'm not asking them to come; they want to do it themselves and give me quite good reasons, but most important is their "will." They really want to do it! . . . At first, I was registering the girls for the courses, but Prywa says that not all of them are qualified, that they will show up once and will jeer at it. Well, I'll ask Surcia . . . Oh, it's so great that I have Surcia and can often seek her advice! Probably on Friday I'll bring her my diary. I'd like my writing to be clearer. I think many things in the diary will scare her . . . Anyway, I don't conceal anything from her, but if there were anything like that, we'd talk about it.

(Today at six the girls from the literature club are coming. As far as that [other] club is concerned, I resigned and somehow they don't ask me to come.) [. . .]

I want to talk about myself . . . Yesterday I wanted to write, i.e., I felt I had something to write, but even if I had time, I wouldn't know what to write, I simply forgot. I have become such a scatterbrain. In the past when I was told something, I remembered it, even woke up in the middle of the night, and today? (Oh, the bell is ringing).

I wanted to write about Tamarcia, oh, sometimes I'm full of remorse. I don't know what's going to happen? Oh, it's so hard . . . In my imagination I see several pictures . . . several . . . even if one of them is pleasant and I find some consolation in it, I can't find a place for myself . . . I'm so exhausted (a few people told me that I looked worse). It doesn't matter, maybe it's because there is no *bajrat*. I have no idea . . . I feel so strange . . . I can't express it . . . I can't find a place for myself.

THURSDAY, JANUARY 6, 1944

Estusia is not well. She has a high fever. That's just what I need. And I . . . I don't know what's happening to me. I don't know what to do . . . I grasp at straws . . .

Yesterday I came to the conclusion that I liked being alone at home. [. . .] I realized that when I was alone I was in a different world, living my inner life. When there is somebody else at home, e.g., my cousins or the neighbors, I feel ill at ease (at a loss). When I'm alone and my girlfriends come to visit, I'm relaxed, and although I don't "go into ecstasies in my other life," I can occasionally share a thought with them (it happens quite rarely and the girlfriends don't come too often). That's why yesterday I couldn't get lost in my thoughts (I had to watch the gruel cooking), but my thoughts were escaping me and I could hardly keep my balance.

FRIDAY, JANUARY 7, 1944

Friday . . . oh, I like Friday evenings! I made a date with Surcia! Lusia wants to visit her, too. All right (we'll talk about Zionism). Mania is to visit me right after lighting the [Sabbath] candles, she has to talk to me . . . When I come back from Surcia's, Fela will come, so my Friday evening is very busy (from now on all my evenings will be busy).

I was at Fela's yesterday. I was very sorry that I didn't visit her when she was sick (yesterday she was already dressed). She was supposed to visit me, but she acted out of wounded pride and . . . I'm glad she didn't come, because I'd be even more sorry. Her father was holding a grudge against me because I hadn't shown up all that time. I really wanted to, but every day I had so much to do . . . Estusia has the flu. Generally, there is flu in the ghetto (an epidemic).*

Oh, really, I describe "external" life so much that I won't have time to write about my "inner" life . . .

A woman from Żydowska Street has just come, the one who disburses money. I haven't received my ten-day payment for three months and I don't have time to take care of it . . . but enough of this . . .† A few days ago I realized that I really was thinking about many problems, but at moments when I couldn't write (it happens mostly when I'm peeling the potatoes). Every time I think about it, I repeat a verse I made (I didn't even write it down):

Oh, to write, to write, as long as I breathe,
About everything, my diary!

---

* On January 10, 1944, the authors of the Lodz ghetto chronicle wrote about the severe flu epidemic, reporting that 50 percent of the factory and department staffs were ill. Nearly all of the afflicted had temperatures of 104°F and were sick for seven to ten days. The ghetto's pharmacies and its physicians could not keep up with the demand for medical care, leaving most of the sick to fend for themselves. See Lucjan Dobroszycki, ed., *The Chronicle of the Łódź Ghetto, 1941–1944* (New Haven, CT: Yale University Press, 1984), January 10, 1944.

† This probably refers to a small welfare grant that Rywka was entitled to as an orphan. It was apparently paid three times a month, every ten days, though it would not have been much money. In general, in the ghetto, money had little value because food shortages drove up black-market prices. Few could afford to buy anything beyond their rations.

Emotions again . . . again the same . . . I think that my diary could be called "Surcia," because she was indeed the person who inspired my writing and . . . generally everything else . . . But I'm losing the thread . . .

[. . .] (As far as the school literature club is concerned, I didn't go to any meetings. When they were preparing a list of the members, Guta asked me if I was planning to attend. I replied I didn't have any time, which was the honest truth. There are not enough days in the week for me.)

FRIDAY, JANUARY 14, 1944

I haven't written for a while . . . Surcia is reading my diary . . . She sent me a letter that I'll be able to read over and over again, and find new things in it. A week has passed and I haven't written anything, so it's not surprising that I have something to write.

On Sunday my tooth was extracted. Horrible, the roots of this tooth were under a different tooth. I don't want to describe it, but I'll add that today (Friday) my face is swollen . . . Flu pervades the ghetto, wherever you go, flu is everywhere . . . in the workshops and offices there is nobody . . . a lot of sick leaves. (Mr. Zemel joked that he would place the sick leaves at the machines so they could continue production.) Mrs. Markus is sick, too, I don't know exactly what's wrong with her (Icykzon will come today); she has a high fever. That's why Minia isn't going to work today. Chajusia has the flu, Surcia's mother, too . . . I'll run out of pages to write down who is sick . . . It affects the assemblies . . . all of them.

Last week I didn't get any soup, although my ID card was stamped (other girls didn't get the soup, either). Every day we went to Żydowska Street. They were postponing it, and on Wednesday they announced that it wasn't their responsibility. Sala Skórecka and I went to the Trade and Control Bureau (TCB) to see Perl (in the beginning I worked for him in the Central

Accounting Office,* but then he moved to the TCB).† He said the inspection was coming . . . When I was there, I stopped by the accounting office. Only Rachelka Bejmówna was in the secretary's office . . . the flu . . . Maryla Łucka and her father are sick, too. In Mrs. Lebenstein's family everybody is sick except her; Samuelson is sick; Jankielewicz has replaced Berg because Berg is sick. Rundberg, half-sick, came in the afternoon . . .

In our literature club we published a little newspaper . . . marvelous, really marvelous . . . I've written two poems. Here is one of them:

Memories . . .

I remember my brother . . .	*I remember him and I sigh*
I remember my father . . .	*Something weighs on my heart*
And a female figure.	*My eyes are foggy*
It was my mommy . . .	*I'm about to cry . . .*
I remember my school,	
my friends,	*I ask myself a question: Why?*
my teachers,	*Isn't there in the world*
And my classes . . .	*a warmer place?*

I remember this question with nostalgia	
It remains a question	*And my heart aches,*
And offers nothing	*Oh, enough, enough*
But a greater suffering . . .	*Of this terrible misery!*

---

* The Central Bookkeeping Office (Main Treasury) supervised the circulation of money in the ghetto, supplied the ghetto currency to all ghetto institutions, and accepted all forms of payment that flowed into the ghetto's institutions. See *Leksykon,* entry "Kasa Główna," p. 309.

† The Trade and Control Bureau (*Fach- und Kontrollamt*), or FUKR, was charged with eradicating economic crimes and abuse in the ghetto. In this capacity, its staff exercised control over the activity of the departments and the Jewish administration in the ghetto, and could summarily dismiss officials and search homes and offices.

This suffering
It's joined by longing
And it's tearing my
heart apart
And it's battering my heart
Horrible longing
Lethal longing
For my brother, my sister.

For my mother and my father.

I have no answer
Maybe this one:
"We Jews! We Jews!"

Something is boiling inside me
I will never know peace!

I ask again: Aren't there enough
Hardships and difficulties?
I cry and cry!
(My voice can't be heard)
What's going to happen?
What's going to happen?
What's going to happen? Damn it!
Right now

[. . .] A long time ago I noticed—and Surcia brought it to my attention in her letter—that I liked suffering . . . but it's hard and I'm afraid I'll break down . . . I'm afraid . . . I remember very well that when something (serious) happened, everybody was going crazy, but deep down at the bottom of my soul there was always a place for some other feeling.

My heart was growing . . . But I can't compare myself to Rabbi Akiba.* [He] was a scholar. He knew how to behave, what to do . . . and . . . [. . .] I know so little that I become helpless, I don't know what to do, I can only see black spots of ignorance . . .

---

* Rabbi Akiba was a major figure in the development of rabbinic Judaism. He is often quoted and cited in the Mishnah and Talmud. He was martyred by the Romans, ca. 135 CE.

SATURDAY, JANUARY 15, 1944

It's horrible . . . I feel I'm losing my balance . . . Both of Surcia's brothers and her mother are sick . . . Chajusia is sick . . . Yesterday I visited Surcia. She showed me some of her poems. Oh, I thought I was reading my own . . . What a resemblance! . . . Today neither Chajusia nor Surcia attended the assembly. Earlier Chajusia had given us an article from a magazine to read: "Tsulib a kleyn bashefernish" ["On Account of a Small Creature"].

On the way back Ewa and I stopped by at Chajusia's to return the magazine. We talked about the *szpera.** Ewa talked to her heart's content and it seems that she got it off her chest. I kept silent, what was I supposed to say? . . . Chajusia told us how they all had managed to save themselves on Czarnieckiego Street.† They were there during the *szpera.* That conversation, the whole thing upset me . . . I don't feel well . . . Oh, I have no strength . . . my heart has become a heavy stone . . . I'm choking, choking . . .

And now a story . . . Fela came over today and told me that Kałmo (a younger brother of Dorka Zand) had borrowed potatoes and rutabaga from her without informing anybody at home. He borrowed from Dorka Borensztajn, too. Oh, he is a swindler. Oh, I feel sorry for Mrs. Zand and Dorka. [. . .]

I really don't want to go to work on Monday . . . well . . . it's unbearable . . . I can't find a place for myself, but will I feel better if I don't go to work? Not at all . . . Yesterday Surcia was reading me some fragments from Psalms. Oh, it's marvelous and so up to date. One can understand it, feel it [. . .] Oh, suffering is necessary. But enough, people suffer in their ordinary lives, too.

---

* *Szpera* (literally "curfew") refers to the tragic events of September 5–12, 1942, when the German authorities carried out a series of roundups to purge the Lodz ghetto of the sick, the elderly, and children under the age of ten. More than 15,000 people were forcibly removed and transported to the killing center of Chelmno, where they were put to death.

† During deportations, those who were designated for transport out of the ghetto were held at the Central Prison located on Czarnieckiego Street.

Everything should have its limits . . . I'm afraid to write a letter to Surcia again, because instead of cheering her up, I'd write something different . . .

[. . .] Oh, I'm so exhausted . . . I'm full of remorse because Abramek and Tamarcia were deported. Oh, God! Bring them back to me, I can't stand it, my heart is going to break . . . Abramek, where are you? Tamarcia! Oh, I can't! I can't! I need strength, oh . . . I feel like weeping . . . I feel like a lump of stone, I can't even cry . . . Oh, go to hell, you plunderers and murderers . . . I'll never forgive you, never. But in the face of "them" I'm helpless . . . What's more, nowadays at home they talk about the dead . . . Today at two o'clock one neighbor died, she fainted and . . . that's it . . . she was a healthy woman . . . when will it end? When will this endless suffering end? I'll go crazy . . . I need strength . . . God! Strength!

MONDAY, JANUARY 17, 1944

Chanusia has the flu . . . Mrs. Markusowa is feeling better. We had a math class at the school today. The best machines were moved to the lecture room and we'll be with the third group . . . There was no assembly yesterday at Maryla Łucka's (we were at her place the whole time), her mother is sick and . . . Generally, it's the flu . . . a serious obstacle.

On Tuesday we have a general assembly with everybody and on Wednesday something like a session, only the old and older. Until now when we have come to the assemblies, it has been so comfortable, we have been like one, but today we feel strangely alienated . . .

Yesterday when I was walking in the street, I was dreaming . . . I had this picture before my eyes: a barely lit room, warm. A few kids are sitting at the table, they are busy with something or they are listening to what I'm reading. I'm reading about the ghetto, I'm telling them stories, and I can see their surprised eyes. It's boggling their minds that something like that could happen . . . Oh, I wish this time would come. I long for it so much . . . I'm cold and hungry. I'm cold not only because of the winter but because I lack inner warmth. I'm hungry not only because I have little food and can't fill my stomach, but because I'm starved and thirsty, because I feel like a vast vacuum, and this place is cold and empty (hunger). Oh, to get warmer! . . . Yesterday in order to get our rations we had to bring our own bags (I was making them yesterday at Chajusia's). They don't give away the rations in *tytkas*˚ anymore. What's more, we have to carry all of them a long way . . .

It's cold around my heart. When I felt it, I recalled a story about a poor boy and an old man. The boy said, "When my feet are cold, I can stamp them, when my hands are cold, I can rub them." So he was enumerating all this and when he got to the heart, he had no advice how [to] warm it up. The old man handed him a coat to warm up his heart and told him, "My boy, take care of your heart, because it's most important. Make sure it never gets cold!" [. . .]

I've written a letter to Surcia but I'm going to upset her. I've written, as I would in my diary, that I can't stand it anymore, that I'm losing my strength.

WEDNESDAY, JANUARY 19, 1944

Again I have very little time. The classes at the school are almost normal . . . But I don't want to write about it . . . When Surcia came to the assembly yesterday, she was cheerful. Her mother is feeling better . . .

At night, going to bed, I involuntarily reached for the pouch filled with photos . . . I looked at a few of them. Oh, God . . . when I saw Tamarcia's picture I suddenly realized that she was [now] six, going on seven years old. At her age I was going to school! . . . Oh, it would be so wonderful if all the children could go to school! . . . My eyes were filled with tears . . . Through the fog of my tears, I saw Tamarcia's frightened eyes (that's how she looked in the picture) . . . Oh, I'm afraid to write about it . . . She looked like she was

---

˚ Small stacks.

calling me, like she was crying for help . . . I did nothing . . . I was in bed, I couldn't even cry . . . my heart was pounding and trying to break free . . . I did nothing . . . Oh, Tamarcia, where are you? I want to help you . . . I'm tossing and turning, well, I'm tied down . . . Oh, how many tragedies are contained in these words!? I'm scared, I miss her, I'm drenched with cold and hot sweat. A drowning person will grasp even a razor . . . I want to become lost in words, think about something different, but this helplessness, this weakness are surfacing . . . [. . .] What's next? One can't live like this anymore! . . . Oh, strength! Strength! Dear God! Strength! All of a sudden I ask myself anxiously if I'll recognize Tamarcia. Years are passing by! . . .

Oh, God! How can I not think about it? How can I take it? . . . I looked into my mama's eyes (in the photo). Oh, God! How much they express and how much Tamarcia resembles her! Oh, I'll never tell you this, Mommy! You've left me forever! I feel horrible, I'm suffocating! God, let me take the place of my mother. Let me suffer for my siblings! Oh, God! It's so hard! . . . And I'm always alone! . . .

THURSDAY, JANUARY 20, 1944

I've noticed that I'm looking for inspiration . . . in memories. Oh, I've just remembered something . . . When I was talking to Surcia about Zionism, Surcia said that in a book the content is more important than the style (i.e., the Torah is the content, but Palestine is the style). If it has both content and style, it's far more beautiful as a whole, but the content is the most important thing. [. . .] That's why I'm not surprised anymore that the Zionists put Palestine in the first place, and the Torah in the second place. Others don't care about the Torah at all. They are not mature enough to understand it . . . In this respect they are like foolishly naive children . . . Poor things! . . .

Oh, God! I feel blessed to have been born in a family like ours, not in any other . . . After all, I was lucky . . . I can appreciate this good luck.

FRIDAY, JANUARY 21, 1944

Friday! . . . Every week I wait impatiently for Friday evening and Saturday . . . I don't know, I can't imagine at all what would happen if we didn't have this one Saturday (and Friday evenings). (This is a winter day.) I feel so good. I can think and dream (I have time then). Oh, dream, dream and forget. [. . .] Let me dream! It's a completely different world. I have some life experience so even a dream isn't something charming and magical for me. In my dreams I struggle with life, with this giant . . . The only difference here is that I'm doing it for somebody; I'm doing it with pleasure and I feel wonderful . . . [. . .] Maybe somebody who is watching me will nod and say, "Poor child, her dreams are really pipe dreams!" But that's what they are. It's a relief for me to move into a dreamworld . . . Dreams, oh, may they come true! . . .

As soon as Chanusia recovered from her flu, Chaja got sick the same day. But she's feeling better, she has no fever anymore . . . Though it's January 21, we haven't had any serious frost yet. To the contrary, it's like March weather, puddles and mud. That's why the flu has spread so widely. Last week we had a little ground frost and the flu disappeared, but when it's slushy it comes back . . . I haven't seen such a winter in my entire life . . .

I'll light the candles in a few hours . . . and then? Oh.

MONDAY, JANUARY 24, 1944

From the letter to Surcia:

Oh, Surcia, I have so much to write to you that I'm afraid I won't write anything.

But let's get to the point! I had a headache on Saturday and wasn't feeling well. Besides, I had a problem, because, as you may know, on Saturday, January 8, I didn't get soup. This Saturday (we're still in bed) Hela Jochimowicz came and said that the TCB inspection was at school. I was on the attendance list and she told me to go to school because they might check it. In ten minutes I was in the workshop. The inspector asked me many questions, wrote down what I said on my behalf, and told me to sign it. I replied that I wouldn't write on Saturdays [because of the Sabbath]. Everybody smiled and the inspector wanted to make sure that I'd sign it eventually. He said he'd come back on Monday. He hoped that the other girl would show up, too (Sala Skórecka wasn't there).

When I entered the classroom, everybody was in a good mood. They asked me what it was about and how things went. I had to repeat myself several times. In other words, I caused a sensation. I stayed until one o'clock because I might be needed and they would have to fetch me again. The girls were all very pleased . . .

I went home and told the whole story. When Minia found out that we're at the TCB (Estusia knew it from the very beginning), she said that because of my soup somebody might be sent to Czarnieckiego Street, that I shouldn't have gone to the TCB. The other girl could have gone, not I (even if I hadn't gone, Sala's father would have taken care of it; he was planning to go there). I was really upset, I felt strange. What could I do? . . . Too bad, after all Sala would go . . . I spent the entire day thinking about it. I had a headache and wasn't feeling well . . . In the evening we didn't go straight home (I wanted to tell you all this but you went away with Chajusia and Różka). [. . .]

Ewa and I (followed by Sala and Cipka) were walking on
Zgierska Street. It reminded me of Piotrkowska Street.* (Ewa
told me that she needed you very much. I replied that you didn't
isolate yourself with me, that she could do what I did.) . . . I
couldn't go home. I was feeling awful. I felt like going to sleep,
I was worn out, but it was nothing . . . If I had gone home then,
I would have needed some warmth, but it would have been the
opposite, everything would have chilled me . . . Never mind, if
I had gone home, Estusia wouldn't have liked it. So I waited
for the sensation to pass . . . And now: as for the diary, I can't
really wait for you to read it. But I want to write a little more
(for a few days).

Besides, you're writing that Estusia is pleased with me.
Are you writing this to comfort me? Recently she has had it
in for me and keeps repeating (a new word) "sluggard" . . .
All day . . . I tell you they are all big children . . .

Oh, I have no time, my dear, and I have so much to tell
you, but it'll be in the diary so you'll know . . .

I'm in a terrible hurry . . . Last night Chajusia sent me some potatoes through
Srulek (quite a lot), sugar and flour, and a letter from Surcia (to which I [just]
replied). There was nothing about it in the letter, and Prywa doesn't know,
either. I'm surprised. Yesterday I took a bath but I had to wait for a long time.
Oh, yes, it's January 24 but the weather is like in April . . . incredible. I'm a
little nervous. After work I have to go to Żydowska Street. Oh . . . I've noticed
that I try to find some comfort in my memories and my pain . . .

Sometimes I want to sleep and forget everything in my sleep or I want

---

* The main north-south street of Lodz from which Jews were excluded after the Germans occupied the
city in 1939.

the night to be long. Oh, there is such chaos . . . I can't dream as in the past because everything has already been dreamed . . . I've put it aside and . . . I'm waiting for the war to end. Oh, this waiting is tragic, too! And then? . . . I'm trembling . . . May I succeed! Oh, God! I believe you'll help me, because who else can? Who else if not you? But if you don't, I don't know . . . (My hand is hurting, I've written so much today.) . . .

TUESDAY, JANUARY 25, 1944

Yesterday I took the bed linen to the laundry. On the way back I stopped at Zemlówna's and I was glad I did. I used to visit her quite often whenever I would need something from her, but when I didn't need anything, I wouldn't even show up . . . I promised myself so many times, "today I will go to her" or "tomorrow I'll visit her for sure."

Later I dropped in at Surcia's and gave her a letter. Right now Mija has just told me what happened at the school. Every day the kids from Group 6 collect potatoes from the soup and leave them in the office. It turned out that Mrs. Perlowa had been eating some of them. Hala, the one who collects the potatoes, found out. (Mrs. Perlowa! . . . I'd never believe it . . . who else is going to disappoint me? Oh, it's terrible . . . hypocrisy, hypocrisy . . . It really hurts! . . .) Hala (a kid) spread the rumor that Mrs. Perlowa was eating the potatoes. Yesterday there was a meeting regarding this matter and Hala was to be expelled from school. There will be some delegations [to appeal for her] . . . maybe Hala will stay after all . . . [. . .]

Surcia reminded me that one day when we stopped at our place to pick up a letter for her after the assembly (which took place at the Dajczes), Estusia said that I should be ashamed because she had to peel the rutabagas since I hadn't done it. Surcia was appalled. Why wasn't Estusia used to doing it? Was she better than me? . . . Well. Am I writing about the facts? Don't I have anything else to do? . . .

Also Mr. Zemel told me and Sala to come to Żydowska Street after work. Yesterday Sala was given her soup there and I was told to come next day.

WEDNESDAY, JANUARY 26, 1944

From the letter to Surcia:

> In your last letter you asked me to tell you what happiness means to me. In my opinion happy is the person who picks himself up—and at that point he is even happier, because first he fell down and now he can appreciate his good fortune! But happiness means many other things, for example, inner peace, relief, etc. But the greatest happiness is when a person is aware of it, when he can appreciate it. For example, for me warmth would be a great happiness . . . and even the hardest work would be [too], if only I knew that I were doing it for somebody close to me. That would be my happiness and comfort. I realized this when Mama was sick. At that time I was so much younger and did everything on my own, and yet I felt so good! . . . I knew that Mama was pleased and this thought gave me more strength. Nobody knew about this. It is still very personal.
>
> True, I had terrible moments, but I knew I couldn't count on anyone. After all, I had Abramek also . . . oh, Surcia, I am telling you, he was so special . . . You can't imagine . . . Together we could lift ourselves up . . . And now? It is not surprising, it is so hard for me . . . And I will tell you something else. You wrote earlier that Estusia was pleased with me and that this should be a consolation for me. I try to do things well, but it couldn't be like that. Now

that you have told me that she didn't mean it, I felt (in the past I had only thought it) that you do understand me and . . . you are always here for me, you always help me!

Well, bye bye, my dear!

Your Rywcia!

The letters I write to Surcia could be my diary. Yesterday I looked through the photographs again . . . but only of Abramek and Daddy . . . Daddy! He appeared in front of me as if he were alive. I heard a whisper . . . your daddy is dead . . . your daddy is dead . . . No, it is impossible . . . he is alive . . . he is alive. Another whisper . . . already a third year runs its course . . . No, it is impossible. I can see his eyes, his wise and expressive eyes, and I suddenly remembered his handshake. I still feel it. It was when they let us into the hospital on Yom Kippur (on Łagiewnicka Street) and Daddy squeezed my hand while saying good-bye. Oh, how much that handshake meant to me, how much fatherly love it had. Oh, God, I will never forget it! My daddy, alive, my loving daddy, the dearest of all the dearest creatures in the world. Now I cannot dream about you . . . it would be just an illusion. Oh, tragedy! The tragedy of my existence! You lie hidden under each of my words . . . under each sigh . . . everywhere, you follow me everywhere step by step . . .

I mustn't have any illusions about my parents . . . they are no more; oh, these words hurt and stab me so much! Like hedgehog spikes. In front of my eyes I see images of my parents' deaths. I wasn't with my father when he was dying . . . when they called me, he was gone. My God! I wanted to throw myself on him, go with him, forget about everything. That was my initial reaction but later I couldn't. I had my mom, my brother and sisters. I had to live . . . I had to . . . for them! But at that moment, for the first time in my life, I showed my emotions . . . I cried, and while crying I spilled out my awful pain without realizing. Until then I had been keeping my feelings to myself . . . nobody knew anything about me, I didn't know much about myself . . .

Only then . . . then I noticed that my mom understood me. Mommy . . . I did feel it. At that moment we got closer and we were living not like mother and daughter, but like best friends . . . The age difference was unimportant (I was twelve then). Oh, God! And then Mom was dead and what she hadn't told me remained a secret forever. After her death I got closer to my siblings (Abramek appointed me as mother. "You are our mother," he used to say). I wanted to fill in, but . . . it wasn't meant to be. I was left alone with Cipka . . .

In my suffering, tragedy is playing a melody. Enough, enough tragedy . . . I cannot get rid of the suffering. Suffering—it is life. If you want to live, you must suffer. Or in other words: Life is a prize for your suffering. I cannot do anything about the suffering . . . but I want to change this melody . . . because I cannot take it anymore . . . I have been through too much! . . .

THURSDAY, JANUARY 27, 1944

Yesterday we had the first class at Bala Działowska's. I think it shows promise. We'll have it three times a week, on Sunday at four p.m. and on Wednesday and Saturday at seven p.m. . . .

I have a headache. It's rare for me, but recently it's been happening more often . . . Yesterday I was at Żydowska Street, because Mr. Opatowski told me to come in order to get some soup. When I showed up yesterday, he told me to come in a few days . . . I'm afraid that nothing will come of this . . .

MONDAY, JANUARY 31, 1944

I'm beginning a letter to Surcia. Surcia let me read the correspondence between her and her friend Miriam. I was so inspired that now I'm writing her a long letter as if it were my diary.

My dearest Surcia!!!

Oh, I have so much to write you that I don't know where to begin. But I'll try somehow. All right, I'll read these letters [between Surcia and Miriam]. When you were both writing about being so joyful, I worried about you. It was a time of such unease . . . and I wanted to remember whether I myself was so cheerful, too. Nonsense . . . I was only eleven . . . (in 1940). Besides I understood a lot from these letters, I felt them. Now I know how much Miriam meant to you and I feel your pain; I know who you've lost (maybe I shouldn't write it but I have to). Surcia, believe me, I feel it, because I've been through the same . . . And . . . I shyly suggest that you confide in me a little. I see how much you need it . . . Oh.

Surcia, I wish you the best. I love you so much, Surcia, let me replace Miriam a little bit. Oh, Surcia, I feel like crying. I've finished these letters—I'm thinking about the last ones. Oh, Surcia, how much I feel it. Surcia, I'm out of words, because what do they mean? Surcia, please, understand me. Surcia, now when I write you that I love you, it will seem as if I'm trying to equal Miriam, that I'm fond of you and that's why I want to have you, but keep this in mind: I love you profoundly . . .

My dearest! Sometimes when I go through my early letters and remember that I wanted you to be my friend, I'm overcome by a strange feeling, but then . . . then we didn't know each other well and what does it mean now? I'm glad to have read these letters because I want you to know about me as much as I want to know about you . . .

Surcia, a father! I really understand it, even more I feel

it . . . Oh, when I was reading it I felt (I'm embarrassed to write it now) like hugging you and having a good cry . . .

Oh, Surcia, I'm so drawn to you . . . Your letters (and mine to you) are in fact my diary. Oh, Surcia, my hand hurts. I was writing so fast—I wanted to tell you everything. I know it's nothing, nothing compared to what I feel and what I want to tell you. Oh, Surcia, I can't write any more words . . . But what do these words mean?

Oh, Surcia, I'll have to write you one more letter. Or better: I'll read my diary to you, all right, my dear? (It's about Friday evening.)

I have to say good-bye (on the paper), Surcia. My love, I think about you all the time, something is drawing me to you. It's . . . well, I can't find the right expression.

Ciao, my love.

Your Rywcia . . .

I couldn't write more at school . . . and now I doubt if I'll manage to do it. I don't want my cousins to know that I'm writing. They'd be gossiping . . . But enough . . .

On Friday evening Surcia and Chajusia took me to the assembly of the older girls. Surcia said she was sorry that I hadn't come the week before; it was so wonderful [. . .] [A]fter the assembly, when we were singing, Różka sang "Shalom Aleichem." It's what you sing on Friday evening before kiddush.* (It doesn't sound good in Polish.) Oh, "Shalom Aleichem" . . . so many memories . . . I see pictures moving in front of my eyes . . . Dad is coming back from the synagogue, Mama is setting the table, everybody is in

---

* "Shalom Aleichem": A Hebrew hymn that traditionally opens the Friday-night meal by greeting the guardian angels who accompany every Jew into the Sabbath. Kiddush: Hebrew for "sanctification" and for the ritual blessing, usually over wine, marking the Sabbath and other major holidays.

a good mood and . . . this "Shalom Aleichem." [. . .] How much it stirred me up. I haven't heard it for a long time. When I listened to it, I was lost in thoughts. In my soul and in my thoughts I went back . . . to those times, the times that will never come back . . . Oh, God! I'll never, never hear my dad saying "Shalom Aleichem." At least I'd like to hear it from Abramek!!! [. . .] Oh, if only there could be peace . . . if only all the Jews had peace . . . God, let me, let me!!! I'm full of longing . . . And I don't know . . . I'm reading these letters by Surcia and Miriam and all this has moved me so much . . . But I have to finish now. It's almost five thirty. They'll be coming back from the workshops soon . . .

TUESDAY, FEBRUARY 1, 1944

It's February 1! . . .

When I read these letters by Surcia and Miriam, I recall the beginning of the war. Oh, how did I look back then? And I'm surprised that they could write such letters. It was not only a time of unease and fear but it happened so suddenly. I was scared, too, but it's over . . . Today is the twelfth anniversary of Grandpa Lipszyc's death. A few days ago Abramek had his twelfth birthday. Abramek . . . today I was dreaming about him. I was still in bed, I had almost an hour. I imagined that they had brought back a group of people deported during the *szpera*. I felt full of energy . . . to do something. I ran there quickly and . . . Abramek was among them. Oh, when I'm describing it, it seems to me so trivial . . . so nothing. I won't write about it. It's a dream, anyway. Oh, if only this dream could come true! God, help me . . . But I'm writing in one style, it's no good . . .

I'm full of longing . . .

It's after one o'clock but we (the school) haven't received any soup yet. Today we get new ID cards and everybody is excited. Fortunately I had the soup for Cipka. There are no classes, either. What a strange day. Until now I have been reading what was assigned for the course at Bala's. I've been reading for so long that I have a headache . . . I hope I'll do well . . .

Oh, I have an enormous appetite . . .
I'm sad . . .
Oh, tears, moisten my eyes . . .
May I feel better . . .
May I cry at night
And . . . may I say: forward! hey!
Oh, it's so far away from me.
How much more to go?
Well, to what's quietly dormant at the bottom of my soul
I want to jump up and . . . run to the one God!
O, God, help me lift myself up
I can't do it on my own! . . .
Don't let me flinch before hardship
And put me back on my feet! . . .
My God! I have such longing . . . God!
And I don't know what to do
I'm suffocating humbly before Your majesty
I want to be pure! . . . To diminish my flaws! . . .
God! I'm full of longing! Dearest God!
I yearn for . . . something better . . .
And the wounds in my heart still hurt
Something is sobbing . . . and fleeing to You the Only One!
My God!
Dearest God, I believe You will help me! . . .

WEDNESDAY, FEBRUARY 2, 1944

Oh! In human life friendship and love are great advantages . . . It's an authentic gift from God and it is happiness . . . Happy is the person who lives in friendship and love . . . It's encouraging and comforting . . . I love Surcia so much! . . . Actually, this is the only strong beam of warmth within this atmosphere that's so icy and cold. I'm so grateful to God for this! When I look back, I think that we came within a hairsbreadth of not meeting at all. Isn't it Providence? Oh, God is so omnipotent, all-powerful, and kind. It's good that I believe in God!

I love God so much! I can always and everywhere rely on God, but I have to help a little since nothing is going to happen by itself! But I do know that God will take care of me! Oh, it's good that I'm a Jewish girl, that I was taught to love God . . . I'm grateful for all this! Thank you, God.

THURSDAY, FEBRUARY 3, 1944

Yesterday during the class Bala asked us to write how we imagined our arrival in Palestine, or rather in *Eretz Yisrael.** I could only guess why she did it: there are different girls in the class and she wants to know what they think, and whether they are Zionists. Oh, *Eretz Yisrael*, the words are so meaningful, how much longing I have for this land! . . . [. . .] Actually, this longing, this attraction has diminished since the *szpera*, but the longing for Abramek and Tamarcia has increased . . . I think about them first.

[. . .] Today we're going to Zemlówna. I like to recall the past. I feel so happy. Oh, happy in a different sense . . . I search for some relief. Relief! Only six letters and they mean so much! I need it! I've noticed

---

* The Land of Israel.

that every day I write almost the same stuff; it doesn't make any sense, really! I'd like to write something substantial. Oh, I'd like that. I'd like that so much . . .

FRIDAY, FEBRUARY 4, 1944

Yesterday Prywa and I visited Zemlówna. A few days earlier her mother had a heart problem and the day before yesterday she went to the hospital. When I asked Halinka how she was doing, she replied, "Everything would be fine if only Mom . . ." When she said it, I really got scared . . . [. . .]

For a few days something has been drawing me to the cemetery . . . apparently some unconscious force. I'd like so much to go there! To Mommy, to Daddy. I'm so drawn to it!* My God! What's going to happen when we are in *Eretz Yisrael*, we'll be so far from my parents . . . But just now I've got quite a good idea. On the gravestones we can write our addresses. Maybe somebody whom we won't be able to find (a relative) will pass by and notice them. But it's not going to happen soon. God! May this war end soon!

Right now it's the course that is ending, not the war. Probably we'll have a week for private work . . . I'll make a pinafore for Cipka, or a different kind of dress. Days are passing by, it's Friday again and February . . .

MONDAY, FEBRUARY 7, 1944

I have so much to write that I really don't want to waste my time on introductions. I haven't written since Friday and a lot has happened. I start with a letter to Surcia:

---

* Rywka's parents would have been buried in the Jewish cemetery located in Marysin, which opened in 1892 and replaced the old one (from 1811) located on Wesoła Street. All those who died in the ghetto were buried in the Marysin cemetery.

My dear Surcia!

I can't wait for tomorrow to come and my duty is to write, I can't wait any longer and I'm writing today. So: I've decided not to ask anybody and on Friday evening I'll go to the assembly. Do you know, Surcia, why? Simply, I feel that I benefit a lot from it and won't allow anybody to tear it away from me. [. . .] Surcia, don't be angry with me, *I have to go!* Oh, Surcia, soon there will be fewer assemblies. Surcia, it's so little. I have to do more! I have to!

And one more thing. Recently I've gone to the assemblies of the older girls and strangely enough (maybe I shouldn't write it) these assemblies suit me better. Oh, the Torah! Although our assemblies have a great link with it, the others are closer . . . I don't know why . . . Don't think, Surcia, that I'm planning to abandon our assemblies in order to come here. Oh, no, I'm not planning to do that. I'm only writing you how things are. Oh, Surcia, I'd like to gain knowledge from all possible sources, our true knowledge. I don't want to waste a single word, and if the opportunity presents itself I have to take advantage of it. I have to!

Surcia, now you shouldn't pay any attention to what the other girls will think and that sort of thing. If need be, I will come alone, but I will come! I will come!

Surcia, don't say anything: you mustn't say it, don't hurt me—understand me! I have this strange feeling, something inside is tearing me apart, I want to grasp anything I can. It's our wisdom, the Torah, it's permanent and lasting, maybe I'll find some comfort in it! Surcia, I have to! Don't be angry with me! Maybe tomorrow I'll write more, so long, good night! Your Rywcia who loves You!

If I hadn't written this, I wouldn't be able to sleep at night. Good night. [. . .]

Now let's get to the point! When on Friday Surcia and I went to the assembly (older girls), Surcia told me that the other girls might be jealous that I was going but they were not going. And she added, "This time only." That means I was supposed to attend the assembly only that Friday. I was a little worried, because it's beneficial for me, but I couldn't argue with Surcia. When the assembly started, I came to the conclusion that I simply had to come again. [. . .] Too bad . . . I was a little upset because I didn't want to defy Surcia, but in this case I decided to do it anyway . . .

I was walking home with Rózia and we talked about the assembly. Oh, it's great to be a Jew, but a true Jew, a Jew in the full meaning of the word! That's why I have to gather this knowledge as much as I can. And I won't let anybody interfere with it. Perhaps Miss Zelicka won't be happy about it, but if need be, I'll talk to her . . .

On Saturday morning I had a dream . . . I'm sitting in the apartment, at the table. Cipka and Mommy are there. Suddenly we hear very familiar voices coming from the street. Mommy came to the window and I saw Abramek behind her . . . In a flash, Mommy jumped out of the window (it was on the ground floor). I couldn't. I felt my eyes filling up with tears, I walked in the room, but my patience was gone and I came to the door. When I got to the door I thought to myself: I'm too calm, I'm not running, I'm doing nothing, I'm walking slowly, almost indifferently. Suddenly the door opened and Abramek came in (at first I thought it was only Abramek), then Tamara and Mommy. I pounced on them. I caught Tamara's hand. I noticed that Tamara was a little taller but she looked the same, the same way we saw her last time. Abramek was decently dressed and he was taller, too . . . Tamara told me that where they had been they were forced to misbehave and if somebody was behaving properly he was punished . . . and . . . I woke up . . .

I regretted that I wasn't [still] sleeping, that [just] when something was about to happen, I had to wake up . . . I was dreaming about them for the first time, for the first time . . . I couldn't go back to sleep, I was feeling strange. Maybe at some other time this dream would be a consolation for me, but this time it was too much, I couldn't find a place for myself. I felt like crying, like screaming . . . Oh, I was suffocating and at the same time I needed to see Surcia right away. I decided to get dressed and look for her after the cholent.* [. . .] Oh, I didn't want my cousins to see my face and to guess what happened.

One other thing is happening, but I won't write at length about it. It concerns food and my cousins. I'm worried about Cipka, because she's weak and with these rations she hasn't even tried a spoon of sugar. Chanusia put some sugar away for *Wielkanoc*, but sometimes a little bit was used for *babka*.† When we took the sugar out, Minia would put it on her bread. There were other things like that. When I told Surcia about it (I went to see Chajusia, Surcia came later), she replied that we had to talk to Miss Zelicka. I'm afraid it's not very feasible. Then Chajusia was reading me *Hovot ha-Levavot*.‡ I learn so much from it. [. . .] When we said good-bye, I felt better. [. . .]

But my mood was spoiled after the assembly, perhaps because I was

---

* Cholent is a Sabbath lunch dish (typically potatoes, meat with bones, beans, onions, and the like) that is kept simmering on a hot stove from Friday afternoon in order to avoid biblically prohibited cooking on the Sabbath. The version of it made in the ghetto was significantly impoverished.

† *Wielkanoc* is Polish for Easter and Passover. *Babka* is a traditional Eastern European Jewish cake, but in the ghetto it was made from minced and baked potato skins or chicory.

‡ *Hovot ha-Levavot* (*Duties of the Heart*) was written in eleventh-century Spain by Bahya ibn Pakuda in Judeo-Arabic and later translated into Hebrew. A very popular set of traditional ethical writings, it was commonly published with an accessible Yiddish translation.

Ruins of Crematorium III,
where members of the *Sonderkommando* buried manuscripts,
Auschwitz-Birkenau, 2012.
(Courtesy of Judy Janec)

Wykaz Spielunów, nie korzystających ze świadczeń

Komisji Spieli nad Młodocianym   XVI

4.   XVI.   2.

Lp.	№ dziecka	Nazwisko i imię Spieluna		Adres		Nazwisko i imię dziecka	
1.	3.	Szczęśliwy	Wigdor	Sulzfelderstr.	56	Sandler	Samuel
2.	4.	Reingold	Zygmunt	Altmarkt	2	Wartsha	Rachela
3.	9.	Lipnowski	Lajb	Sulzfelderstr.	10	Widelgux	Estera
4.	10.	Mirc	Szyjosz	Mühlgasse	15	Seideman	Paul
5.	11.	Białorybska	Mania	Franzstr.	28	Piotrkowski	Szmul
6.	13.	Gerszowski	Gibus	Am Bach	14	Lanski	Hemel
7.	30.	Lipszyc	Ebaja	Rawagasse	38	Lipszyc	Rywka
8.	47.	Gerbler	David	Brunnengasse	16	Brewer	Salek
9.	48.	Kaufman	Jerson	Franzstr.	30	Rabinowicz	Michał
10.	59.	Nowak	Eliasz	Hohensteiner	15	Gutman	Emanuel
11.	56.	Ramkowski	Mordcha	Hanseaten	63	Stein	Stanisław
12.	89.	Grynszpan	Zygmunt	Bierstr.	43	Markowicz	Rachela
13.	93.	Braun	Jakub	Franzstr.	20	Braun	Mara
14.	124.	Gulis	Dora	Hanseaten	63	Klein	Wygda
15.	137.	Rosenberg	Izrael	Cranachstr.	23	Szymała	Natan
16.	152.	Perle	Szala	Franzstr.	47	Mawela	Jenta
17.	248.	Fajolewicz	Naftali	Hohensteiner	84	Wajsztejer	Rachela
18.	261.	Kirszer	Mania	Hohensteiner	84	Kan	Hanka
19.	273.	Wajntraub	Luber	Cranachweg	14	Wajnajker	Herse
20.	282.	Cycowska	Mania	Alexanderhof	17	Cycowski	Rywen
21.	301.	Prusber	Barud	Matrosengasse	1	Berman	Stela
22.	306.	Lenga	Symha	Rawagasse	40	Glübsman	Jakub
23.	326.	Ast	Abram	Hanseaten	15	Glyser	Szmules

Opposite: Rywka's name appears in this adoption list on line 7. Her aunt Hadassah (Chaya) adopted Rywka after the death of her mother on July 8, 1942. *(Courtesy of Archiwum Państwowe w Łodzi)*

Above: The Bergen-Belsen Memorial.
(Courtesy of Judy Janec)

Above: The section in the Jewish cemetery in Lübeck, Germany, where eighty-seven Holocaust survivors were buried between 1945 and 1950. *(Courtesy of Judy Janec)*

Opposite: An article, "In Lübeck verliert sich Rywkas Spur," published on February 19, 2012, in the *Lübecker Nachrichten*, about the search for what happened to Rywka.

NORDLICHTER

Curd Tönnemann
norddeutschland@ln-luebeck.de

Stegner zwitschert

Eigentlich kann es nur einen im Land geben, der fürs höchste Amt im Staate geeignet ist: der unverwüstliche SPD-Mann Ralf Stegner. Mit seinem glasklaren Verstand hat er uns wieder durch diese Woche geleitet. Was wären wir ohne seine bahnbrechenden Analysen?

Nachzulesen ist das alles bei Twitter, jenem Medium, dem sich der fortschrittsliebende Stegner alltäglich bedient. Zunächst half er dabei mit, der Bundesforschungsministerin Annette Schavan die Ehrendoktorwürde der Lübecker Uni zu verleiden. „Wenn Frau Schavan den Ehrendoktor der Uni Lübeck bekommt und der Uni-Lübeck-Terminator de Jager mitfeiert, könnte Pokerweltmeister aus Kiel Ehrendoktor der Uni Sylt werden. Festredner: Arp und Kubicki", lästerte Stegner. Und sparte zwei Tage später nicht mit Häme: „Na also, geht doch: CDU-Ministerin Schavan verzichtet nun doch auf peinliche Ehrendoktorvorwahlshow in Lübeck."

Nur am Tag des Wulff-Rücktritts war Stegners morgens offenbar nicht hellwach. Sein Musiktipp, meistens eine Anspielung, war diesmal ein Song von Joe Cocker: „You can leave your hat on" (Du kannst deinen Hut auflassen). Haben wir das alle nicht gewusst: Stegner ein heimlicher Wulff-Fan?

Es ist einfach zu schön. Was brauchen wir einen Vorabend-Langweiler wie Gottschalk? Wir im Norden haben den ganzen Tag unseren Herrn Stegner! Der hat nach wie vor großen Unterhaltungswert. Ohne sein Engagement wäre das Abkommen zwischen CDU und SPD, einen fairen Wahlkampf zu führen, wohl nie zur Unterzeichnung gelangt ...

IN KÜRZE

Brand auf Campingplatz – Wohnmobil brennt aus

Stove – 50 000 Euro Schaden ist in der Nacht zu gestern bei einem Brand auf einem Campingplatz in Stove im Landkreis Harburg entstanden. Ein mit Holz verkleidetes Wohnmobil sei komplett ausgebrannt, teilte ein Polizeisprecher gestern mit. Personen seien nicht verletzt, der Besitzer des Mobils sei zur Brandzeit nicht auf dem Platz gewesen. Die Brandursache sei noch ungeklärt.

Studentenmagazin „heuler" ausgezeichnet

Rostock – Das Rostocker Studentenmagazin „heuler" bei der jährlichen Ausschreibung des Pro-Campus-Presse-Awards den ersten Platz belegt. Es wurde zusammen mit dem „Ottfried" von der Universität Bamberg als bestes Studentenmagazin Deutschlands ausgezeichnet. Der Pro Campus-Presse Award wird jährlich verliehen. 2011 bewarben sich bundesweit 34 Studentenmagazine.

TV TIPPS

15.15 Uhr Vox Auf und davon – Thema u. a.: Isabel Gülcks Weg zur neuen Miss Germany
19.30 NDR Schleswig-Holstein-Magazin – Themen u. a.: Gibt es ein Rezept gegen Bevölkerungsschwund? / Tischtennis-Verein aus Siek mischt die 2. Liga auf
19.30 NDR Nordmagazin – Themen u. a.: Straßenkarneval in Dömitz / Maybebob in Schwerin

Montag

17.30 Sat.1 Regional – Thema u. a.: Karneval in Dithmarschen
18.00 RTL Guten Abend – Thema u. a.: Gentest in Schwarzenbek
19.30 NDR Schleswig-Holstein-Magazin – Themen u. a.: Streit um verschimmelte Wohnungen für Senioren in Albersdorf / Hilfe bei der Schulausbildung für Alleinerziehende
19.30 NDR Nordmagazin – Themen u. a.: Hansa gegen Ahlen / „Tag der Norddeutschen"

In Lübeck verliert sich Rywkas Spur

In den USA ist jetzt ein Tagebuch der Jüdin Rywka Lipscyz aufgetaucht. Historiker hoffen, dass ihr Schicksal in Lübeck aufgeklärt werden kann.

Von Oliver Vogt

Ein britischer Offizier überwacht den Einzug jüdischer Flüchtlinge in ein Transit Camp in Lübeck. Das Bild ist 1947 im Lager Pöppendorf entstanden, wo die Passagiere der „Exodus" untergebracht waren. Foto: Corbis

Lübeck – „Oh Gott, wie lange noch? Ich glaube, nur wenn wir befreit werden, können wir noch einmal einen richtigen Frühling genießen. Ach, ich vermisse diesen wunderbaren Frühling." Mit diesen Worten endet das Tagebuch von Rywka Lipszyc, das im März 1945 von einem sowjetischen Arzt in den Ruinen des Krematoriums von Auschwitz-Birkenau gefunden wurde. Es ist nicht bekannt, ob seine Verfasserin jemals wieder einen Frühling erlebt hat, wie sie sich ihn hinter den grauen Mauern des Ghettos von Lodz erträumt hatte. Sicher ist aber, dass die junge Polin den Holocaust überlebte. Nach ihrer Befreiung durch die Alliierten wurde Rywka Lipscyz zusammen mit anderen überlebenden KZ-Häftlinge in einem Transit Camp der britischen Armee in Lübeck untergebracht. Hier verliert sich ihre Spur.

Das Tagebuch, in dem die 1929 in Lodz geborene Frau die Schrecken von Verfolgung und Deportation festgehalten hat, ist wiederaufgetaucht, beim JFCS Holocaust Center in San Francisco. Eine Enkelin des sowjetischen Arztes hatte es dort abgegeben. „Eine unglaubliche Entdeckung", sagt Judy Janec, Archivleiterin beim JFCS. Mittlerweile sei das 112 Seiten starke Tagebuch ins Englische übersetzt und soll 2013 veröffentlicht werden. Was aber bleibt, ist das Rätsel um seine Verfasserin.

Bis zu ihrer Befreiung durch die Briten teilt Rywka Lipscyz das grausame Schicksal von Millionen Juden unter der Terror-Herrschaft der Nazis. Gemeinsam mit ihren Eltern und den drei jüngeren Geschwistern Tamara, Abramek und Cipka wird sie 1940 im Ghetto von Lodz interniert. Mutter und Vater sterben an den im Ghetto grassierenden Krankheiten; die kleinen Kinder Abramek und Tamara fallen im September einer Massendeportation zum Opfer. Bei der „Aktion Gehsperre" werden die Patienten des Ghetto-Krankenhauses sowie Kinder unter zehn Jahren in das Vernichtungslager Kulmhof verfrachtet und ermordet.

„Ich bin sehr aufgebracht. Heute morgen kam die Erinnerung zurück, dass Abramek und Tamara deportiert wurden und Mutter tot ist. Ich wurde so traurig, überwältigt vom Schmerz", schreibt Rywka, selbst erst 14 Jahre alt, am 13. Oktober 1943 in ihr Tagebuch. „Konnte ich mir je vorstellen, dass wir getrennt würden? Niemals wäre mir das in den Sinn gekommen. Vor dem Krieg habe ich einige traurige Bücher gelesen und mich gefragt, ob Schicksale wie in den Geschichten wirklich passieren können. Heute weiß ich es, ich habe es am eigenen Leib erfahren."

Rywka muss noch mehr Schmerz ertragen. Im Sommer 1944 wird das Ghetto aufgelöst, Rywka und ihre Schwester Cipka nach Auschwitz-Birkenau deportiert. Unmittelbar nach ihrer Ankunft werden die Schwestern von den SS-Wachen auseinander gerissen, Cipka in die Gaskammer geschickt. Vielleicht war es dieser herzzerreißende Moment des Abschieds, als Rywka ihrer Schwester das Tagebuch, das später im Krematorium des Todeslagers gefunden wird, zusteckt. Weil für Worte keine Zeit mehr ist.

Rywka bleibt der Tod in der Gaskammer erspart; die Nazis verfrachten sie in das Konzentrationslager Christianstadt, wo sie als Zwangsarbeiterin Munition für das NS-Militär herstellt. Als die Rote Armee im Februar 1945 immer weiter nach Westen vordringt, wird das Lager aufgelöst, die Insassen auf einen 800 Kilometer langen Todesmarsch nach Bergen-Belsen geschickt. Rywka überlebt die unbeschreibliche Tortur. Krank und völlig entkräftet kommt sie am 6. April 1945 in Bergen-Belsen an. Neun Tage später wird das Lager von der britischen Armee befreit.

Die Überlebenden werden von den Alliierten in sogenannten Transit Camps untergebracht, die über ganz Deutschland verteilt sind – auch Rywka. Das letzte Lebenszeichen, das es von ihr gibt, stammt aus dem Transit Camp Lübeck, das in der Waldersee-Kaserne eingerichtet war. Auf dem Registrierungsformular vom 10. September 1945 ist vermerkt, das Rywka nach Palästina auswandern wollte und man sie wegen der Strapazen des Todesmarsches im Krankenhaus Niendorf behandelt hatte.

Was danach aus ihr wurde, ist unbekannt. Sollte sie im Krankenhaus gestorben sein, müsste ihr Name auf offiziellen Sterbeverzeichnissen auftauchen. Doch das ist nicht der Fall. Dass sie wie so viele andere jüdische Überlebende nach Israel ausgewandert ist, gilt als unwahrscheinlich. Bei ihren zwei Cousinen, die heute in Israel leben, hat sie sich zumindest nie gemeldet. Ist sie stattdessen nach Polen zurückgekehrt, in Deutschland geblieben? Vieles ist möglich, nur fehlt es an Beweisen. Das Rätsel um Rywka Lipscyz bleibt vorerst ungelöst. „Vielleicht ist sie nicht gestorben und hat es geschafft, sich ein Leben aufzubauen", sagt Judy Janec vom Holocaust-Center. „Ich hoffe es."

Wer kennt das Schicksal von Rywka Lipscyz?

Das Holocaust-Center hofft, mit Hilfe der Bevölkerung in und um Lübeck das Schicksal von Rywka Lipscyz zu klären. Gesucht werden unter anderem:
Informationen über das Krankenhaus in Niendorf, das von der britischen Hilfsorganisation „Save the children" betrieben wurde. Wo wurden verstorbene Patienten begraben? Wer hat dort gearbeitet? Was wurde daraus?
Informationen über das Transit-Camp in Lübeck 1945: Wer erinnert sich daran? Ist noch jemand bekannt, der dort gearbeitet hat oder untergebracht war?
Hinweise an die Lübecker Nachrichten, Redaktion Norddeutschland, Herrenholz 10-12, 23556 Lübeck, E-Mail an norddeutschland@ln-luebeck.de oder Telefon 04 51/144-2328.

„Wir sind Maschinen mit tierischen Instinkten"

Auszüge aus dem Tagebuch, das Rywka Lipscyz mit 14 Jahren im Ghetto von Lodz geschrieben hat.

17. Januar 1944
„Gestern habe ich geträumt. Ich hatte dieses Bild vor Augen: Ein schummriger, warmer Raum. Ein paar Kinder sitzen an einem Tisch, sie sind mit irgendwas beschäftigt oder hören mir zu, während ich ihnen vorlese. Ich erzähle ihnen Geschichten vom Ghetto. Ich sehe in ihren Augen, dass sie verwirrt sind, dass sie nicht fassen können, dass so etwas wirklich passieren konnte. Ach, ich wünschte, diese Zeit wäre schon da."

28. Februar 1944
„Mutter!? Was bedeutet dieses Wort? Wer ist diese Kreatur namens Mutter, die mit so viel Vergnügen leidet und neues Leben gebärt ... neues. Und da ist ein Teil von ihr in diesem neuen Leben. Ist diese Mutter nicht kraftvoll? Unglaublich, mächtig? Ohne Zweifel, ja! Niemand kann tun, was sie tut. Werde ich eines Tages eine Mutter sein? Werde ich auch so mächtig sein? Ich weiß nicht, warum ich das gerade jetzt aufschreibe. Ich denke schon eine ganze Weile darüber nach ... aber es aufschreiben? Vielleicht, weil ich mich gerade erinnert habe. An meine geliebte Mami!"

12. April 1944
„Das Wetter ist so schön! Schön! Schön! Oh, ich bin so glücklich, es ist so ein großer Trost. In Momenten wie diesen will ich so gerne leben. Aber es sind diese Momente, in denen wir uns auch unserer schlimmen Lage bewusst werden, in denen unsere Seelen traurig sind. Man muss wirklich stark sein, um nicht aufzugeben. Wir blicken auf diese wundervolle Welt – und im selben Moment sehen wir uns in diesem Ghetto, von allem beraubt, ohne die kleinste Freude. Wir sind Maschinen mit tierischen Instinkten, wir sind Sklaven. Doch ich versuche, diese Gedanken zu verdrängen, um nicht diesen kleinen, fröhlichen Moment zu stören."

Aus dem Englischen übersetzt

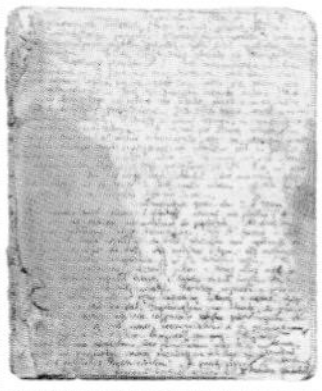

Das Tagebuch von Rywka Lipscyz, das 1945 in Auschwitz gefunden wurde. Foto: JFCS Holocaust Centre

Darf der SSW sich zu Rot-Grün bekennen?

Kieler Politik-Professor: So ist die Befreiung von der Fünf-Prozent-Klausel nicht gedacht. CDU unterdrückt Ärger.

Kiel – Der Südschleswigsche Wählerverband SSW soll die dänische und friesische Minderheit im Land vertreten. Jetzt hat er sich parteipolitisch klar positioniert. Mit SPD und Grünen will man nach dem 6. Mai gemeinsam eine neue Regierung bilden, verkündet SSW-Frontfrau Anke Spoorendonk. Damit hat sie die Debatte, ob der SSW weiter von der Fünf-Prozent-Hürde befreit sein sollte, allerdings auch gleich wieder neu entfacht.

„Da stellt sich schon die Frage, ob das noch systemgerecht ist", sagt zum Beispiel der Kieler Uni-Politikprofessor Joachim Krause. Der SSW werde nur deshalb von der Fünf-Prozentklausel ausgenommen, weil er die Vertretung der dänischen Minderheit sei. Tatsächlich positioniere er sich mehr und mehr als eine generelle linksliberale Partei, die es schaffe, mehr Stimmen von deutschen Wählern zu bekommen als von dänischen. Das Thema Wahlrechtsänderung sei aber derzeit tabuisiert. CDU und FDP fehle der Mut dazu, SPD und Grüne wollten vom SSW profitieren.

Anke Spoorendonk (64).

In der Tat waren die Reaktionen heftig, als CDU-Politiker den SSW zuletzt 2005 angingen, als er die rot-grüne Simonis-Regierung mit einer Stimme im Amt halten wollte. Norbert Röttgen zum Beispiel, damals CDU-Bundestagsabgeordneter, hatte vor einer „Belastung des Verhältnisses" zwischen Minderund Mehrheit im Norden gewarnt. Solange der SSW keine fünf Prozent erreiche, dürfe er keine Regierungsmehrheit herbei führen. „Wir haben ein vollwertiges Mandat", konterte der SSW, und das betont Sprecher Lars Bethge auch heute.

Die Dänen-Ampel scheiterte am „Heide-Mörder", der Simonis viermal die Stimme verweigerte. Dessen ungeachtet umwirbt heute auch SPD-Spitzenkandidat Torsten Albig die Partei: Reiche es für Rot-Grün alleine nicht, werde man mit dem SSW regieren. Grünen-Fraktionschef Robert Habeck kann sich das sowieso gut vorstellen, man arbeite mit keiner anderen Fraktion so gut zusammen.

Bei der Union unterdrückt man den Ärger nur noch mühsam. Es sei schon „ungewöhnlich", dass sich der SSW, „der den Minderheiten-Status hat und deshalb von der Fünf-Prozent-Hürde befreit ist, so eindeutig zu einem Lager bekennt", sagt Landesgeschäftsführer Daniel Günther. „Der SSW verabschiedet sich davon, die ganze Minderheit zu vertreten", klagt Axel Bernstein.

Lauenburgs CDU- Kreischef, Innenminister Klaus Schlie, will zwar „die rechtliche Situation des SSW nicht infrage stellen", hat aber „politisch null Verständnis". Die einseitige Positionierung werde zwangsläufig zur Diskussion über die Angemessenheit der Fünf-Prozent-Hürde führen. *Wolfram Hammer*

Pannenserie bei Volkszählung im Norden

Kiel – Bei der Volkszählung 2011 ist es im Norden zu einer Reihe von Pannen gekommen. So wurden Briefe an verstorbene Hauseigentümer verschickt und massenhaft Bescheide ohne die notwendigen Fragebögen (die LN berichteten). Das geht jetzt auch aus der Antwort der schleswig-holsteinischen Landesregierung auf eine Kleine Anfrage des CDU-Abgeordneten Werner Kalinka hervor. Dem Papier zufolge ist der Norden dabei kein Einzelfall: Die genannten „Ereignisse" seien nach Erkenntnissen des Statistikamts Nord bei allen Statistischen Ämtern in vergleichbarer Größenordnung aufgetreten. Der Zensus war die erste gesamtdeutsche Volkszählung.

Rywka's cousins Mina and Esther
were the only members of their
immediate and extended families
to survive the Holocaust. This
photo was taken in 2012.
(Courtesy of Hadassa Halamish)

Below: Sisters Esther and Mina with their families in Israel in 2011. *(Courtesy of Hadassa Halamish)*

Following page: Jewish cemetery in Lodz, 2012. *(Courtesy of Judy Janec)*

standing next to Lusia and Edzia. The assembly was wonderful but if I had been sitting somewhere else, or if they hadn't been there at all, I would have benefited from it much more. They were disruptive. Lusia had had to burn her violin (in the ghetto all the musical instruments had to be surrendered) and occasionally she burst into tears. I felt so strange . . . [. . .]

There will be courses for older girls. My cousins registered; so did Surcia and Chajusia. Everybody is excited; it's very encouraging. Oh, if I were older, I could register, too, and could gain more knowledge. But what can I do? I'm so helpless! Oh, God, help me! Help me. Also hunger is increasing, this horrible and hopeless hunger. It's colder, it's freezing. Oh, why shall I even write about it? Words are so insignificant and they express nothing, Oh, always oh and oh. Enough . . .

Nevertheless I'm grateful to God that I'm a Jewish girl! That He let me understand it. God! I know so little, I hear so little, but what I've heard means so much to me, it has fulfilled me a lot, that . . . Oh, that's why whenever the opportunity presents itself, I have to take advantage of it, I have to . . .

[. . .] I've always wanted to study, but I didn't know exactly what. Now I know, now it's different, now I know that I want to study, but to study the Torah, our dear, beloved, always new, and yet so old Torah.

Our life-giving Torah!

Mother Torah!!!

THURSDAY, FEBRUARY 10, 1944

I haven't written for a long time . . . (from a rough copy!). I couldn't write in my diary because I didn't have any ink. Estusia took an ink bottle to the workshop and was supposed to bring me back some ink but every day she kept forgetting . . . Finally, she has brought some. It's already evening.

I knew that a lot was happening and it was difficult to remember everything, so I was writing rough copies:

9 Feb.: on Feb. 8 a command, or rather an order (from the Germans), was issued that the ghetto had to deliver 15,000 men aged eighteen to forty from the offices. Today is Feb. 9. Mr. Wolman received the summons, too. Oh, God, the deportations have begun again . . . Minia said with a smile (stupid) that after men they will deport women, including her. Nobody is sure, neither we in the ghetto nor they over there. But You, God, You are omnipotent and I believe You will direct us to the right path! Oh, I wish everything were all right!!!

Today's postscript: There is terrible hunger in the ghetto, I don't know what's going to happen . . . and the deportations . . . oh, all this . . .

Besides . . . besides . . . Ewa is going to write a diary (she's writing already; we're writing together), maybe Fela and Dorka will write, too, and that pleases me a lot. I've written them letters, because I have so many thoughts and nobody to share them with. Surcia is too far (it's better to share them with Surcia), but I can't be limited to one person; it's impossible. I've written to them because I want to know what they think about human life . . . [. . .]

Yesterday I stood in line for briquettes [of coal]. Everything has to be picked up by Sunday, so the lines were huge. A line, or rather a queue. How much could be written about it! But I won't write anything, that's it. I'll only write that I wish all this tsuris* were over forever. This is too much for me . . . Hunger has always had a very bad impact on me, today is the same. For Cipka and me last year it was, so to say, a challenge to fight hunger. Oh, it's so exhausting! It's a terrible feeling to be hungry. I don't like to stay at home. I prefer to be in class . . . or I don't know where, but not at home, it's almost dangerous at home. [. . .] Nowadays it is different than before the *szpera*. Nowadays I'm hungrier when Cipka doesn't eat and fuller when she does . . . Oh, God, it's so hard!!!

---

* Aggravation.

When will the time come when all the hunger is satisfied? And all the thirst? And when won't it be cold anymore? Oh, God!

I've so much to write now. So, let's get to the point! [. . .] I met Surcia in the street. She was going to see me. She was taking her shoes to the shoemaker and she has a letter. [. . .] She wrote that Miss Zelicka would allow me to attend their Friday evenings. When I read that I thought, "What? Only that? So little? Nothing more?" Oh, what kind of person am I? When they let me do one thing, I want more. Also, she wrote that she had talked to Miss Zelicka about the problem of ours (Cipka's and mine) that we had discussed at Chajusia's on Saturday. Right now Miss Zelicka is at our place, and I'm writing this at the Dajczes. I'm trying to eavesdrop and I can hear: the voice gets louder, then softer. Cipka came in a minute ago. She was asked to leave—just now they are starting to talk. Oh, I'll be so sorry . . . I can't imagine what will happen. God, God, help me, You are the Only one, the Only one who can do it! Oh, God! . . .

Miss Zelicka called me. Oh, she took care of it so well, so wisely. I admire her because I wouldn't be able to do it myself, certainly not . . . So, we are to divide the food products into portions. Oh, the ghetto . . . my dear God! . . . and those deportations. It's so depressing, but as Surcia wrote: *Hazak.*˚ We shouldn't let ourselves be depressed; we have to overcome this depression . . . Oh, what do I care? Tomorrow I'm going to Surcia and to the assembly. Why should I care about other things? I shouldn't care. But I'm only writing this—I do care. [. . .] What's more, Miss Zelicka is going to teach a course for the older girls and my cousins will attend. They are so glad! I shouldn't be wasting any time, whenever I have a moment in which I'm not sad. Oh, damn it! [. . .]

I've just noticed that I wrote almost nothing about Cipka—I haven't even thought about it. But now . . . at this moment, I've thought, Cipka, something

---

˚ "Be strong!"

whispered into my soul, this name is so sweet. Oh, Cipka, I'm taking delight in it. Cipka, she's really so sweet . . . I remember that this morning I looked at a photo of her when she was three (1936). It was winter, she was in the street. Her little face hasn't changed much, it's almost the same, but her figure, her figure has changed a lot. In the picture she looks like, or rather she resembles, Tamarcia so much! So many years! Now Cipka is eleven, oh, time is going by so fast! [. . .]

FRIDAY, FEBRUARY 11, 1944

Write! . . . Only write! . . . Then I forget about food and everything else, about all the trouble (it's an exaggeration). May God grant Surcia health and happiness, at least for suggesting to me this wonderful idea that I write a diary. Sometimes when I'm about to write I think I won't write anything, and when I start writing, there is so much to tell about and I don't know where to begin.

I want these two weeks to be over, so I could go to Miss Zelicka . . . Sometimes I feel I have something to say, but (there is always a "but"), I'm simply shy.

Oh, it's Friday again! Time goes by so fast! And for what? Do we know? What's waiting for us in the future? I'm asking this question with both fear and youthful curiosity. We have an answer to this, a great answer: God and the Torah! Father God and Mother Torah! They are our parents! Omnipotent, Omniscient, Eternal!!! It's so powerful!!! In front of this I'm just a little creature that can hardly be seen through the microscope. Well . . . oh, I'm laughing at the entire world—I, a poor Jewish girl from the ghetto—I, who don't know what will happen to me tomorrow . . . I'm laughing at the entire world because I have a support, a great support: my Faith, because I believe! Thanks to it I'm stronger, richer, and more worthy than others . . . God, I'm so grateful to You!!! . . .

There was an inspection by a hygienist in the school. But don't be afraid, my diary, I was and am clean.

SATURDAY, FEBRUARY 12, 1944

Oh, God, what's happening in the ghetto? Resettlements* again! There are many children, even five years old, at Czarnieckiego Street. They are held hostage for those who received the summonses . . . Mrs. Krochmalnikowa (she's a relative of "K" and our neighbor) said that it was just the beginning and nobody knew how many people would be deported . . .†

Last night I was at Chajusia's (it was Friday—I went to Surcia but she wasn't there). Mania Bardes's father was there, too. When we walked down I found out that Mania was at Czarnieckiego Street as a hostage for her father . . . God! It hit me like a bolt from the blue. Mania at Czarnieckiego Street! No, it isn't possible! We didn't go to the assembly and Surcia said that such was my unlucky beginning. After all, Miss Zelicka allowed me to attend. I guess she read my letter to Surcia, because Surcia told me that Miss Zelicka had stated that my "must" can't be refused. She added that in my case it was very healthy . . . [. . .] But enough of that, there is no time for this today.

I must add, however, that Surcia and Chajusia were very upset—one might even say crazy and downcast. Today's assembly has been canceled, but I think that during such a terrible time we should get together, because we are totally scattered. Oh, God! Today as soon as I got dressed I went to Chajusia. We continued with *Hovot ha-Levavot* and we talked about duty.

---

* *Wysiedlenie* (literally "resettlements") was the euphemism used by the Germans to refer to deportation. Although the term implied relocation to another area, in reality it often meant transport to a concentration camp or killing center.

† The Krochmalnik family (mother Sura Rywka and daughters Bela Perla and Fajga Rachela) lived in the same building at 38 Wolborska Street as the Lipszyc family.

[. . .] Later Fela and I went to our place. They all chattered only about food. Indeed, the cousins are managing very badly with bread . . .

[. . .] Later Mrs. Bardes came and said that Mania was not at Czarnieckiego Street anymore but at the police precinct. Who knows? May everything be all right with God's help . . . Later we got a food ration and . . . I have no idea why but the mood became more cheerful . . .

I decided to write letters to Surcia and Chajusia. Oh, because they are so dispirited, it's awful, but it's not surprising. The war has been going on for five years and people are exhausted by all those ordeals, and who knows? And it isn't over! Oh, God, protect us from evil!

Today I have a lot to write. I've just given a notebook to Fela. She will write a diary, too. As a model she's now reading *Pamiętnik Laury*,* but in my opinion you don't need any models to write a diary. It's true that it's hard in the beginning. I'm the best example of that, but later one gets more experienced. On Saturday evening, when I was at Chajusia's, those deportations made me think about some things. I even talked about them with Chajusia. Chajusia told me to get closer to Cipka, to talk to her, to ask her what she thinks about this or that. I'll try, after all it's my duty, I have to replace her mother for her as much as I can. I haven't started yet, although I think about it. True, I can't do much for everybody, but I have Cipka with me. (Oh, God, I'm trembling. I don't want any enemy to get her, to lay a hand on her. I want her always to be mine. Oh, God, help me, I can't write in Polish now, I simply don't have the expressions.)

I'm stopping now—I'm talking. Mrs. Marcus is having an argument with me, claiming that such hunger has never existed before. Maybe not for her, but for us? For me? Oh, God, what we've been through. When Mommy was

---

* A novel for teenage girls by Felicja Szymanowska, published in 1930. Probably adapted from a German book by the author.

sick, I'd boil 20 dkg [about 7 ounces] of potatoes for four people, without any *kolonialka*.* Mommy would get the potatoes and we would drink the boiled water and each of us would receive a piece of potato just "for taste." I'm writing about food again! What's happened to me? When I think about food, I'm both disgusted and delighted! Two extremes! What a contradiction! And yet they go hand in hand! But enough! Enough about food!!!

Tomorrow (Sunday) there will be some soup in the workshops. I'm going to be there at nine thirty . . .

I'm so sleepy! I'd like to sleep through the rest of this war and wake up when it's over. After all, I could read about what happened. Though it might be interesting—I have experienced so much "kindness" that I don't look forward to more. Well . . . but does anybody ask me? No. The current of life brings it, and then it rushes away. It rushes away, ahead, forward. How many people have wondered: why, what for, and slowly, step-by-step, they lose their faith and have been discouraged with life. Oh, it's so terrible! Discouragement with life. That's why I'm grateful to God three times over, even four, for giving me the opportunity to believe. If it weren't for my faith, I, like other people, would lose my will to live. However, I was saved just in time. Surcia contributed to this a great deal. [. . .] At that point I started to think about it more, to wonder, contemplate, and inquire more often and more deeply. Maybe it's like that with other things, but . . . have patience, with God's help everything will be all right. You can't do everything at once! Yet, you want to do it so much!

Oh, well. I've written all this at such a terrible time—how can I? I must write a letter to Surcia! I feel so sorry for her, I don't know, yesterday I felt so sorry for her and Chajusia and . . . generally for everybody . . .

---

* This term, meaning "colonial items," was how people in the ghetto referred to flour, groats (kasha), spices, fats, powdered soups, cleansers, and so forth. Before the war, the expression designated imported products such as citrus fruits and spices (10 dkg [decagrams] is 100 grams, or about 3.5 ounces).

Oh, God, speedily redeem Israel from exile! *Oy, G-t, leyz shoyn oyz yisroel fun goles! O, G-t, ven vet shoyn zayn di geule?**

One is so full of longing (as Chajusia said today—we are one big lump of longing) . . . Oh, it's true, it's true! [. . .]

SUNDAY, FEBRUARY 13, 1944

Sunday . . . I'm sitting at the school now and like all my friends I'm waiting for the soup. It is terribly cold—there is snow outside and the classroom hasn't been heated. I'm writing, or rather scribbling; my left hand is in a muff. I'm sleepy. [. . .] I'm full of remorse . . . maybe if Abramek had looked well they wouldn't have taken him. He was such a good kid. How many times, when I was short of bread, would he give me his? Oh, how many times? That's why he looked bad. I'm full of remorse . . . I feel like crying, crying, crying, even screaming.

Today I spent some time with Cipka—I talked to her a little. I asked her to think and later tell me what she thought about people. Oh, I love her so much. Strange, I feel sleepy—it's such a sleepy longing. I don't feel comfortable sitting like this and writing; it's terribly cold. Oh, what does my discomfort matter now? I mustn't write it now. At night I have a place to lay my head, may I be content with that. How many people don't have even this? Do I know, can I know, whether Abramek and Tamara have the same? Oh, God, bring us back together! Oh, I'm full of longing and I'm writing this over and over again . . . To write! It's such a gift. Thank you, God, for letting me write! [. . .] When is it going to be all right? I don't know . . . What an answer! Oh, I'm going to fall asleep on the school bench writing this—I'd better put it away and visit my friends from the other benches. Will it be

---

* "Oh, God, when will the redemption happen?" The Yiddish original is not standard spelling, but likely reflects Rywka's pronunciation in Lodz dialect.

better? I don't know it, either. But really I shouldn't be fooling around . . . I'm full of yearning!!! God . . . My words are falling apart . . .

MONDAY, FEBRUARY 14, 1944

Dearest Chajusia!!!

I'm worried because of you. You are too concerned with this deportation—come to your senses, Chajusia! Good heavens! It can't be like that, Chajusia, I understand you very well. I know what this means to you, but everything has to have its limits . . . Chajusia, because of this big worry . . .

Now I'm going to tell you some of my observations. Well, in normal times (if we can call them something like this at all), I can go through different states, different moods, but now? I mustn't do it now! . . . Now I have to keep on going . . . I have to know how, God forbid, not to be out of my depth. And I'm telling you: keep on going! Don't be angry with me for this preaching, or for the fact that I, being younger than you, allow myself to say something like this. But believe me, I'm writing this from the bottom of my heart for your own good. In any case, you know it very well!

Dearest Chajusia! Is Surcia as concerned as you are? Show her this fragment with my observations. And you must come to your senses! Don't stay at home all day! Take a walk! Maybe you'll feel better! You understand that you go from one extreme to the other. Oh, Chajusia, you may think that I can't understand it, but believe me! Believe me,

I'm in it myself—I have this terrible reality before my eyes, but believe me, I can't lose heart. The trick is to control yourself and not to let the evil control you . . .

But enough! Bye for now!

Your Rywcia . . .

[. . .] Last night we had an assembly, or rather "a party," at Maryla Łucka's. A better time could have been chosen for that, but what can we do? Two boys came: Józio and Paweł. Generally they are bearable . . . I keep myself in the background. They come only on Sunday, so I'd like to go somewhere else. I'd like to find an excuse not to go there on Sunday. If I could only go to Surcia and read some parts of Psalms—oh, it's so delightful!

But I shouldn't digress from the topic!

—I had to stop. Mr. Zemel came and delivered a speech, or rather he repeated what the chairman had said before.* And: those who are to be deported but are hiding are being aided by other people. This is forbidden . . . Apparently, this is going to be some kind of easy labor. But who knows? What's more, during the working hours between seven a.m. and five p.m. nobody will be allowed to walk in the streets. The ghetto is turning into an *Arbeits Lager.†* The apartments will have to be locked. Only the bedridden with medical certificates will be able to stay inside. Nobody else. Now I don't know what's going to happen to Saturdays . . . after all, an apartment can be locked with a padlock. What's going to happen with attendance at the workshops? God! What's going to happen? Only You know. I was so upset

---

* Rumkowski delivered a speech to the factory managers on February 13 at five p.m. saying that he was required to send 1,500 men "to work" outside the ghetto. People started to hide en masse in order to evade the deportations. He attempted to convince people to report for the transports, assuring them that they were in no danger while at the same time threatening that if the ghetto itself did not deliver the required contingent, the German authorities themselves would do it. See Dobroszycki, ed., *The Chronicle of the Łódź Ghetto,* February 13, 1944.

† Labor camp.

that I wrote a poem. I don't know what will happen to the assemblies. The provisions department and the other departments will be open from five p.m. so people will be able to get their food.*

What I'm worried about most is Saturday . . . It's getting worse and worse . . .

My God! Isn't it enough? . . .
How much longer are we going to suffer?
We are full of longing, something is choking us like a bone
What's going to happen tomorrow, we don't know! . . .
Oh, God! Help us at last!
This ghetto is a monstrous machine! . . .
God, how long will this poisoned life last?
We are doing worse and worse . . .
There is no hope . . . it's getting darker . . .
Do we have to be alone?
To waste our lives in the closed ghetto?
Our life is miserable . . .
But it could have been so fabulous! . . .
I'm burning! . . . I can't put out the fire,
I'm entangled by this eternal suffering! . . .

O God! Everything is in Your hands!
Calm our bleeding hearts! . . .
Put an end to our torment!
Oh, how to satisfy these hungry souls!

---

* These rules were introduced to prepare the ghetto for unexpected visits by German commissions. The organizational changes—such as the compulsion to stay at work and restrictions on moving about—were designed to make the ghetto appear highly functional. Fearing the attitudes of the German commissions, Rumkowski even introduced a ban on women making themselves up with cosmetics. See Dobroszycki, ed., *The Chronicle of the Łódź Ghetto*, February 13, 1944.

TUESDAY, FEBRUARY 15, 1944

As usual what is tragic is also funny, but on the other hand, for example, people work at the coal yards or vegetable yards from five p.m. until midnight!* Could you imagine something like that in the past? Certainly not! Oh, it is so tragic! At least spring is coming and days are longer. I've had enough. For example, I can imagine people working at the yard in the middle of the night. Cold, dim light, a terribly long line, chaos, everybody is sleepy. Oh, God! . . . In the face of such forces, my life at home is diminished. However, there are things we can't get over in silence . . .

So: yesterday [. . .] [t]here was no water at home. There had always been water at 31 Wolborska Street, but today it's broken. I had to carry water from 21 Wolborska Street. I was in a hurry because I wanted to pick up some briquettes, the last ration, instead of wood . . . I wanted to be there before five p.m. When I left, dinner was being prepared. I came back at seven p.m. I stopped by at Ewa's, we talked (about the diaries). I wasn't terribly hungry and I thought that if they wanted to eat, they would call me. At eight p.m. they still hadn't called me. I realized that by then the dinner must have been ready. I entered the apartment. Estusia and Chanusia were still eating. I wanted to get some food but to my surprise the pot was empty. They all smiled and Estusia said, "I wish you had come three hours later. What would happen if I left the pot on the stove? Everything would be cold and you would be chopping the wood now." I was about to reply, "Oh, really, that's too bad. If I had known, I would have come three hours later." But I didn't say a word . . . Is it up to her to decide when I can eat? Was I supposed to eat when I wasn't hungry, and later would eat only bread? . . .

---

* There were two coal yards in the ghetto: at 10 Mickiewicza Street and at 47 Łagiewnicka Street, operating in the framework of the Coal Department that began functioning on May 8, 1940. Vegetables were stored at the vegetable yards, which were managed by the Provisioning Department.

[. . .] While I was eating, Estusia said, "Someone has to take a bucket of water down." It was said to everybody, but I felt she was referring to me. Then Minia went to sleep. I made a bed for Cipka. I was very tired . . . Although I wanted to do some darning in bed, I rejected this thought very quickly and wanted only to sleep . . . sleep. When Estusia noticed that I was taking off my clothes, she said, "Take the bucket down!"

"I won't, because I can't," [I said].

She started making a fuss and ran toward me. I told her that I had carried enough (Minia was in bed and Chanusia was standing by the tile stove crocheting).

"What? I want to know what!" Estusia was yelling.

"I won't tell you, because you know!" I showed her that I didn't have to be so submissive, that I could be tough. She smacked me . . . Oh, now I won't do what you want for sure! She was like a child; she was hitting me on the head, the idiot. I wanted to push her away; I tore an apron; she lost her ring. Finally she left me alone; I went to bed.

"I'll make sure you're better off in some other place," she declared.

"Oh, I've heard it so many times!"

Oh, God, I am so lonely! I don't know if she will do what she promised, but I thought she would go to Miss Zelicka. How will it look? She keeps saying that she is pleased with me, but now? Right now, would she say that she doesn't want me anymore? It seems so unbelievable. Oh, is this the right time to think about it? Not only are the times horrible and tragic, but I don't even have a shelter called "home." I recall a sentence from A *Light in the Darkness*, "Even the most modest place, but your own."* Oh, it is so true! That's why I am so cold! . . . I feel like crying! Cry, scream from this vast pain surrounding me! Oh, God! Things feel so constricted here! So stuffy!

---

* A new edition of C. E. Weigall's book, *Swiatło w mroku. Powieść dla dorastających panien* (A Light in the Darkness: A Novel for Maturing Young Ladies), was published in Lodz around 1935.

Oh, God! Something is about to happen. I don't know. [. . .]

I stopped at home to pick up a booklet and some money. Minia was at home. Since the money was not in the dress, I asked Minia if she had cash. No answer . . . I ask again . . . No answer . . . I ask if she can hear me . . . No answer . . . I asked her over and over again but she didn't answer me, not even once. I got angry and informed her that I was going to the assembly. I left. I had no doubt that she could hear me . . . at least once. I was about to cry. What is she thinking? [. . .] I had no idea what to think. My crying was choking me. Horrible . . . Later Cipka told me that Minia had asked her what I was telling her. I can't believe that she didn't hear it, but even if she didn't? She didn't say a word to me! I can't grasp it . . .

When I came back, Chanusia was already home. I wanted to bring some water (one bucket was full), but she said it wasn't necessary. Again I didn't understand anything! [. . .] But I don't know, everything is putting me in a bad mood, it's awful. Oh, God! This mood in the ghetto, at home. Oh, I can't stand it . . . so what? I'm only writing and in fact I will hold on . . .

At night the Jewish police knock at the doors of the apartments. They are looking for those who are hiding. Last night they were at Prywa's and asked about the men. Oh, God! Nothing like that has ever happened in the ghetto. We've been through many terrible periods; each of them was different; this one is different, too. Yesterday when Zemel was talking about the people who help other people hide and don't want to denounce them, I realized that we, the Jews, suffered these deportations and their effects so much that now we were grasping at straws and didn't want to turn those people in. Unfortunately, we are helpless. We aren't up to it. Oh, suddenly I felt so bad. I was suffocating! I saw the *szpera* in its full colors . . . Abramek . . . Oh, God, I almost blacked out!

[. . .] Oh, I want to pour all my sorrows over the paper—will I be able to feel better? Oh, what now? Now, when so many people suffer in these terrible and tragic times, is there a place for my silly sorrows and suffering?

By writing this I'm not diminishing my sorrows at all; to the contrary, I'm increasing them. And it's getting colder. Cold! I'm shaking at the mere mention of this word.

Yes, first Srulek has brought me a letter from Chajusia. She seems to be much better and it pleases me a lot. Surcia was probably at her place, but apparently she didn't have a letter for me . . . I'd love to see her! There will be a class tomorrow. Maybe afterward I'll stop by at Chajusia's. I miss everybody! I don't know what's happening with Mania Bardes, and the Wajskols, and Dorka Zand, I don't know anything . . . [. . .]

Oh, today we were at Edzia's and we saw a batch of men (one).* They were going to Czarnieckiego Street—we could hear them crying. Oh, it's heartbreaking! It is! We are all in shreds . . . we are in shreds! God, unite us! Blend us into one big and inseparable whole! Oh, when will it happen? When will *Geula*† come?

WEDNESDAY, FEBRUARY 16, 1944

Today we came to the school at seven . . . We saw a change of "décor" . . . The lecture room was filled with tables and machines. So what? I don't care! But one more thing! In the morning the guard didn't want to let me in. I never show my *Arbeitskarte*,‡ but today he didn't want to let me in at all. I showed him my food (dinner) ID instead of my work ID card . . . but it didn't help, either. What is more important to me is that I miss the girls, the assemblies and all . . .

And . . . one secret . . . my cousins are almost out of marmalade and brown sugar, but Cipka and I still have quite a lot. This morning we were

---

* A group of men designated for deportation from the ghetto.

† Redemption.

‡ Work identification card.

going to work (Cipka and I) and she told me that on Sunday when we went to get our rations, Chanusia said to Estusia that we'd finish our marmalade and sugar very quickly and they'd have to share theirs with us. Estusia replied, "I surely wouldn't think otherwise."

Stupid cousins, you were so wrong! I have my own satisfaction. I haven't thought of being as "generous" as you! I don't even think about it. Ha, ha, ha, at the bottom of my heart I'm sneering at them. Anyway, it's not worth pondering over! Times are terrible . . . many people have left . . . there is hunger . . . but I've already written about it. I feel something, but I can't express it, though I'd like to. I'd like to help everybody . . . I'd like to be helpful . . . I'd like to be useful! I'm full of these inexpressible emotions. I don't know . . . it's connected with my longing and I'm so sad. But I can't be overwhelmed by sadness, because I know that nothing good will come out of it. I'm against evil . . . I want kindness! I do want it! There is a saying, "Where there's a will, there's a way," but it doesn't apply in my case . . . because I want to do so much . . . so much, but what can I do? Little, very little, almost nothing . . .

(I'm writing at home) a letter to Surcia.

My dearest Surcia!
I have to write to you now because I can't wait any longer.
And so: about September 20 you wrote a poem, do you
remember? The assembly was at our apartment. You
brought two poems, showed them to my cousins, and
they were delighted. When I asked you to show them to
me, you said with a wave of your hand that I wouldn't
understand . . .

You see, Surcia, today by sheer happenstance, I was going
through some poems (collected by Minia) and suddenly
I started reading, "Life, life, life." I immediately thought

it was one of your poems . . . I think you know! . . . Oh, Surcia, I think you know that I've understood it well (oh, it's wonderful!). I've understood it, right? You know! In the past you couldn't show the poems to me because you were sure I wouldn't understand them (at that time I'd have understood them, too), but today you know! Right, dearest?

Beloved Surcia! What shall I write you? Maybe that I have a lot to tell you and when we see each other I won't know where to start. Oh, it's so much, there is a lot in the diary, too! Oh, Surcia!

Today at school I had a little talk with a Marysia Glikson (an *apikoyres*)* about Miss Zelicka. You can guess what she could say about her! . . . She was adopted and Miss Zelicka is the one who checks up on her. Other girls who know Miss Zelicka joined the conversation and none of them agreed with Marysia. Finally Marysia said to me, "She was made of the same clay as you!" When I heard it, I had the feeling that a non-Jewish girl was talking to me. And besides . . . Oh, I can't write you more, the rest is in the diary . . .

My aunt sends her compliments! Ciao, for now! Kisses (now I can!).

Loving you a lot,
Your Rywcia

Something happened (or rather is happening) at home. [. . .] Cipka noticed that every day her marmalade was missing. She told me today, and when

---

* The Yiddish/Hebrew word *apikoyres* comes from the name of the Greek philosopher Epicurus (341–270 BCE). According to the Weinreich Yiddish dictionary, the term is translated as a Jewish heretic. It could also be understood as a term to refer to a Jew who did not believe in the divine revelation of the Torah and rejected Jewish religious principles.

Minia came back, she told her, too. We suspect . . . no, I can't write it yet . . . It became clear to me, I realized, that one couldn't accuse a person without being sure. Even during the time when we were sharing everything together, I noticed that things were disappearing. Estusia was talking about it; perhaps she suspected us (Cipka and me) . . . and I thought it was Minia . . . although Minia used to lick a little bit of marmalade, but too much was always missing and I couldn't believe it was her.

Today we found out. But I can't believe it at all. Oh, God, what a disappointment with people! It's unbearable! Cipka added that one day, when she was to go to the workshop at twelve in the morning, she pretended to be sleeping and "that person" (Cipka sensed it) took out the sugar jar. Cipka heard some munching. Today Minia noticed that their sugar jar was moved to a different place and her coffee *łatki* were spread all over the plate.* In the morning when she was leaving for work, everything was together. I can't get it out of my head. Oh, God! If you can't trust people like that, then whom can you trust? Whom? Oh, trust! It's so ugly! God! Oh, such rotten tricks! It's disgusting! It's unbearable! It's what the ghetto did! The best people were taken away . . . the worst remained . . . God! Your advice! Your help!

THURSDAY, FEBRUARY 17, 1944

Yesterday during class Fela told me that apparently Mania was about to be released. Her father was at home and they took him away. Anyway, it's not certain. There is so much bitterness. Oh . . .

Surcia visited us in the evening. When I came back from class Minia was talking to Estusia about those disappearances. For a few days, until Saturday, we are going to set "traps" for the thief and then we'll see. Oh, it

---

* This was probably what ghetto inhabitants called "coffee cakes," a black concoction prepared from chicory, grain, or the like (but not including coffee), mixed with water and cooked in a pan.

would really be terrible. When Surcia was here, the cousins started talking about it but in some sort of code. I couldn't tell her myself, but she'll find out anyway. It made a bad impression on the cousins and Estusia was very disappointed, all of them were . . . But enough. What's more, Surcia brought me a letter. I'm glad that I had written a letter to Chajusia and I don't have to mention that it was honest, from the bottom of my heart. I'm pleased that I could do something, even with a few words. Oh, this letter from Surcia encouraged me so much! I do want reciprocity! Only reciprocity! Once you give something to me, then I give something to you . . . and so on . . . That's the way it should be, but it isn't, or rather it is extremely rare. At least we should want it (I'm lacking a word), we shouldn't demand this reciprocity from others, but from ourselves, from ourselves! As much as we possibly can, we should try to repay those who deserve it. At the same time we can learn a lot and find out more about ourselves. In my opinion true reciprocity is not like this: I have to repay you immediately because you've done something for me—if I do something for you, it's only because I expect you to repay me. No! In my opinion reciprocity should be selfless! I'm not going to keep accounts and I'll reciprocate or better, repay, when I'm able to, when it's from the bottom of my heart. This is the kind of reciprocity I have in mind! Like with Surcia . . . reciprocally, reciprocally!

When I came home, the first thing Minia told me was to check Cipka's bread. I did so and (oh, God, how hard it is to write it) a piece of bread was missing. I can't write about other things because bread is most important. We were bitterly disappointed . . .

I can't even look at this person, I'm so disgusted. Bread . . . when I found out, I simply wanted to, well, I don't know what to do to this person . . .

Oh, God! . . . *Far guts, varft min shteyner.* Unfortunately, in this case it's true. One has to be a terribly rotten person to do something like that . . .

---

* In return for good, people throw stones.

135

and this innocent. Oh, this disappointment hurts so much . . . Estusia was terribly disappointed, more than all of us. Oh, I'd rather not write or think about it. It's all because of the ghetto! This ghetto! Really, it's unbearable!

What's more in our school (not school anymore, because its name was changed to *Fach Kurse**), we won't have any Hebrew classes or math, only five hours of productive sewing and one hour of technical drawing.[†] Neither books nor notebooks are allowed at work. It's all secret, they (the workshops) must cover up for us, us—the children—because studying is forbidden. It hurts so much (for them we are not humans, just machines). Oh, pain! But I'm glad that I can "feel" that it hurts because as long as it hurts, I'm a human being. I can feel—otherwise it would be very bad. God! Thank You for your kindness toward us! Thank You, God!

Tomorrow we are having an inspection by a hygienist again, like every Friday . . .

SUNDAY, FEBRUARY 20, 1944

The *szpera*! How many tragic memories, how much pain and longing, how much anxiety (I can't even enumerate all of them) are contained in this single word? Oh, God, how much horror? Just a single memory . . . and what if there's a *szpera* again?[‡] Is it a *szpera*? Fortunately it's not, thank God, like the other time. It's Sunday. We are at home. I tried to finish my household chores as soon as possible, so I could start writing . . . really, I have so much to write. Probably there will be a *szpera* today and we won't be able to go out

---

* Vocational course.

† The shift in schooling toward vocational skills was designed to prepare children for skilled and useful physical labor.

‡ On this date, February 20, the ghetto authorities issued a ban on moving about the ghetto. Only watchmen were able to stay in the workplaces. People designated for deportation were then taken from their homes and moved to the collection point at the Central Prison on Czarnieckiego Street. See Dobroszycki, ed., *The Chronicle of the Łódź Ghetto*, February 19, 1944.

in the streets. This morning we were woken up by a knocking at the door. Minia opened it. A policeman came in and asked about men (we wanted to tell him that he was the only one in our apartment, but it was no time for joking). He walked a little ways into the room, moved Minia's bed and opened a closet and . . . realizing that nobody was there, he left.

To tell the truth, we could hide a lot of men here and they wouldn't find anybody. But never mind: although this *szpera* is not as terrible as the previous one (which doesn't mean it's not terrible at all), the truth is that it doesn't affect us personally . . . but . . . just say "*szpera*" and . . . enough! Oh, God! This word makes me afraid, even this word by itself, and what about . . . oh, what about the reality? I don't want to write further . . . because, oh, because . . . no, I can't! . . .

Yesterday, on Saturday, I had to be in the workshop for the first time (may it be the last time!). Chanusia and Estusia were there, too. Minia stayed in bed (before five p.m. an official from the bank brought her a *stam karta** for Saturday and Sunday soup). Yesterday we all got our soup that was for today. But I don't want to write about it.

Oh, God, it was so awful to get up so early on Saturday! I was choking! When I was crossing the intersection of Jerozolimska Street and Francisz-kańska Street, I saw a soldier near the barbed wire looking at the ghetto.† It seemed to me that he was looking only at me and was pleased that I, too, was on my way. Oh, God! I'll never forget this feeling, I felt so bad, I was suffocating, I felt like crying! Crying . . . crying . . . I watched people going to the workshops as usual. This day, this holy, sacred day is for them an ordinary and normal weekday. God, and I'm among them? And I'm like them? (Maybe nobody thought about it.) For me, going to the workshop on Saturday was a terrible agony. I thought involuntarily: If I have to do it again

---

* Ration card.

† Most probably this refers to a member of the German uniformed police, armed with rifles, stationed at a sentry post along the perimeter of the ghetto fence.

(I wish I wouldn't), will it become commonplace for me, will I get used to it? Oh, God, do something so I wouldn't have to go to the workshop on Saturday! I felt so bad! I wanted to cry! It seemed to me that everybody was laughing at me. That they were laughing because I came. God, I'll never forget these feelings. Oh, I felt so bad. In this respect our class is all right. There are many girls who don't work on Saturdays . . . but so what? What good is it for me?

Mrs. Kaufman showed us how to cover the gusset and the lapels. That's what I need! I kept whispering inwardly, "Saturday, Saturday," in order not to forget, God forbid! One more thing: it was the Saturday of *men hot gebentsht rosh khoydesh*° and I was in a hurry to go home.† I kept saying to myself, "May I not forget it!" Oh, it's so difficult.

What's more, Friday evening, as usual, I was at Surcia's. I had to wait a little bit for her. I was waiting and (it's hard to write this) her brothers weren't behaving as they should. I thought to myself: poor Surcia! It must be difficult for her. How much she has to fight! Oh, I feel sorry for her and I admire her at the same time. *Dos iz a shtiler held!*‡ (I have a topic for the class.) I wish I could help her! I wish I could make it easier for her! She let me read some of her articles. One of them (published before the war) was entitled, "On the Edge of a Precipice." Oh, it was so true! Whenever I think about it, I can't imagine that I've read it in Polish. When I recall a sentence, it's always in Yiddish. For example, "There is no Jewish father" . . . always in Yiddish it is, *Nisht do, keyn yidishn tatn!*§ It sounds different . . .

When we left, Surcia was somehow looking for excuses, [saying]

---

* The blessing for the new month.

† On the Sabbath preceding the start of the new month (called Rosh Chodesh), there is a special blessing recited in synagogue. Religious Jewish women, in particular, observed Rosh Chodesh as a women's holy day since it marks the renewal of the lunar cycle.

‡ "That's a quiet hero!"

§ "Not here, I have no Jewish father!"

that it was like that in her house and I shouldn't follow suit. Her oldest brother was a ladies' man. I thought to myself, "Oh, Surcia is suffering so much—it's so difficult for her. Yet, she doesn't complain and even warns me . . . it's heroism!" Rywcia, you have to learn from her! And for that I loved her even more!

Last night at the dinner table I had a sudden need to read my cousins the last letter written after Mr. Zemel's speech. Estusia said it was written by Surcia. Oh, they liked it . . . for me it was enough that she said it was written by Surcia. Well, I have to stop for now, maybe more later!

TUESDAY, FEBRUARY 22, 1944

Thank God! Mania Bardes's father has been released!

Perhaps this coming Saturday we'll have an assembly. Oh, I'd like it so much. We haven't had a real assembly for a long time. Since yesterday Franka Wajskol has been coming to work, but I don't know anything more about it . . . I only know that every day we collect soup for her.* But enough! We don't belong to Żydowska anymore; we are a workshop now and it's Mr. Szuster who is our boss, not Mr. Zemel. After all, it's better . . .

I was sitting with my head down and reading. I don't want to waste a moment. I decided to read more. And I have a problem. I don't write anything special besides the diary, sometimes a poem, but what about prose? Oh, I can't write prose at all. Have I become incompetent? Oh, I thought I had nothing to write, but in the course of writing . . . everything in the course of writing. I've written an essay for the class and thanks to Surcia I have something special . . . maybe I've written it a bit clumsily, but truthfully!

At the moment we're organizing a library. (The Zonenberg Library was

---

* A manifestation of solidarity that was fairly common in the ghetto. Not receiving soup in the ghetto was equivalent to a death sentence. Therefore, factory workers often set aside a few spoonfuls from their portion of soup for sick or absent colleagues.

closed.)* Every girl is donating one book, so we'll have a collection. I've joined the library, too, and I'm offering volumes III and IV of *War and Peace*. Probably we'll have good books. Today I have (I borrowed it from Surcia) *Yesterday and Today* by Żeromski.† I'd like to read something good . . .

WEDNESDAY, FEBRUARY 23, 1944

I feel strange! I don't know . . . I was reading when I had nothing to do and Mrs. Pilcewicz came over (I didn't notice her) and took away my book . . .

Oh, damn it! I have nothing to do, but I have to sit and do nothing. Now, I have work. I'm to make some book inserts. I wasn't paying attention—I sewed it on a slant and now it's creasing. Oh, never mind the workshop stories! I feel strange and no longer like doing anything. But yesterday I spent an hour and a half or two hours in Cipka's company. Nobody was at home . . . we were alone, we talked, I read her some fragments from my diary.

Perhaps today will be the same? Chanusia is coming back home later, so we'll be alone longer. I like it so much! Oh, I have so much to do . . . and I have to pay many visits. I wanted to go to my cousin Balcia Zelwer. We hadn't seen each other for a long time. I have to go to Zemlówna, I should visit Mania . . . really, I feel we are both connected—I feel I love her, I love all of them. Oh, when is it going to be better? It's already so dark that it's easy, very easy to trip and fall down. Nothing can be seen, not even the little lights flickering far away. Not only are they weak, they just go out . . . and how do you turn them on?

I'm helpless! Totally helpless! What else shall I write? Everything is the same! I feel that precisely at this moment I should write a lot, I feel it . . . oh, if I poured it out onto the paper, would I be better? But how can I do it?

In Żeromski's book I found some good parts . . . namely: there was so

---

* There were several libraries in the ghetto, although Jakub Wolf Zonenberg's Lending Library at 19 Zgierska Street was the only one that had operated before the war.

† Polish author Stefan Żeromski (1864–1925).

much longing, so much, in the heart . . . but with the arrival of the son, with his one hug, all the longing melted away. The arrival of the son took it out of the heart and when it melted it went through the eyes in the form of tears of happiness. How much we need something like that!

Bits of longing have been accumulating in my heart for years, but any time my brother or sister shows up with one hug, one look, those bits could disappear and turn into tears of happiness. But for now I don't have any tears. However, I cry, I scream, but in silence. I'm so unhappy.

My longing is growing . . . there is more and more longing . . . the only thing that could stop it is so far away . . . and it's receding . . . What shall I do? Blow myself into pieces? No! I can't do that! Wait patiently? Oh, it's too much! It's nerve-racking. Oh, I'm afraid I can't take it anymore! I cry with all my might, "Hold on!" Because it's most important! And most difficult! God! What a struggle! What a terrible struggle!

I'm more and more exhausted! It's not surprising! But it can't be like that! It mustn't be like that! It mustn't . . . I can't give up! But who's thinking of giving up? Never mind . . . it's so hard! What else shall I write? Perhaps "hard" yet again. Oh, I feel that I'm sinking more and more into a swamp and mud . . . and . . . I can't get out. Maybe somebody is pushing me? That somebody is going to be stronger than me? No! I won't let it happen! I'll do my best! But again I'm overwhelmed by exhaustion! Oh, how can I stop it? Who can help me? This ghetto is a terrible hell.

Oh, the bell is ringing. I have to finish now, but I'd like to continue writing . . .

THURSDAY, FEBRUARY 24, 1944

There is some unease in the ghetto. They say that the women will be deported, too . . . they haven't got all the men yet. Tomorrow we are to bring a bread card and some other document. In order not to forget we have written little notes: "Remember about bread, a card, and some other document!" Oh, a tragicomedy . . .

It seems to me that the ghetto is getting empty—it's empty everywhere (right now only in my mind). God forbid that something bad should happen. Unfortunately, the prospects are not good. There is a bad mood everywhere. Oh, I'm not even thinking what it was like in the beginning of the war. Oh, I'm so experienced . . .

Chawka Gr[yn]wald has come and says that she has seen a batch of women. Good God! It's so awful! There will be some *Folkszeilung** on Sunday and again we won't be able to go out. Terrible!

If I only knew that we'd be together, it wouldn't be so bad, but a separation. Who knows about the cousins? Oh, really. And Balcia Zelwer? And all! It's so hard! So very hard! We are in darkness . . . somebody is pushing us . . . and pushing . . . we can't resist . . . and we're sinking . . . and we're getting stuck . . . God, help us get out!!! Unfortunately, help isn't coming yet. Who knows if it's going to come in time? Oh, everything is in God's hands! What can we do? It's dark and empty around us! It's terribly dark and foggy! And this fog is getting into my heart . . . I can hardly breathe. Oh, impossible . . . we'll suffocate. Oh, more fresh air. Oh, we miss it so much . . . God! God! It's so tragic, hopeless, bad.

It's even tragicomic. Unbelievable things are happening. For us it's daily bread, but when you think about it, you'll see the extent to which it's comic. God? For example, various dishes made of coffee, *lofiksy*.† Prywa's sister calls them "muzzle-stuffers," because they can stuff your muzzle. Oh, if only this were the worst! Oh, it's so tragic . . . tragic . . . tragic . . .

---

* Probably a reference to a census of the ghetto's population.

† *Lofiks* was a small black pastry made from ersatz chicory coffee and cooked in a frying pan. It was called this because it resembled a type of briquette kindling with the commercial brand name Lofix.

FRIDAY, FEBRUARY 25, 1944

I have a lot to write. But first things first! As for the deportation of women—Marysia Glikson has had a registered address since 1925, but because she was adopted she can stay there only until March 1. After that she won't have a place to stay . . .

Because I had to be at Juvenile Protection, too (later I was sent off), I went with her. Her situation is very unpleasant. If this chaos went away, she could perhaps stay in an adolescent home, but at the moment nothing is happening.* On the way she told me that she came from a very religious family, but she was brought up by her brother (he was an officer and completed his studies in France) and lived among the Poles. Lately in the ghetto she has been disappointed with the Jews and that is why she is the way she is. I wanted to help her (at least to show her that people from our milieu were capable of helping others). I took her to Chajusia (she'll talk to Miss Zelicka in secret); I also went to Balcia Zelwer, thinking that maybe Marysia could move in with her for a while. It didn't work, because in the winter Balcia moved in with her neighbors. Marysia expects the worst.

Right now I shouldn't complain that she isn't one of us, but I have to help her as a human being as much as I can. She's also looking for some access to the chairman. I told her that if she wanted anything from my cousins (they are in touch with Rozenmutter),† she could visit us. I doubt anything concrete will come out of it, but what can they do? But enough!

Besides (it's a secret), Lola and Majer slept in our place last night. I would like so much for everything to be better! I feel I have so much to write and . . . I only feel it! It's something very difficult. I have a strange feeling.

---

* Polish *bursa* is a home for young people, most often those who were without family.

† This could be a reference to Mendel Rozenmutter, who in April 1943 was a member of the committee that granted relief benefits to the needy. See Dobroszycki, ed., *The Chronicle of the Łódź Ghetto*, March 4, 1943.

What's more, I'll have to wait a long time to read Surcia's diary. [. . .] Well, I need to be patient. It can't be done in haste. Damn it! It's morning . . .

SATURDAY, FEBRUARY 26, 1944

It's Saturday evening. I'm dead tired, but so what? I can't say I'm cheerful—I'm far from that, but for now the mood of yesterday is gone, thank God. Oh, last night I was in a terrible mood. I learned from Surcia that several girls from Bnos are at Czarnieckiego Street; some are still in hiding. Oh, it's so horrible!* Surcia says that we have no idea how terrible it is. She's right! But if we had any idea, it would be worse for us.

Last night a few girls (including me) gathered at Mrs. Milioner's. We were talking. [. . .] We only asked God to take mercy on us and help us. (Oh, I can't express myself in Polish.) Besides, they are collecting bread and provisions for those whose cards are blocked.† Oh, it's so dark! When I think about it, I always recall the *Ayelet ha-shahar* from Psalms.‡

Today [Saturday] I didn't go to the workshop. Instead of experiencing the feeling from last week again, or getting used to it, I decided not to go. I didn't count on getting any soup. Prywa was not there, either, because yesterday she had a fever. However, I got the soup, but it was the ration for the sick. Never mind! I couldn't stay in bed any longer—I had to go to Chanusia's workshop to leave the doctor's note for her. She had a tooth extraction and later her other tooth was swollen. She got a fever of 38.5 Celsius

---

* Bnos refers to Bnos Agudas Israel, the Orthodox girls' organization or club that was sponsored by the Orthodox Hasidic political party Agudas Israel.

† The food ration cards of those evading deportation were blocked.

‡ *Ayelet ha-shahar* is biblical Hebrew for "Gazelle of Dawn." The phrase is associated with Queen Esther, who is said to have recited Psalm 22, in which this phrase appears as the title, when she went to King Ahasuerus to plead on behalf of the Jews, who were being persecuted by Haman.

[101.3 degrees Fahrenheit]. Today she's feeling better but all this disrupted my entire Saturday. I had to be in the workshop twice. Then I went to Chajusia's. She read me something about Dr. Birnbaum* and I learned a lot . . . it's very precious!

Last night was quiet. Nobody was taken, but one has to be cautious . . . perhaps it's a trap? Who knows? Better safe than sorry. [. . .]

Oh, I still have so much to write! Saturday evening I went to my uncle's in order to pick up Cipka's coat. I didn't see Tusia. Oh, I miss her so much! Oh, recently I haven't thought about her, haven't written to her . . . well, I think about her. I wanted to see her several times but time doesn't permit. After the end of havdalah,† we (Minia, Cipka, and I) went to get 20 kilos [44 pounds] of briquettes (two rations). The weather is good for a sled, so we took it with us. Wonderful! We were walking, holding the cord in our hands. We were to go out again, but dinner was ready, and we didn't feel like it, so we didn't go. [. . .]

I'm sitting here. I've just gotten "permission" to write. Almost everybody is sleeping and I'm waiting for Lola and Majer. Tonight they are coming later, because they have to pick up their rations. I'm very sleepy . . . my right leg is cold . . . I'm wet . . . my shoes are soaking wet . . . I'm cold.

Oh, yet, on Thursday Surcia wrote a poem, marvelous and so well crafted. I'm sleepy. (I'd like to write, but it's not going well and I'm only scribbling.) I'd like, oh, very much, to wake up in the morning in a different, better time! I'd like it so much!!! I'd like something substantial! Something rich in kindness! Something encouraging! Something soothing! I'd like it a lot. I'd like to learn the Psalms because they are so encouraging! And so

---

* Probably an allusion to Dr. Nathan Birnbaum (1864–1937), who went from being a secular university student in Vienna (and who coined the word "Zionism") to being a pious Orthodox Jew, an advocate of the Yiddish language, and an active member of Agudas Israel, whose girls' movement was called Bnos.

† Havdalah marks the end of the Sabbath and the division between the sacred day and the regular days of the week. The ritual includes blessings over a cup of wine, a spice box, and a braided candle.

soothing! . . . so wonderful! . . . Perhaps tomorrow there will be Psalms at Mrs. Milioner's. I'm going . . .

Not only Psalms, but also our beloved Torah. Oh, it's so good to be an open-minded person, to be a Jew. So good to be skilled, to know (it's difficult). Oh, it's so good! The Rossets have just arrived. I'm going behind the curtain.

SUNDAY, FEBRUARY 27, 1944

When I was out in the street earlier, I wondered why a human being is always unhappy and always wants more and more. He makes demands all the time. For example, when he's at a lower level, he wants to be at a higher level. It has its positive and negative aspects . . . if he climbs higher and higher, and wants to learn more and achieve a higher level, then it's positive . . . but . . . there are limits! (I don't know whether it's suitable for a diary.) For example, when you show one finger to a dog, he'll grab the whole hand. There are people who want more and more, if they are allowed to do something. (Oh, I don't know if this is what I mean.) A human being, in the full meaning of the word, should always remember that but he's so narrow-minded! Out of spite, he doesn't remember what he should. Eh, I can't write it, because I'm getting more fresh and chaotic thoughts. Oh, if I could only shape it somehow!

I'm feeling awfully bad. I feel like crying! Oh, perhaps crying would calm me down? Oh, tears! I don't have them on demand—I don't even have them when I need them. God, what's going to happen to me? I'm suffocating! I can't find a place for myself. I don't know what's going to happen!

First, I went to see Mania. She told us (I was there with Ewa) what happened to her.* Oh, what an experience! I told her that she had to write a diary. It would be a pity if she didn't write it down. (Estusia is annoyed that

---

* This surely refers to her experience of being held in the Central Prison as a hostage for her father.

I'm writing now . . . oh, if she only knew what writing means to me!) God! I can hardly breathe! I can hardly do anything! Something very heavy falls on my heart . . . squeezes it. Oh, it hurts so much. Oh, it clasps it tightly! [. . .] What can I do, I, one of the smallest pieces of dust on earth. What do I matter at all? What do I matter (I won't say: before God), but before all the people living on this planet. What do I matter at all? What does my life matter? Oh, these questions! I know that I can't do much for those who are far away, but for those who are near I can do a little. I have to . . . I can't just sit on my hands and do nothing. Oh, if I could only do as much as I want! God! I'm sad, I'm full of sorrow. I'm full of longing! . . . and I can't breathe! Oh, God, help me! Help me! I'm sleepy. I'm in a stupor. Oh, I don't know . . . I don't know anything. [. . .]

What's more, my shoes are soaking wet and this has a bad effect on me, oh, it's like having a bath . . . I'm shivering . . . I'm so cold. It's an awful sensation to have wet shoes. But it's not the worst . . . only all of this combined is . . . Oh, a mishmash . . . A hodgepodge! All of this makes me dizzy. Oh, what a chaos! Oy, it's unbearable. What am I saying? Unbearable? . . . I'll hold on . . . but even if I do, so what? I can't see beyond this unreal deep darkness like an Egyptian night . . . I can only see black! Oh, God! When will I see?!!! When will I see?!

MONDAY, FEBRUARY 28, 1944

Today I thought I wouldn't write anything, but obviously I changed my mind. I couldn't write in the workshop, because I was busy with Cipka's dress. I had a small problem with the soup, so my break was rather sad (because of the soup). But to the point! Sewing something gives me a lot of pleasure and when I finish it I'll know that I'm stronger . . . I'll know that regardless of the conditions I'll be able to move forward. I'll have a profession. I won't depend on my fate, but my fate will depend on me. I feel stronger.

A few years ago, in my dreams, when I was imagining my future, I could see sometimes: an evening, a studio, a desk, there is a woman sitting at the desk (an older woman), she's writing . . . and writing, and writing . . . all the time . . . she forgets about her surroundings, she's writing. I can see myself as this woman. Another time I could see a modest apartment that I share with my sister—earlier I thought it was Tamarcia, but today it's more probable that it's Cipka. Some other time I can see: an evening, a modest room with lights, all my family sitting at the table. It's so nice . . . so warm, cozy . . . Oh, it's so good! Later, when they all go to bed, I sit at the sewing machine and I'm sewing . . . sewing . . . it's so sweet, so good . . . so delightful! Because everything I make with my own hands is our livelihood. It pays for bread, education, clothes . . . almost everything. The work I do with my own hands . . . I'm very grateful to Mrs. Kaufman for this . . . and then (obviously only when I think about it, because it's not a reality yet), then I feel that, that I can be useful, and not only can, I have to, I have to! (I have to stop now and bring some water.)

Will I be able to write now as I was writing before? I have to try. (Oh, damn it! Cipka took my pencil case and a pen. I had to try four nibs. None of them is good and I can hardly write.) I know, because I've said it to myself many times that work is essential in human life, at least in mine. I'd like to dream up work for myself, difficult but rewarding so I'd know that I'm doing it for somebody, that there is somebody. This is most important: I'd like to give but also to take. It doesn't come easy. [. . .] Oh, to interrupt writing is not good—I'm writing completely differently now. (Mr. Dajcz brought some paper and notebooks from the paper products factory.* Sala is going to write a diary, too.) . . .

I wish this dress for Cipka were ready. I'd be very pleased. Yes, but what

---

* An adult Lodz ghetto diarist, Jakub Poznanski, worked and lived with his family at the paper products factory [*Papier-Erzeugnisse*].

does my little pleasure mean compared to all these problems and failures we face here? Oh, it's partly because people don't try to get to the core of the situation of others, they don't understand one another. But what can be done? The world was created this way. But in abnormal times evil grows bigger. Everybody is anxious . . . [. . .]

Just a while ago I was a bit glad, but now? Maybe because the cousins are at home (first Chanusia was here . . . but we hardly talked, it was all right, and now?). Their frequent anxiety and annoyance have a negative effect on me. Enough of this! Everything in moderation. When I repeat this, I always recall Mommy. Oh, I'm so happy to resemble her just a little bit. I'm always remembering her. My beloved Mommy!!! [. . .]

Once upon a time when I was five, maybe six, or maybe younger . . . it was in the evening. Mommy was sitting at the table and I—I don't know why—was a little irritated and was saying stupid, childish things that hurt Mommy a lot. I said, "I don't need such a mommy; you are not my mommy; my mommy was much better; in the other apartment the wall was painted with pretty figures, dolls and flowers, but here? . . . I don't want to be here, etc. . . ." But when I looked at my mom, I saw something that I'll never forget in my life. Never in my life will I forget her face . . . I immediately felt a stabbing pain in my heart. After all, at that time, I understood so little. Oh, even today I'm full of remorse for those words, although I was a child who understood almost nothing. Oh, God! Did I renounce my mommy at that moment!? If I had understood what I said, I surely wouldn't have done it.

What pushed me to write this? One thing leads to another. Oh, now Mommy would be very happy with me . . . she'd be so glad! It wasn't given to her. She only knew pain, suffering, and destitution. In short, she only knew this terrible, terrible life struggle . . . unfortunately . . . she was defeated.

Oh, I feel like sighing. I remember a song: "Only a Mother's Heart." Oh, if someone doesn't know what a mother is, he can come to me to find out. I know . . . I know what I had and what I lost. Oh, will I ever be a mother?

And . . . it's the same over and over again. That's how the world was created. But wise after the event . . . unfortunately after the event . . .

(Am I fooling around now?) Well, I'd like to write a little about it . . . Mother!? What does it mean? Who is this creature called mother, who with great pleasure suffers and gives birth to a new life . . . new. There is a part of her in this new life. Oh, isn't this mother powerful? Extraordinary, mighty? No doubt, yes! Nobody can do what she can do. Nobody. Even pain and suffering make her happy, there is evidence of that. First: how much she suffers before and after she gives birth to a tiny creature, hoping that in the future that tiny creature will be her pride. Or when this tiny creature gets sick? She will fight this sickness day and night, until she beats it . . . or until she drops. Oh, only a mother can do that! She can understand and sense everything. This outwardly delicate woman . . . but at the same time an all-powerful mother! [. . .]

Will I be a mother one day? Will I be powerful? I don't know why I've written this just now. I've been thinking about it for a long time. [. . .] I feel like a mother to my brother and sisters. Perhaps there is a difference between those things—a factual, tangible difference. I haven't created them (my siblings). They were created by the same person who created me; she gave us life (why am I even writing this?).

WEDNESDAY, MARCH 1, 1944

Marysia's case took a positive turn. She visited us yesterday (after all, she had nothing else to do). She talked with the cousins about various things. Quite accidentally she mentioned that she'd like to reach Rozenmutter, so he could talk to the chairman about the dormitory. Minia promised her that when everything calmed down, she'd take her to him. I'm glad that Marysia is in a better mood. She's more self-confident. Estusia told her that if she needed anything (a chair or a bowl), she could always come back and she'd get help. Marysia likes my cousins very much (she's surprised that they are a rabbi's daughters). [. . .] I'm writing standing by the tile stove, but it's cold. I have no patience to sit down and I have to check the pot every now and then. Today in the workshop I was very upset, because I couldn't sew until Mrs. Pilcewicz checked if I had made a good cut and later I could hardly get a sewing machine. I was walking around as if in a haze and felt dizzy. I let one girl use my thread, and then other girls borrowed it, too, so yesterday and today I used two spindles and now I have no thread at all. I don't know what's going to happen.

My eyes again . . . I blink a lot . . . I'd like to get out of this habit, but I can't. I know when I do it: when I'm sleepy or upset, like this morning in the workshop. I was half-conscious . . . and those eyes. Besides when I ran out of thread and asked my friends to lend me some until tomorrow, they found a thousand excuses. That's the way it is . . . here is your human gratitude. When they needed it, they got it from me right away, but in reverse? You can go crazy. I had a machine, nobody was rushing me, I could sew but I didn't have any thread. But what am I writing? It's so chaotic! Today I'm generally chaotic. [. . .] I'm writing nonsense. In the letter to Surcia I asked her whether I should be writing about this.

Oh, preparing food at home is . . . Chanusia says, "Don't add water, it's thin," or "Pour some coffee." You can't do that . . . Oh, she knows so little about "ghetto households"! What? The thin one doesn't taste good? Thicker is better . . . heh, heh! Ghetto! Ghetto! What have you done to us? Oh . . .

THURSDAY, MARCH 2, 1944

There is some unease in the ghetto. Apparently a German commission is visiting Czarnieckiego Street. Anytime soon there will be deportations . . .

tonight we will be on "high alert." Oh, we don't realize how tragic it is. Tragic . . . tragic. I'm cold. Something is chilling me. I miss warmth . . . oh, warmth! [. . .] Oh, living is so hard! In the moments like this I don't want to be among people. I'd like to be in a secluded spot. But people attract . . . and people repel. That's why there are conflicts, wars, etc. If we only had normal times! But no . . .

One more thing. I'm still impressed by last night, or rather by my dream. Oh, what was my dream?! It was dark . . . Chajusia came and said that she reported for a deportation out of honesty. Not only she . . . others did the same thing. I remembered Miss Zelicka and Surcia. Oh, I can't express the feeling I experienced. I know I saw darkness in front of my eyes. I was choking. I wasn't able to utter a word. I fought an internal struggle whether I should report, too, or stay . . . I had to be with Cipka, but I couldn't part with Surcia. Oh, what a horrible feeling! I don't remember the dream well, but everything reminds me of it. It still has me in its grip. It has a terrible impact. Oh, God, I see darkness in front of my eyes. [. . .] Oh, nerves . . . nerves . . . I'm exhausted. It's horrible . . .

First Cipka brought (she borrowed) a book from the sixth grade entitled *A Window to the World.** [. . .] When I look at this book, old memories come back to me. Already by then the schools had been closed. Mommy was sick but I was able to dream and I felt so good! Oh, it seems so far away. Today I have only memories! Only painful memories. Oh, my legs are growing stiff with cold—I'm terribly cold. All this. I know I have to hold on. I think I hold on—at least I appear to.

It's dinnertime. They're already grumbling about something. Apparently I poured the wrong *pulwer.*† Oh, all those stories. I'm impatient (though I don't show it), but most of all, I'm exhausted. I'd like to write about my

---

* Probably a reference to a sixth-grade elementary-school textbook.

† *Pulwer* is German for powder. In 1944, powdered soups and seasonings were provided to the ghetto.

thoughts and feelings, but it's not going well. I feel a grip on my throat . . .
sobbing. Oh, oh . . . maybe I shouldn't write anymore? [. . .]

SATURDAY, MARCH 4, 1944

I thought I wouldn't write today. I have a good book entitled *Les Misérables*,
which I'm sharing with Chanusia. This book has fallen apart. Some chapters
have more pages and we have to wait for each other. Right now, I'm waiting
for Chanusia. That's what reading in the ghetto is like . . . (it's late at night,
everybody is sleeping). Besides, it's not good when you have something to
write but you can't. It happens to me every Friday evening. When I come
back from Surcia's, I always have a lot to write but it's the Sabbath. Thank
God I'm not going to the workshop on Saturday. I was there only once
and . . . enough . . . enough . . .

What's more, there are posters all over saying that people who are hiding
and whose cards are blocked should report as soon as possible. They shouldn't
think they'll get away with it, etc.* It's terrible. And everything is under threat.
Yesterday when I was at Mrs. Milioner's (I was looking for Chajusia), I noticed the
faces of the people who gathered there, and they didn't herald anything good.
Oh . . . it's so hard! Besides, I'm glad that tomorrow (Sunday) I'm not going to
Marysia, but to Surcia. We'll take "a walk," which means: we'll be totally alone.

Oh, my soul is full of something . . . it's elusive . . . unidentifiable . . . I
don't know . . . [. . .] (Chanusia is rushing me to bed, she says I can finish
tomorrow. Oh, does she even know what writing is? She apparently has no
idea. Time? Estusia received a coupon and told me to pick it up tomorrow
and to take the bed linen to the laundry and this and that and this generous
Chanusia tells me to go to bed and finish tomorrow.) I'm writing about triv-
ialities. Well, good night!

---

* Proclamation No. 414 was posted in the evening hours of March 3, 1944.

SUNDAY, MARCH 5, 1944

I can't write more, only that I feel awful and downcast. I'm so sad . . . instead of going to Marysia Łucka I went to see Surcia. I told her about my mommy. In her letter Surcia mentioned a friend. Oh, I was so moved! Oh, I'm crying! I'm really crying. I can't write because of tears. Oh, I'm suffocating, I'm choking! My dear God . . . what will happen to me? Such incapacity . . . Surcia wrote that first of all we had to calm ourselves down. I turned to her for help. Oy, oy, I'm not feeling well! I'm helpless!

Enough. It's always the same. I have to do an examination of conscience . . . to persevere. The Rossets are not coming; they won't probably come today. Unrest in the streets.

MONDAY, MARCH 6, 1944

It's not good . . . they're taking young women and girls even from the workshops.* Chanusia has just come from the workshop and says that a lot of her friends were taken last night. She's expecting the same . . . she said it with a smile. Strange, but she's like that. Oh, it's awful. A group of men is coming from the bathhouse. I'm stepping aside . . .

TUESDAY, MARCH 7, 1944

I'm very sleepy. Although it's daytime. In her last letter Surcia quoted a fragment from *Jean-Christophe* about a friend.† She said I should go to

---

* On the night of March 6, 1944, 350 people, mainly single women, were delivered to the Central Prison. See Dobroszycki, ed., *The Chronicle of the Łódź Ghetto*, March 6, 1944.

† *Jean-Christophe* (Polish: *Jan Krzysztof*) was a novel written between 1909 and 1912 by the French author Romain Rolland, for which he received the Nobel Prize for Literature. It was translated into Polish by Leopold Staff.

sleep and she'd be watching over me. I don't even know how to do it. Yesterday was a bad day for me—I was so absentminded that I forgot to send a letter to Surcia.

Today I'm writing a letter to Mommy. Yes, I have to—I'm overwhelmed with a strange feeling . . . unnamed . . .

I've finished a dress for Cipka. She's going to try it on and later Mrs. Kaufman will take a look. God forbid there are any mistakes! Who knows? Oh, everything is flashing before my eyes. I seem to have a cold and the sniffles . . .

But right now it's not important. What do I matter? Nothing. I've to get back to work, which is very difficult, namely: I've fallen, or rather I'm falling; I have to lift myself up. It's important . . .

WEDNESDAY, MARCH 8, 1944

Tomorrow is Purim.* Purim! What kind of holiday is that? . . . And what times are we living in? . . . *Ven s'volt geshen aza neys vi demol[l]t?!*† . . . But do we deserve it? Although we suffer so much . . . well, why shall I beat about the bush? I'd simply like a miracle to happen. Yesterday I saw Surcia and Chajusia. Well, it's no good. They take people from the workshops at night. Besides Berka, Kon's sister, has been released today. Really, nobody could believe that. It's destiny. [. . .]

I've made a dress for Cipka and now I'm making one for myself. Enough of that. I go back to Purim. Cipka was the only one who remembered to give *mishloyekh mones*‡ to everybody from the Dajcz family, to the cousins. For

---

* Purim is a Jewish holiday commemorating the deliverance of ancient Persia's Jews from the annihilation planned by Haman. It is observed with a day of rejoicing, including costumes, celebratory meals, and gifts, as well as public readings of the Megillah, or book of Esther.

† "Oh, if only such a miracle would happen like back then."

‡ Gift parcels.

Mrs. Markus she's sent some little things: washing powder for Rózia, hair curlers for Nadzia, and a book for Pola. She's enclosed little notes on which she wrote "Trinkets." I have to admit that it was partly my idea. But it doesn't matter now . . .

Chanusia has just come back. In the morning she was at Czarnieckiego Street to see Rysia (a friend from the workshop). She says that if somebody wants to get sick, he should go there. I don't feel strong enough to write about it. If I had gone there myself, I would have to write about it, but in this case I can't . . .

Besides, what's important and unimportant is that I feel very bad . . . and physically, too . . .

THURSDAY, MARCH 9, 1944

First I went to Surcia. I read some fragments from her diary but later I had to stop because of Purim. Estusia didn't let me go (I had to be at Miss Zelicka's). Estusia wanted to have the Purim dinner together, but it didn't work, because when I came back, Cipka wasn't here (she is still not here). But that's not what I wanted to write about. So I read a little about Surcia's life. It resembles mine. Oh, this life! Oh, if only we had known then (in 1940) that it wasn't the worst, that something far worse for us was waiting, then, who knows, maybe we wouldn't have been able to stand it. [. . .]

What's more—I feel very bad. I have a sore throat, I'm hoarse and . . . is this the place to talk about it? No! There are more serious problems now and I have to step aside.

As far as my dress is concerned, today I haven't made a single seam, simply because most machines are broken, some are missing needles, and one can hardly get to those that are working. Well, just during this private work I recognized the selfishness, egoism, and anger of the girls. They are so young, and yet . . . oh, so awful. After staying with them for a while you can lose the will to do anything. And with this amount of evil, can we see a little bit of kindness? (Can we even call it kindness?) To know how to live is difficult! It's so difficult to be a true Jew! So difficult . . . difficult!

(Right now my throat scratches.) We are a little bit familiar with these hardships, because they are ours! They enter our lives, they become our lives. Oh, God! Help us walk a true and good path and ease our suffering now! It's high time . . .

*S'iz shoyn purim . . . un . . . vi iz di neys tsu velkhe vir bengin azoy?** Actually, I didn't expect anything, but . . . but I wish everything would end well! Oh, how much I want that . . .

MONDAY, MARCH 13, 1944

Dear little sun! I miss you so much! . . . but you're hiding. It's rotten weather. Wind, wet snow, mud . . . and obviously when there is mud, your shoes are soaking wet. I don't remember any winter in my life when my shoes were soaking wet. This pair is from Juvenile Protection. Today when I came back from the workshop, I couldn't stand it. I had to take off my shoes, my stockings, I had to take everything off.

Besides, it's not good in the ghetto. In the cooperative office they register people for work in Marysin.† A list has been sent from the bank to Bałucki Square.‡ Minia is on this list. Minia is (I've noticed this) a big cynic . . . she laughs all the time . . . oh . . .

Why were my first words today "dear little sun"? Oh, may your beams

---

* "It's already Purim and where is the miracle which we so long for?"

† In this period, the German administrator of the ghetto, Hans Biebow, supervised an initiative to construct prefabricated, temporary housing units that would be shipped to Germany to house victims of the Allied bombings. The work took place near the Radegast train station in Marysin. Administrative employees were registered for this labor because they were in better physical condition than many others in the ghetto.

‡ Rumkowski had one of his principal offices in Bałucki Rynek or Balut Marketsquare.

warm us from all sides! Oh, we need them so much! Little sun! Soothe us! Instead you are hiding! It's time, high time. Brr . . . it's so cold. Yesterday I didn't feel well. I had a terrible headache . . . and . . . recently my ear has been oozing, which worries me . . . you can't get cotton wool even in the pharmacies, Oh, this ghetto!

I remember that on Friday evening Surcia told me a saying attributed to King Solomon. She said that physical suffering is worse than moral suffering because physical suffering affects morality. (Did I express myself correctly?) That's the way it is. I'm experiencing it today. It makes every particular thing difficult for me. Oh, I wish at least we had our assemblies! At least something we could resort to in confidence. Recently there has been nothing, nothing. We're busy analyzing our stomachs (I don't like it), we've simply become animals . . . we're more like animals than humans. How horrible it is . . .

Yes, nowadays we learn more about people and, unfortunately, we're very disappointed. [. . .] Oh, it's so terrible, so impossibly terrible. We can only do one thing: ask God for mercy! Oh, God, help us!!!

WEDNESDAY, MARCH 15, 1944

It's a pity that last night I didn't write, because now I have really a lot to write and I don't want to stop, so I'll write it in order . . .

So, last night we agreed that three of us (Chanusia is a little sick, yesterday she had a high fever, today she's feeling better) would go to pick up some coal.* We were to collect 100 kilograms [220 pounds]. The entire ghetto

---

* The inhabitants of the ghetto were obliged to collect their entire coal ration—20 kg [44 pounds] per person—between March 11 and 17 so that the coal yard at 29 Łagiewnicka Street could be cleared out in advance of construction of quarters for metal factories. It was also announced that there would be no additional coal rations issued until May 31. Such a short time for collection of the coal caused huge lines, even though the coal yard was open until three a.m. See Dobroszycki, ed., *The Chronicle of the Łódź Ghetto*, March 10, 1944; March 17, 1944; March 20, 1944.

has to do it by Saturday. I went alone, because on the way I wanted to visit Chajusia. At 9:40 p.m. I stood in line . . .

The line was very long! Very long! Accidentally I stood among several women, who were very talkative. [. . .] One was saying, "It looks like the line is shorter at seven to seven thirty p.m. because people are having dinners." "Yes," confirmed the other one. "And at nine to nine thirty, after the meal, they leave their houses and start hunting. Oh, we live like the primitive people, we come home after a day's work, eat our meals in a hurry, and go hunting . . ." Something inside me sobbed and hurt. Yes, we're wild and primitive people and . . . we go hunting. Oh, it hurts so much! We, the people of the twentieth century—we, who just a few years ago had a relatively high standard of living, we are now compared to the primitive people! Oh, God! We lived and worked so that after a few years we could face such a comparison. Oh, it's so tragic.

Yes, I stood in line for a long time. The mud was horrible. I don't wear these leaking shoes anymore, but I wear the shoes that are very tight and I can't put on more than one pair of stockings. No wonder my feet were freezing and I was shivering. Brr. Finally . . . finally (I won't elaborate on that) I entered the coal yard. It was eleven thirty p.m. I met Estusia, Minia, and Cipka in front of a pile of coal (oh, they had to also bring Cipka). We came home at one o'clock. I had a little adventure in the street. In the Old Square, a sack (20 kilograms [44 pounds]) fell off my back (I couldn't pick up more). There was a hole in it and pieces of coal were scattered all over. I was walking alone and without any help, so I wanted to wait for Estusia. Estusia did not arrive. What to do? I had no other choice but to take out a needle, a piece of thread, and stitch it. But I couldn't lift the sack up again. As if out of spite, nobody was coming. A sled would have come in handy for me. I had been waiting for Estusia too long, so I decided to pull the sack. I walked a little bit and . . . stop . . . I was halted by a large puddle. I wanted to lift the sack up (I didn't succeed), when I suddenly heard Estusia calling me. She had been looking for me everywhere; she didn't know where I was. She went home and brought a sled. We went to bed at one thirty a.m.

Now I'm not feeling well. But enough of that. I have to collect 40 kilograms [88 pounds] more. Yes, I can see how much we're humiliated—how far we've departed from humanity. Oh, God, how stupid, hopeless (I can't find a better phrase), miserable our life is. Oh, God, how dark it is! Please, send us a beam of light! Help us! We're so wretched!

And now about today. There will be an exam in the school on Sunday. Mrs. Kaufman selected Kornela [*sic*] Kopel, Estusia Borensztajn, Henia Wajsbaum (Group II), and me to organize a program and decorations. Oh, now I have to write something for them. I have so much work. Tomorrow is Thursday. For now we've stopped private sewing, but after the exams we'll continue. Well, I have to write something.

FRIDAY, MARCH 17, 1944

I'm so absorbed with this exam that I have no more time for my diary. Yesterday I wrote a poem in Yiddish for the school performance but probably it'll be recited by Juta Alperin. I'm curious how it'll work out (because certainly people will applaud), [but] whom will they applaud? Mrs. Kaufman said that before the recitation of the poem they would announce that I was the author, so now it's a little different . . .

[. . .] I must admit I have a little problem with that but I think it's natural. Besides Juta is not a good speaker, she's started so many times . . . but what can I do? That's the way it is in the world and I have to reconcile myself to it. I was told to write it, to make some effort, etc., and after all that I'm disposable? If I were a bad speaker and Juta a good one, then it would be understandable, but it's not like that . . . anyway, why should I write about it? I have to get rid of this thought and not be so selfish!

On the other hand . . . I don't know whether anybody else has put so much effort into it, has written so much, and all this, even at home, and now? In this performance it's Kornelia who reads the essay, although it was I who was supposed to memorize it for today, well . . . I haven't read it for them even once . . . I won't lie if I write that it's *unjust*.

Unfortunately, injustice is a frequent visitor to this world. I'll get used to it and I won't be disappointed anymore. The Wajskols' cards have been unblocked.* Finally . . . after five weeks. Their father must look terrible . . .

SUNDAY, MARCH 19, 1944

The exam is over. I'd like to stay for the next course. I don't know, but it always happens to me that wherever I am, in the beginning, nobody knows me, and only later or in the end I become close to other people, like at school. (Our Bnos group is an exception; here I became close to other girls right away.) Today I asked my uncle to talk to Szuster. I will also go with Prywa to Zemlówna. It's very important to me to stay in the school. Now, I want to write about the exam. The exhibit was wonderful, everything was—guests' speeches and the performance. When Juta got to the end of reciting, Mrs. Kaufman asked her (although by accident), "Who wrote it?" "Rywcia Lipszyc," answered Juta. I had to go to the middle and show myself. I don't have the patience to write about this . . .

Besides, on the Sabbath we are going to have an assembly. Tomorrow a few girls from our group will join the older girls, because it's the *yahrzeit* of Mrs. S[arah] Schenirer's death.† And Passover is coming . . . Passover

---

* The food ration cards were blocked, probably due to the failure of a family member to report for deportation. In practice, lack of food cards meant inability to buy (collect) any sort of food from the official allocations. It was possible to count only on the help of other residents of the ghetto, although such aid was certainly not large in view of the unusually meager food rations, as well as the risk of punishment in case the help became known.

† Sarah Schenirer (1883–1935) created the network of Beys Yaacov schools affiliated with the Agudas Israel movement of Orthodox and Hasidic Jews. This date marked her *yahrzeit* (anniversary of her death, according to the Jewish calendar). She died on March 1, 1935.

is coming. Unfortunately, I'm not looking forward to it as I did every year before the war (or even during the war). I'm overwhelmed by horror thinking about it, because no doubt we'll be starving. It's a holiday that has always been welcome and yearned for, this holiday . . . well . . . ? Nevertheless I wish it were here now. Who knows? Who knows, maybe it will be better? It has to be better! It's time! High time! We're longing for this spring with nostalgia! May it come soon!

TUESDAY, MARCH 21, 1944

Because of the starvation in the ghetto people steal food from other people when they are at work, or when they aren't at home. It happens in our place, too. Unfortunately. We thought we had gotten rid of it then, but we suspect it's our tenants because "that person" is working today in the morning. Today I stayed at home, just in case somebody would come (yesterday we noticed that things were missing). I was in bed and every single murmur made my heart beat faster. I was imagining various things (I must admit that I was also full of anticipation), but nobody showed up. This doesn't mean, however, that nobody will show up. Tomorrow, probably, I'll stay at home again, maybe I'll get a doctor's note . . . but . . . mum's the word!

I have to admit we suspect one person (right now it doesn't matter whom). Oh, suspicions are terrible. A suspicion . . . a disappointment. Oh, awful things. Today in bed I had to be quiet, I couldn't move. I couldn't read all the time so I was musing. When I thought that it was murder—worse: a slow killing of somebody, making him die slowly—when I thought about it, I was so furious at "him" or "her" that if they had been at hand, I'd tear them into pieces. Animal instincts . . . God! God! What happened? How can we live in this morass, this mud, in this air filled with infectious germs. I've wondered many a time whether life was worth living. Fortunately, I know that despite everything it is. But the lives of such people are truly worthless. [. . .] Oh, it's so hard, so hard, I'd like it to be resolved so I could get rid of this suspicion. Suspicions are terrible . . .

Minia says she doesn't feel like living. What more shall I write? Perhaps once again that it's terrible. I have a lot to write, but today this is most important. Chanusia has just returned from the workshop and says that such things are "in fashion" now.

WEDNESDAY, MARCH 22, 1944

It's like yesterday. I was supposed to receive a doctor's note but I didn't and I don't know if I will. I don't know whether I'll go to work tomorrow. Anyway, I have to stand guard and the fact that nobody is showing up today only means that the rations are coming to an end. Oh, I'm so tired of this . . .

At first I thought that the weather was getting better, but we got wet snow again. Spring is not in a hurry, although we're longing for it. What will come out of this? Is it possible to hold on any longer? I can't . . . really, I can't. I'm losing my strength (not necessarily my inner strength), but that's enough. I'm so weak that sometimes I don't feel any hunger. It's awful (hunger used to have a bad effect on me). A skirt that was made for me at the beginning of the course (a few months ago) is hanging loose on me. I don't exaggerate . . . what will happen? What will happen? And on top of everything—Passover. I don't know. God! God! Send us some help! When will You finally? My heart is tearing itself apart . . . my thoughts are scattered all over . . . it's impossible to collect them . . . there is chaos . . . everything has a bad effect on me. I miss a mother's warmth, love, and heart terribly . . . oh, how I miss them! I'm very cold . . . brr . . . so cold! It's so tight around me, I don't know where to turn, I'm feeling so bad! You, my diary, must be feeling bad, too, because you have to absorb so many sorrows. [. . .]

I want to hold on, stand firmly, and not to lose my balance, but that requires some strength that unfortunately I don't have. If only we had the assemblies, I could draw some strength from them . . . and now I'm feeling so lonely, so helpless *az ikh broykh nisim!*[*]

God! Help me now! Help us now!

THURSDAY, MARCH 23, 1944

I'm in the workshop. Nobody stayed at home. Now Cipka is with me; they are not letting people out, probably there is some commission in town.[†] There is still some unease. Oh . . . Last night I was feeling so bad, so weak! What has happened to me? I've changed so much! I decided not to give my diary to Surcia tomorrow, because she'd be upset by all this. I'll give it to her next week, but I don't know, maybe I'll give it to her after all . . . [. . .] We can't leave the workshop. This commission must be very important.

FRIDAY, MARCH 24, 1944

Yesterday Prywa and I went to Zemlówna. She said she'd talk to her brother about my request (to stay for the next course). Besides, her mother is at home. She spent seven weeks in the hospital and I conclude from the conversation that she was and is seriously ill. We stayed there long, until nine thirty p.m. She told us a lot about the hospital.

---

[*] "That I need miracles!"

[†] According to an entry in Dobroszycki, ed., *The Chronicle of the Łódź Ghetto*, dated March 23, 1944, a commission of about forty men from the Anti-aircraft Defense Service (*Służba Obrony Przeciwlotniczej*) arrived in the ghetto on that date to visit nearly all of the more important enterprises.

SATURDAY, MARCH 25, 1944

A letter to Surcia: My beloved Surcia!

. . . You write that it's love (*I wrote to Surcia that I had this feeling of affection*). It's possible. Do I love? It's possible! But I must love very little indeed, because whom can I love? There are so few people whom I really love. Perhaps . . . perhaps I love, but . . . does anybody love me? Certainly, there are fewer people like that! Yes, after your letter I can see it more clearly. That's what I desire—I'd like to make a cozy little place, full of love. I'd like to offer my love because I know that everybody needs it. I know how much I need it, how much I desire it, so I can identify with a situation and understand how much love is needed. I tell you, I was, and still am, so moved when I read it. You have no idea.

And now about people. I thought about it for a long time. (Now, after your letter I can see it more clearly.) I love people! Yes, I do love them, but not each person separately, just all of them together. Besides, I feel sorry for them. I feel sorry for them, because they see and know so little; because they are so narrow-minded (I mean the people from the ghetto); because they don't care what they do; because they are reckless. It doesn't mean that this is my opinion about all of them, but the majority are like that. (I'd like to help them so much!) [. . .] Besides, you know that recently I've been disappointed with people and still am. It makes me distrustful and more cautious (it won't hurt). I don't trust people. When I meet somebody, I'm not the way I usually am, I have to know this person better, I must know what kind of person it is. In the beginning I'm just polite (if I can call it like that) and then . . . it depends . . . I can see (I've noticed) that people have many defects and in many cases they hurt themselves. Egoism is one of those damaging characteristics. (Oh, dear Surcia, I can feel now how much I'd like to help them, because I can see that people don't notice certain things, they don't let anybody instruct them or tell them what to do, and I'd like them to help one another.) That's why it's so hard for me. I can't do anything now, really, but I should hope that in the future, when I'm older, I'll have some influence on people, that I'll succeed. But I don't want to write about this.

(I can see that we need a conversation, I have so much to write to you and to tell you, but somehow it's not working.) Oh, dear Surcia, it doesn't mean that I think I'm superior to those people, not at all (I'm the same human being), but it's based on the facts. I must have bored you to death. I feel I have something to tell you from the bottom of my heart and . . . I don't know, it's not working . . .

Good night for now, I kiss you strongly and sincerely.

Your loving Rywcia

Perhaps tomorrow I'll visit the two sick Dorkas. We'll talk about the assemblies . . . I'm going to sleep. Good night!

TUESDAY, MARCH 28, 1944

I have little time. Yesterday (the first day after receiving the ration), Estusia stayed at home, but nothing happened. Last night we were baking matzos. Minia and I were rolling them out. Last year we were baking them, too, but what a difference between those two holidays! First of all, last year we had more flour, more strength, and even the weather was different! It was pleasant and warm, even hot, and today? Oh, it's more like winter! Everything has changed! (They predict a hot summer, let it come quickly, faster!) But I'm not going to spend my time writing about it. We came home at three a.m. And for this reason I didn't go to work today. [. . .]

Finally after four p.m. Minia came back. I found out that yesterday Rozenmutter talked to the chairman and they needed people to roll out the matzos in the bakery, which had just opened. Minia was to be among them.* She was to report to the bakery (at 14 Pasterska Street) at six p.m. with a note she was about to receive. However, she didn't get the note before six and she went to see Rozenmutter without it. It turned out later that it was Dwojra who had the note. When Estusia brought it to Minia, it was too late. She was told to come back the next day. Now Minia, totally upset, has gone to one bed and Chanusia, equally upset, to the other.

Today was so idiotic for me. As for the food, I have no idea what's happening. Could it be an illusion? Moreover, there was no snow today. The sun was shining. I asked God not to make it set . . . maybe, maybe finally, the longed-for spring will come! May it come! There are letters coming from the recently deported. They write that they are doing well, etc., but I don't believe it. God forbid! Maybe they were forced to write those letters.† God forbid! May it not be true! Who knows? . . .

Oh, yesterday I caught a nasty cold. When I got up first, I almost fell down. Despite everything, despite this hunger, I'm looking forward to Passover. I want this holiday to come as soon as possible. Oh, I have so much, so much

---

* Assignment to work in a bakery was a special privilege in the ghetto. In this instance, employees from factories and workshops were sent to work on the baking of matzo for a period of ten days, or about as long as production was to last. It was especially helpful during Passover, when the matzo ration was 1 to 1.2 kg [2.2 to 2.64 pounds] (as compared to a standard loaf of bread in the ghetto, which weighed 2 kg [4.4 pounds]). Such an assignment would give the privileged persons the opportunity to significantly increase their food intake during that period. See Dobroszycki, ed., *The Chronicle of the Łódź Ghetto*, March 28, 1944.

† Rywka's suspicions were right. These letters were written at the command of the Germans in order to calm the Jews in the ghetto.

to write. After all, this is the first time I'm writing this week! Yes, one more thing, our workshop is moving to 25 Młynarska Street and I'll have quite a walk. Almost everybody is happy about this move, but I'm not [. . .] What, shall I finish now? But I feel I have so much to write. Estusia wants the pen. There are rumors that it's going to be better. Oh, I'd love to believe it, I'd love it to be all right, oh, at least better, a little better, a little comfort . . .

I'm worried about my health (naturally, nobody at home knows about this). I'm downcast. I need a little bit of life, a vital life, something concrete. It seems that I'm like a lonely tree in the field. There are storms and wild winds around it. The tree is standing and it's slowly losing its strength, but it's outliving other trees growing in better conditions, because its organism is strong. I must, I want to believe that this is the way it should be. It's not so easy! [. . .] I'm going to sleep. I'm feeling very bad! What's going to happen?

WEDNESDAY, MARCH 29, 1944

Today I have to write about it. I mentioned that in the letter to Surcia I wrote about an overwhelming feeling; I couldn't name it, I didn't know it, it was a burden to me. If it weren't for Surcia, I still wouldn't know it. Surcia wrote me (I forgot to add: it's some feeling of affection), that I was filled with love. (I replied to her letter on Saturday evening.) Oh, how grateful I am to Surcia. Yes, now I know for sure it's love! When I'm overcome by this feeling, I'd like things to be all well and for it to be warm. When I think about it I'm overtaken by such affection that . . . I feel like crying! (Unfortunately it's suppressed, because I don't cry, I suppress my crying.) At this moment I'd like to embrace the entire world, hug it, warm it. At this moment I'm not jealous that others are doing better, but I feel sorry for those who suffer. Oh, at this moment I totally forget about myself, as if I didn't exist. At this moment I'd like to do so much for the world. I see many, many defects and I feel so sorry that I can't find a place for myself. And when I realize that I don't matter in the world, that I'm just a speck of dust, that I can't do anything, at this moment I feel much worse, I'm suffocating and I'm helpless . . .

In order to screw up my courage I tell myself, "After all, I'm still young, very young. What else can happen?" But time is passing by. It's the fifth year of the war. Sometimes I ask myself, "What do I care? Why am I so interested in all this? I don't do anything, after all." But there is always a little voice whispering, "But you do!" And it always wins. [. . .] The only thing that's encouraging me (as I've mentioned before) is the hope that it won't always be like this and that I'm still young. Maybe I'll grow up to be somebody and then I'll be able to do something. Because I am Jewish, I believe and hope. I hope that this "hope" has some strong foundation. God, make the time go faster. (What time?)

. . . The weather has deteriorated, it's terribly windy, although yesterday the sun was shining. If it weren't for Passover, I would think it's January. I borrowed a sheepskin coat from Prywa because I'm very cold. Yes, Lola R[o]sset was laid off from the kitchen; what a pity!

THURSDAY, MARCH 30, 1944

Yesterday after I ate the soup, I definitely got a fever. I was about to go to the doctor, when Mrs. Kaufman called Kornela, Estusia, and me to her office. What is happening? On Sunday on Żydowska Street there will be a repeat of the exam, a skill demonstration. We (from Franciszkańska Street) are to join it and add our program. Probably about ten girls from our group will be in a delegation. But what's most important, we have to organize a program and take it to Żydowska Street at three p.m. When we announced it in class, there was a rebellion. Why only ten girls? As for the program, we had very little time because it was Wednesday, and they have been getting ready for weeks. We didn't want to be embarrassed. We talked to Mrs. Kaufman and tried to convince her. Finally we gave up, but Mrs. Kaufman promised to find out whether she should send only ten girls or all of them. I was feeling awfully ill and didn't want to think about it. [. . .]

After work I decided to check my temperature. If I had a fever, I'd go home without any "but," although it would be good if I didn't. [. . .] I went down to see a doctor and . . . I almost burst out in laughter. He prescribed some pain relievers, but he didn't have a thermometer. At last at the committee for the sick I checked the temperature, but it was 38.5°C [101.3°F]. It has dropped so much in a few hours! [. . .] At three thirty p.m., I was already home. I didn't know what happened to Minia. Chanusia came back after five p.m. She had paid for the matzos and they were to be collected the day before. I told her I couldn't go, because I wasn't feeling well, but I felt sorry for her. She had been in line to get canned meat. What a surprise! She believed me. Estusia did, too. I almost didn't go to the workshop today. But I can't miss work every second day. [. . .]

After all, I wish it were the holiday now. I'd have some rest. Maybe by thought I could wander somewhere . . . where I could find some comfort. To find some comfort?! At least for now. Or to hold on to hope. O hope, don't leave me! Oh, there are so many things I have to do during the holidays, the assemblies or the classes. Oh, when I think how much I have to learn, how little I know, I'm so eager to have the classes that . . . I don't know.

MONDAY, APRIL 3, 1944

Yesterday we worked so hard! Especially Estusia and I. In the evening we're baking matzos. Thank God, thank God, a hundred, a thousand times for this miraculous change of weather! Yesterday we opened the balcony. Oh, one wants to live! It's so different now! On Saturday I got up earlier (I was waiting for Surcia), I simply couldn't stay in bed. Young blood flowed in my veins. Youth! Youth full of life! Something in me was calling! (After all, my little poem had some effects! On Friday I wrote a poem about spring.) God.

Thank you, thank you for this miraculous change of weather. My hope is revived. Oh, really, I have no words of gratitude for God! I wish the holiday were here now! I wish the summer were here! I wish . . . I don't know. I only know that I want to live! I want to live!!! Yesterday when we were baking the matzos, it wasn't so cold. Oh, all of this! I'm afraid that it may disappear soon. But I'm driving this thought away. To live now! To live!

[. . .] Oh, I want to live! I want to sing! Spring! Beloved spring! (I can't recall a day like that in my diary. Oh, this awful ink. Everything runs together in one word! Little spring! Little spring!)

WEDNESDAY, APRIL 5, 1944

Because of the holidays there is a lot of commotion. But not everything is positive, unfortunately. Yesterday those who registered for matzos didn't get any bread.* They can starve for a few days or eat matzos. Well, it's not so easy to be a Jew. At every step there are difficulties. And the weather is capricious, too, although no doubt it is much better, but . . . children who were adopted receive coupons, so Cipka and I do, too. What we'll get, I don't know, that will become clear today. Some kitchens were registering people for the holiday soup. A few girls from our group are leaving at ten a.m. Today, we'll find out. Anyway! I wish it were a holiday right now! During the holidays I won't know where to go first, to Dorka Zand, to Mrs. Lebensztajn, to Dorka Borensztajn and . . . and I don't know myself, and now . . . I've planned to write tomorrow, but I don't know whether I'll be able to or whether I'll have an opportunity.

Three years ago the holidays fell on the same days. It was the last holiday, the last Seder with my daddy. Oh, time goes by so quickly! Daddy was

---

* Between March 11 and 18, 1944, it was possible to register at the bakeries for matzo in place of bread. In place of one loaf of regular bread one could receive 1 kg to 1.2 kg [2.2 pounds to 2.64 pounds] of matzo. See Dobroszycki, ed., *The Chronicle of the Łódź Ghetto*, March 9, 1944. See footnote, page 167.

supposed to be released from the hospital for the holidays. *Erev Peysekh,*⃰ like this year, fell on Friday, so Daddy came back on Thursday (like tomorrow). We, the children, were very impatient all day and every few minutes we would approach the window or the balcony to see if an ambulance was coming. [. . .] I couldn't stay still in one spot but I remember how happy I was that Daddy was coming back. We, the children, weren't allowed in the hospital, so we would write letters and Mom would take them to Daddy. I discovered so much love for us in Daddy's letters. God! Perhaps because of this separation, because of these letters, I loved him even more.

In the winter I saw Daddy in the hospital window. He was cheerful, he could easily pour his own reassurance into me, he said he was better, and soon we'd see each other. Didn't I see for myself that he was doing better? Yes, that's why I still believed his words. I was full of hope and reassurance myself. Later, Daddy took a turn for the worse, the hospital itself was getting worse, but nevertheless Daddy was supposed to come home for the holidays.

On that Thursday I didn't remember or I didn't want to remember that Daddy was feeling much worse than in the winter. However, I was very happy that finally he'd be at home. At that time I remembered only the good things, like Daddy holding my hand on Yom Kippur, the letters and the visits. [. . .] In the evening, at last the ambulance stopped in front of the gate. I was on the balcony and my heart totally stopped for a second. And then it started to pound so violently that I thought my chest would explode. I had no idea what to do: stay in place or run to the door. I don't exactly remember what I did. I only know that it seemed forever when my daddy was climbing the stairs. Finally, finally, Daddy was in the room and . . . how disappointed I was . . . it wasn't the same daddy as the one in the hospital window. He didn't even smile, didn't respond to our greetings. He was upset and visibly tired. He wanted to go to bed as soon as possible. We had to leave the room.

⃰ Passover eve.

God! This feeling! It was in the evening, but the light wasn't on yet. In that darkness everything was black in front of my eyes. I simply didn't see anything or anyone. Like a drunk, I stumbled into the other room. I felt like sobbing, but I didn't. I remained silent. Various thoughts were running through my head: what's wrong with Daddy? Why is he so different? I didn't expect this. [. . .] I was telling myself that he was only tired, but I was overcome by a strange anxiety. I was bothered by the thought that Daddy wasn't thinking about us. [. . .] It is true, later I calmed down about the change in Daddy. We even talked to him, although I was very shy, but in my heart . . . there was a pain, a sorrow in my heart. I don't know, I don't know what to call it. Such feelings always wear me out, reduce my energy. I'm unable to do anything. When Daddy wanted a cup of tea, I brought it for him with great difficulty. I had to bring it, because it would look bad that here he is from the hospital and I'm disobedient. The next day I tried to do everything right, although Daddy was very upset. I tried to make every good moment last and not irritate him. Oh, nobody will ever know how hard it was for me and how "cold" I was feeling. And yet nobody knew. [. . .] I withdrew into myself. Nobody could get anything out of me. After all, nobody even supposed that I was worried. Oh, how much I needed a kind word, how much I wanted to be alone with Daddy. I wanted him to be like he was in the past. I missed all that and I felt so helpless, so helpless.

After a few days Daddy regained his cheerfulness and good spirits, but I didn't have any more opportunities to fulfill my dreams. We were all very happy to be in one room with Daddy. We didn't talk much, but we exchanged looks. Oh, those looks! I couldn't say anything at all, not even that I wished him to get better, nothing . . . simply nothing. I was very awkward. But I wanted to, I wanted to. Only God knows this, because I didn't tell anybody.

Oh, now I'm remembering it all. I can't even look at Daddy anymore, only at his picture. But I'll never see Daddy alive, never see him alive again, never again. God! How terrible it is! It's going to be the third Seder without

Daddy, and the second one without any man at all. Last year Aunt Chaiska was here, and today . . . today there is Estusia. Oh, it's so tragic! If only Abramek were here! Oh, God, precisely on Pesach, at the Seder, Daddy will be missed most. Oh, he'll be missed so much . . .

FRIDAY, APRIL 7, 1944

Yesterday I did the right thing to write. But to the point: God does not abandon. *G-t farlozt nisht. Ven me tut zikh nisht fablozn un s'geyt zer in dem ver zol ophitn helft G-t!** Apart from the coupons (for the adopted children), we received a coupon from the Rabbinate.† Wonderful coupons! It's late, I have to finish my breakfast!

TUESDAY, APRIL 11, 1944

I have so much to write that I don't know where to start. Well, never mind. It's the second day of the holidays. How was the first day? How was the Seder? The Seder? How could it be?! *Nebekh!*‡ Oh, Daddy's absence made our life miserable. The Seder without Daddy, but without not only Daddy, without men at all . . .

Last year there were no men, either, but our aunt was here. She could replace a man, because she was an adult and knew a lot, but today? She's gone. The Seder was celebrated by Estusia. It's true that she did it very well,

---

* Yiddish: The aphorism appears to be garbled. It seems to mean: "God does not abandon. If one does not become agitated and it really depends on whether one observes [the Torah], God helps!"

† There was no official rabbinate in the Lodz ghetto after September 1942. However, certain rabbinical functions, like conducting weddings, were taken over by Rumkowski himself. This might refer to a part of Rumkowski's administration that distributed coupons to religiously pious Jews who were considered worthy of extra privilege. Rywka and her sister received a coupon, probably because of their family connection to the late Rabbi Segal and other former local rabbis.

‡ "A pity!"

but . . . oh, this "but" is so sad! God, was I really at fault, that you punished me so much? I have friends in the workshop who have fathers, but their fathers don't celebrate the Seder. But why? I could have had the Seder, if only Daddy . . . Oh, God! This is what it's like in the world!

If my daddy had celebrated the Seder, I'd have been so happy! Others have their fathers (they are lucky), but they don't want the Seder at all. After the second Seder I became so sad! Oh! I wanted to burst into tears. Just to think that Daddy will never celebrate the Seder for us, never. It's been the third year, and I still can't reconcile myself to this thought. Daddy will never celebrate the Seder for us. It sounds so painful. It hurts so much! [. . .] I prayed to God so that the next Seder would be celebrated by Abramek . . . [. . .]

What's more, yesterday (Monday) people didn't work in the workshops. It was a day off.* We picked up the rest of the coal, or rather the briquettes. In the evening there was an assembly at Mrs. Milioner's. There will be courses for the older and for the younger girls. Oh, what excitement. One must admit that the weather has its effects.

Thank you, God, for the spring! Thank you for this mood! I don't want to write much about it, because I don't want to mess it up, but I'll write one very significant word: hope!

Besides, we probably will have a plot of land.†

For the holidays, Chanusia took sick leave and stayed home, and yesterday

---

* The *Chronicle* of April 8, 1944, refers to the two free days (Sunday–Monday, April 9–10): "The labor departments were informed by the Central Bureau, Bałuty Marketplace, that Easter Sunday and Easter Monday will be days free from work. This is the first such case in the existence of the ghetto that people will not work on both days. Moreover, today the end of work was set for 12:00 noon. People have no concept how this instruction should be understood. [. . .] In reality what is involved is that the gentlemen of the Ghetto Administration this time wanted to have off on Easter and that the population of the ghetto has nothing to fear in relation to this."

† In the ghetto, every fragment of soil was taken advantage of for farming vegetables and fruits. Most of the plantations were in the Marysin area, where before the war there were garden plots and parcels of land. Individual families could get a parcel to farm with the obligation to supply vegetables to the community but with the privilege of saving a portion for themselves. Due to continual shortages of food, there were many eager to farm the allotments.

I had a lot to deal with because of her soup rations. We had an assembly on Sunday. I'm so happy. Maybe it'll be better, maybe finally it'll be all right? Oh, as soon as possible! Oh, this excitement. It seems to be overcoming everyone. In a way it's because of this wonderful change in the weather. Yes, no doubt about it. [. . .] Only the Lord knows what we need and . . . Oh, God, give us what we need! Give it to us!

(Oh, summer rain is falling!)

WEDNESDAY, APRIL 12, 1944

Oh, the weather is so beautiful! Beautiful! Beautiful! Oh, I'm so happy, it's such a great comfort . . .

Yesterday Prywa and I went to see Zemlówna. It's not clear yet, but I hope that everything will be taken care of, if possible. It's almost a month since the exams. Not only don't we work on producing anything, but we come as we please, we go as we please, and we take care of our private affairs as we please. Freedom, paradise. Oh, it would be great if it lasted longer (at least through the holidays). But who knows? These are workshop matters and there's no time to debate them now (I just don't want to work with the machines in the summer).

Last night I was walking home. After we saw Zemlówna, Prywa, and I visited Fela Działowska. We registered for the courses and decided to join the library. It will be better than the literature club. I think Bala will help us. I'd like it to work! Because of this, when I was walking home I realized how beautiful youth was. If I only had a piece of paper, I'd have written something. Later, I recalled the "Ode to Youth" and it happened that I had this very volume of Mickiewicz with me.* At moments like this I want to

---

* Adam Mickiewicz (1798–1855), Polish national poet, was the author of "Oda do młodości" ["Ode to the Youth"].

live so much. There is less sadness, but we're more aware of our miserable circumstances, our souls are sad, and . . . really one needs a lot of strength in order not to give up. We look at this wonderful world, this beautiful spring, and at the same time we see ourselves in the ghetto deprived of everything, we're deprived of everything, we don't have the smallest joy, because, unfortunately, we're machines with well-developed animal instincts. They're visible everywhere (mostly during the meals). It all affects us so much that we become duller and duller. Looking at us, one can see how much effort we need to create a better daily life, in which . . .

Why shall I even write about it? I want it, I want it so much. When I realize that we're deprived of everything, that we're slaves, I try to put off this thought in order not to spoil this joyful little moment. How hard it is! Oh, God, how much longer? I think that only when we are liberated we will enjoy a real spring. Oh, I miss this dear spring . . .

First, Ms. Hania (from the office) informed us that those born in 1926/27 could work for ten hours and have *Lang*. But they would need a document from the Registration Department stating their dates of birth. I'm afraid nobody will apply. For now, I'm glad about this turn of events, because I was born in 1927, but actually . . .*

---

* Rywka was actually born on September 15, 1929. It is unclear why she wrote her birth year as 1927, unless she either made a mistake or was thinking of giving a false birth date in order to register for long-shift work to get the supplemental rations that came with it.

Part III

AFTERMATH

The Family Remembers

More Than a Name

HADASSA HALAMISH

I only knew Rywka by name: Rywka Lipszyc.

As the Israeli poet Zelda said, "Every person has a name that was given by his parents, and one that was given by God."

All I knew about Rywka was that she lived during the war. Beyond that, I knew absolutely nothing; I could only imagine. What kind of girl was Rywka? Was she pretty? Was she outgoing? Did she have braids? Did she have dreams? Was she skinny or fat? In my mind, I could picture her any way I liked.

No matter how much I asked my mother about Rywka, she couldn't tell me anything. My mother knew her very well; they belonged to the same generation. They spent the hardest years of the terrible war together, all the way until the end. They even slept in the same bunk, on the same bed of misery. Still, my mother couldn't tell me about Rywka, just as she couldn't tell me about the other members of her family who no longer existed, who rose to the heavens through the ovens of Auschwitz.

My mother, Mina, was born to Hadassah and Yochanan Lipszyc in the Polish city of Lodz in 1926. She was the third daughter in the family, after Esther and Channah. The house she grew up in belonged to her grandfather, Moshe Menachem Segal of blessed memory, who was the city's rabbi. Grandfather had five children, but it was his oldest, Hadassah, who stayed with him, even after she married Rabbi Yochanan Lipszyc of blessed memory. Rabbi Yochanan was a judge in the Lodz rabbinical court. Mina's grandfather, Rabbi Moshe Menachem, and her father, Yochanan Lipszyc, served the community with great dedication.

Mother used to tell us about a house full of life, full of Torah. She spoke of the cabinets filled with holy books, and of the dining room tables that, on Sabbath and holidays, were adorned with silver platters laden with all kinds of delicacies. She also talked about the needy people who relied on their support. She told us about her grandmother, Tseluva Leya of blessed memory, and how she ran the household with a firm hand. People used to come to the house, she said, to ask the rabbi questions, not only about Halacha (Jewish law) but about worldly matters as well. She spoke of a home that was focused on giving to others, and, above all, to steadfast faith in God.

When Mother spoke of home, she mostly talked about her *yichus*—her prestigious ancestry. Her maternal great-grandfather was Eliyahu Chaim Mezul [Maizel] of blessed memory, who was the rabbi of Lodz. Rabbi Eliyahu Chaim was known for his skill, his wisdom, and his keen mind. He led the Jews of Lodz with modesty and kindness, and he was recognized by the Polish government for his many accomplishments. In fact, the city of Lodz recently dedicated a garden in his memory, on the hundredth anniversary of his death.

Mother didn't say much about the family of her father, Rabbi Yochanan Lipszyc, perhaps because nobody from his family survived, at least not to my knowledge. The pain of loss is unbearable, and therefore rarely discussed. My questions were generally answered in a matter-of-fact way. Mother remembered the names of the uncles, but not those of their spouses or children.

In 1990, my daughter Tamar went to Poland on a youth mission. When she came back, full of experiences to share, she asked to write a family history. This was the first time Mother

Rywka's cousins, Esther and Mina (right), at Mina's wedding in 1949. *(Courtesy of Hadassa Halamish)*

was willing to help us with our family tree, to bring all her relatives who had died in the Holocaust back to life, at least on paper. From this large and re- markable family, only two girls survived, Esther and Mina, and, thank God, they created new families to carry on the names of those who died.

Avraham Dov and Esther Lipszyc had eight children. Yochanan, the third son, married Hadassah. Yankel, the fifth son, married Miriam Zelwer (Rywka's mother). All of them lived near each other in Lodz and saw each other fre- quently. When the war broke out, and the sense of uncertainty was enormous, everyone tried to save their families and themselves. There was an atmosphere of panic and chaos; some people tried to run away, without knowing where. Their lives were filled with fear, anxiety, and a desperate search for solutions.

Yankel Lipszyc tried to run away with his brother-in-law, Noach Vladmirsky. A bomb fell on a house near Lodz and buried Noach. Yankel waited for his proper burial, then went home. One day, he went outside and was caught by Germans, who beat him mercilessly. The volley of blows that rained down upon his head and body left him severely injured. He was taken to the hospital, where they did their best to restore him to health, and he was able to return home (as Rywka describes in her diary). But he continued to have pulmonary problems, and a year later he died of his injuries. He was buried in Lodz on June 2, 1941.

Miriam was left with four children: Rywka, her sisters Cypora (Cipka) and Tamarcia, and her brother, Abramek (Abram)—four small kids, living in the squalor of the ghetto. Despite the help of her many relatives still living in the ghetto, starvation exacted its cost, and Miriam succumbed on July 8, 1942—a month before the *szpera* (mass deportation).

Now there were four orphaned children between the ages of two and thirteen. Three weeks after the death of their mother, the deportation took place. Abram and Tamarcia were taken to their destruction, and Rywka (thirteen) and Cypora (ten) were left all alone. They were supposed to go into the ghetto's orphanage, but family members took it upon themselves to rescue the girls. Rywka and Cypora were adopted by my grandmother, Hadassah.

Hadassah, too, had lost her husband, Rabbi Yochanan of blessed memory, who had been taken to Chelmno and murdered there. In addition to Rywka and Cypora, Hadassah had also taken another niece under her wing, a three-year-old girl named Esther. Hadassah was now living in her house with six girls; her three daughters: Esther, Channah, and Mina; Yankel's daughters Rywka and Cypora; and little Esther, the daughter of Tova Vladmirsky, the sister of Yochanan and Yankel Lipszyc.

My mother told me that her mother was so devastated by the loss of her husband that it fell to Esther to look after the home and the children. Hadassah became severely ill due to hunger, and the girls took turns tending to her. My mother told us how they took on extra work to get food for their mother, and how they dedicated themselves to saving her life, until on July 11, 1943, her heart stopped.

Now there were five girls living in the house by themselves: Esther, Channah, Mina, Rywka, and Cypora. (Little Esther had gone to live with another aunt on her father's side at the age of three; she died along with the rest of her family.)

What was it like for them? I had no idea. What was life in the ghetto like? "Hard." That's the only answer I would get. Esther, who was not yet twenty-one, was the oldest and served as a surrogate mother to the rest of them, but I never really understood what losing their parents, or fighting for survival, had meant for her and for my mother. My impression is that Esther felt responsible for the rest of them, and Mother felt that she had someone she could depend upon.

About a year ago, someone from Yad Vashem contacted me and asked if I had ever heard of Rywka Lipszyc. I knew that she existed, but I didn't know anything else about her. That's when I found out that a family from Moscow had held on to a diary their grandmother had found in the ashes of Auschwitz. It was a diary kept by Rywka in the Lodz ghetto. In it, she described her experiences during this difficult period.

> Write! . . . Only write! . . . Then I forget about food and everything else, about all the trouble (it's an exaggeration). May God grant Surcia health and happiness, at least for suggesting to me this wonderful idea that I write a diary.
>
> (FEBRUARY 11, 1944)

In this stunning, personal testimonial, Rywka writes about the suffering and excruciating hunger she experienced. She describes the life of a growing girl who is learning things about the world and about people, who watches the world around her and tries to understand the impossible reality that exists in these crazy circumstances. Most of all, she writes about how much she misses her mother, her father, and her little brother and sister. She saw her parents die, but she has no idea what happened to her brother or younger sister. She realizes she will probably never see them again. Who can she share her thoughts with? Who can she talk to about her pain? She finds comfort in her diary; the diary is her secret self. She writes that she has to hide it from her cousins. This is the only way she can preserve her soul: to hide her authentic self from everyone else.

Is it possible to be authentic in an impossible reality?

In the reality of war—a reality too unstable to rely upon—Rywka looked for something to anchor her, and she found it in God. It was to God that she addressed her prayers and her faith. Had she not grown up in a home that was built on faith, a home in which religious life was the greatest liberty of all, she would have been devoid of any comfort during these incomprehensible times. Reading her diary, we see that her pain and hunger were getting increasingly difficult. The food supply was dwindling, she had no tools to work (all the sewing machines were broken, and there was nobody to fix them), and time was becoming a precious resource. She had no time for herself or for her writing; she lived on prayer and faith. She found comfort in Torah study and in preparing for the Seder. She regretted that her need for work compelled her to break Shabbat, and she asked that never again would she have to go through a terrible experience like this.

Oh, it's Friday again! Time goes by so fast! . . . Do we know? What's waiting for us in the future? I'm asking this question with both fear and youthful curiosity. We have an answer to this,

a great answer: God and the Torah! Father God and Mother Torah! They are our parents! Omnipotent, Omniscient, Eternal!!! . . . I have a support, a great support: my Faith, because I believe! Thanks to it I'm stronger, richer, and more worthy than others . . . God, I'm so grateful to You!!!

(FEBRUARY 11, 1944)

Through the diary, Rywka reveals herself as a Jewish girl full of faith in God. She sees God in everything she does.

I am amazed that such a young girl—she was only fourteen—could be so incredibly aware of her emotions. Rywka was fighting for her life. She didn't want to simply survive; she was choosing life! She knew that this choice would bring sorrow and pain, but to her it was better than choosing to live without feeling.

Last night I thought: happy is a person who is unaware, totally unaware, like a child. Unhappy is a person who is aware of his unawareness . . . I belong to the latter category. I'm miserable. What's worse, I can't find any solution. I don't know what to do . . . it's the same over and over again . . . I have only one answer to everything: Surcia. Oh, Surcia . . .

(DECEMBER 23, 1943)

The way Rywka analyzes her life through the prism of her emotions is astounding. She is always studying people: how they behave, and how they embody the divine image. She watches them and scrutinizes their actions. She even advises her younger sister, Cypora, to keep a diary of her own and teaches her how to observe people. And in the cruel reality in which she lives, she discovers, to her dismay, how people can turn into beasts, into cheaters and liars, how they will steal your food, how they will sacrifice their friends in order to survive. These observations weigh heavily upon her, and sometimes—when life becomes meaningless or intolerably cruel—she wants to die.

Living with her cousins is hard for her. She knows she is there as an act of kindness. She doesn't feel like it's her home, and she bemoans the fact that she has no home. She doesn't feel like she belongs where she is, and as a result, she doesn't help out as much as others may expect of her. This makes her cousins angry—none more so than Esther, who runs the household. The others get angry, and she doesn't respond. They complain to her teachers. She tries to do her best and hopes that all will be well. Rywka thinks they don't understand her. Her diary becomes her sanctuary. The paper endures everything.

Esther remembers one day when Rywka disappeared from the home just when her help was most needed. She remembers how Rywka would close herself off from everyone else and write. Mina, on the other hand, didn't always believe that Rywka kept a diary, because she had never seen her writing. Rywka felt like a stranger in the house. Poor girl.

Rywka decided to go to school; she was such a curious child. She loved to read and write, to ponder the meaning of life. School was a refuge for her. There she studied literature, exchanged books with others, wrote plays, and composed songs. School became her workplace, and it was there that she received her food rations. It was also in school that she found love—love of Surcia (Surcha). Surcia was her counselor, and like all growing girls who admire the people they want to emulate, Rywka admired Surcia.

We now know that Surcia is Sara Selver-Urbach. She was a member of the Lodz Jewish Women's Association, and she was Rywka's spiritual mentor. She, too, kept a diary, and she published a memorial book for her relatives: *Through My Window: Memories from the Lodz Ghetto*. Sara's diary, it seems, was destroyed in the flames of Auschwitz. In her book and her autobiography, she writes that after the agony of Auschwitz, she was sent to a work camp. There, she wrote the story of her life on random pieces of paper that she found lying around. These fragments of paper survived and remained in Sara's possession. They can be found in her book. Reading these assorted pages, you can see a strong similarity to Rywka's writing style.

We (my aunt, my mother, and I) met with Sara after Rywka's diary found its way into our hands. I hoped she could tell us about Rywka. Sadly, Sara's condition prevented her from speaking clearly about Rywka, and I was left with the question: Was Sara related to Rywka on her mother's side? Did Sara know how much Rywka loved her, or was her love concealed?

When I finished reading Sara's diary, I felt very sad about this missed opportunity. I still didn't know Rywka. I had tried to get more information from Mother in the past, but whenever I asked about Rywka's fate, her only answer was a terse "she died." Mother left the dead to themselves so that she could build a new life.

Still, I persisted. I asked Mother to tell me about what happened to them after they left the ghetto. Mother told me her story, and Esther told me hers. Their versions were similar, but different, too. Memory is subjective, and each of them remembers things differently.

In August 1944, after the ghetto was destroyed, five girls stood together in the train station for a journey to the unknown. One of them was given a loaf of bread, which they took with them to Auschwitz. I asked them what else they brought with them. Mother said she didn't remember; Esther said she brought photographs of her family members. Rywka, it seems, took her diary. When they got to Auschwitz, they went through Mengele's (may his name be wiped out) infamous selection process. Cypora was sent to the left. Esther, in her role as protective "mother," tried to go with her but wasn't allowed to do so. Now there were the three cousins and Rywka. After seven days of indescribable hell, they were all sent to a work camp in Christianstadt for six months. They worked laying down sewage pipelines. Mere skeletons, they toiled in hard labor, with nothing to shield their bodies from the freezing winter of 1945. Miraculously, they survived this brutality. With the defeat of the Germans, they were taken on a death march. Over the course of six weeks, they walked forty to fifty kilometers (twenty-five to thirty miles) a day until they reached Bergen-Belsen, where they were left to die. They were very ill.

Esther, Mina, and Rywka were put in a bunk together; Channah, who was in critical condition, was taken to the hospital. Every day Mother would go to the hospital to see how Channah was doing and to tend to her. She tried to lift her spirits, urging her to hold on until liberation. But on the day of liberation by the British army, April 15, 1945, Channah died. When Mother saw that Channah had passed away, she went back to her room and lay down on the bare floor next to Rywka and Esther; they tried their best to warm each other with their bodies. When Esther asked her if she had seen Channah, Mother told her to go visit her herself. Esther went and learned that Channah had died; she, too, returned to the bunk and lay down on the floor next to the others. They didn't speak. There were no words to describe their grief. The loss was immeasurable, the pain unbearable. Even today, nobody talks about the pain. It is buried deep inside us; it gets passed down from one generation to the next.

The liberation and rehabilitation plan for the survivors at the camp was to transport them to Sweden, where they would receive further care. Everyone was very sick. Mother said that the moment she found herself in the hospital, lying next to Esther, she lost consciousness for two weeks. Esther was very sick also, and was unlikely to survive the trip to Sweden. Mother was required to sign a form stating that she would take responsibility for the trip. Before the departure, when she was feeling a bit stronger, Mother went to look for Rywka. She remembers that when she got to the hospital, the doctor told her that Rywka was dying and had only a few days to live. Mother left her, knowing that her cousin would not survive this cursed war. And so Rywka, too, descended into the depths of oblivion and forgetfulness.

Until the discovery of her diary.

"Now that I've finally managed to forget her, she has suddenly come back to me." This was Mother's reaction when I told her that Rywka's diary had been found by a Soviet doctor during the liberation of Auschwitz and finally made it to America sixty years later. Because of the documents that Mother had filled out after the war, in which she listed the names of her relatives who had died in the Holocaust, we had been tracked down as the next of kin.

"How do you remember her?" I asked my mother. She replied that Rywka looked older than her, even though she was actually two years younger. She remembered that during the selection at Auschwitz, there was no question about Rywka, since she looked old for her age and able to work. With Mother, the choice wasn't so clear. Esther remembers that Rywka's belly was distended, and Mengele, may his name be wiped out, asked if she was pregnant. Esther explained that her belly was swollen from hunger. Mother said that they all shared the same straw-covered bunker, both in Auschwitz and at the labor camp, but she didn't remember their relationship.

We received the diary from Dr. Anita Friedman, executive director of Jewish Family and Children's Services in San Francisco. The granddaughter of the doctor who had found it delivered it to JFCS's Tauber Holocaust Library for safekeeping. The library's director, Judy Janec, has been leading an investigation to find out what happened to Rywka. Her explorations of the paper trail led to the discovery that Rywka survived the war. As for Rywka's fate after the war, nobody is certain.

In the course of the investigation, a document with Rywka's handwriting was found. It had been filled out five months after Mother said good-bye to her, sure that she was going to die. When we saw the document, we were filled with doubt. Mother talked about the impossible choice she had to make: whether to stay at Rywka's bedside when the doctors were certain that she wouldn't make it, or to go to Sweden with her sister and start the rehabilitation process. She made her choice! Now, with this new information, she was plagued by doubt.

Rywka's cousins' families at their maternal grandfather's gravesite in 2012; Eliyahu Chaim Mezul [Maizel] was the chief rabbi of Lodz for forty years. *(Courtesy of Hadassa Halamish)*

Was Rywka still alive? Had she moved to Israel? Why hadn't she looked for Mina and Esther? Did she think they hadn't survived, just as they thought about her? Did she have a family? Did she die? Where?

These questions remain unanswered.

And me? I feel very sad that I didn't have the opportunity to know her. I'm sure she and I would have found a common language. I feel that she taught me how one can, and must, *live*, regardless of the situation. Even under impossible circumstances, under Nazi rule, Rywka never lost the divine image within her. The strength that she drew from God, from her faith, from the Torah, from the physical life that went along with her spiritual life, was the knowledge that eternal life is rooted in the spirit.

Rywka had the good fortune to come back to us. To this day, I feel her inside me. I feel a pressing need to tell her story, to bequeath it to future generations. Esther and Mother were lucky enough to build large families. In Israel, they have grandchildren and great-grandchildren, which allows them to keep the memory of their loved ones alive. Rywka was blessed with a name—a name given to her by God. All those who read Rywka's diary will keep her name alive.

Hadassa Halamish is the daughter of Mina Boyer, one of the two older cousins who lived with Rywka Lipszyc in the Lodz ghetto and survived Auschwitz, Christianstadt, and Bergen-Belsen with her.

A Meeting with the Past

ESTHER BURSTEIN

It's hard to believe! After so many years, we saw the journal of Rywka, which had been buried at Auschwitz!!

When I learned of the journal's existence, I was in shock. I couldn't believe that such a miracle as this could have happened. While reading it, I was transported to the times in the ghetto—to the fear, hunger, and difficult work without end. I don't think that a person who wasn't there could grasp the hell that we experienced during those war years.

I was a child in the ghetto, only nineteen years old—however, I grew up fast. I was responsible for all of the girls in my family—two sisters and two cousins—and this was not easy. It was especially hard since Rywka, who had been the oldest girl in her house, also thought that among us she was "a big girl," and she found it very difficult to accept my authority. She wrote in her journal about the arguments that we had. It's clear to me now that these circumstances—my being the eldest and the one in charge—were not comfortable for her.

Rywka joined us in September 1942, after both her parents died. She was a very talented girl and loved to read and write. It seems that her journal would have dated from the beginning of 1943, while she was influenced by her mentor, Sara Selver-Urbach. However, the notebook that was found at Auschwitz dates from October 1943 to April 1944. We left the ghetto for Auschwitz in August 1944. Perhaps there was another notebook?

The writing gave Rywka a lot of satisfaction. She was able to forget about the hunger and pain. In the journal, one sees tremendous faith, and this is what sustained her and gave her the hope that tomorrow would be a better day. Without such faith, one was liable to go mad.

Today, it is difficult to believe that all of this suffering befell us. We have *our great revenge* in that we've survived against those who wished to destroy us. We have a big family . . . *a tribe among the glory of Israel*. To my great sorrow, we still don't know what happened to Rywka. In 1945, my sister Mina and I went to Sweden to recover, while Rywka remained, very ill, in a hospital. With the finding of the journal, and through subsequent investigations that were made as a result of it, it was revealed to us that she remained alive for a number of months after we left. In a document from September 1945 that was found, she wrote that she wanted to come to *Eretz Yisrael*. However, we still don't know where she went.

Perhaps this book, once published and publicized, will help reveal her fate.

Esther Burstein is the elder of the two cousins who lived with Rywka Lipszyc in the Lodz ghetto. She and her sister, Mina Boyer, are the only two members of their families to have survived the Holocaust.

Rywka's Family

Rywka Lipszyc (pronounced Rif-ka Lip-shitz):
   Born September 15, 1929; date of death unknown

RYWKA'S FAMILY

Yankel Lipszyc (Father):
Born October 14, 1898; died in the Lodz ghetto, June 2, 1941

Miriam Sarah Lipszyc (Mother):
Born December 15, 1902; died in the Lodz ghetto, July 8, 1942

Abramek (Abram) Lipszyc (Brother):
Born January 13, 1932; deported to Chelmno, September 1942,
   and died there

Cipka Lipszyc (Cypora) (Sister):
Born October 9, 1933; died in Auschwitz, August 1944

Rywka's cousins Mina and Esther were the only members of their immediate and extended families to survive the Holocaust. These photos were taken in 1948. *(Courtesy of Hadassa Halamish)*

Tamarcia (Estera) (Sister):
Born September 10, 1937; deported to Chelmno, September 1942,
 and died there

RYWKA'S COUSINS AND THEIR FAMILY

Yochanan Lipszyc (Father):
Born October 31, 1894; deported to Chelmno, September 1942,
 and died there

Hadassah Lipszyc (Mother):
Born March 8, 1903; died in the Lodz ghetto, July 11, 1943

Estusia Lipszyc (Esther Burstein):
Born October 31, 1923; lives in Israel

Chanusia Lipszyc:
Born January 3, 1925; died in Bergen-Belsen, April 15, 1945

Minia Lipszyc (Mina Boyer):
Born June 18, 1926; lives in Israel

RYWKA'S MENTORS IN THE LODZ GHETTO

Surcia:
Sara Selver-Urbach; lives in Israel

Chajusia (probably Haya Guterman):
Friend of Surcia; fate unknown

Miss (Fajga) Zelicka:
Teacher; fate unknown

What Happened to Rywka Lipszyc?

JUDY JANEC

The last passage of Rywka Lipszyc's diary was written in April 1944. We know that she was deported to Auschwitz during the liquidation of the Lodz ghetto in late summer 1944. After all, the diary was found there. But how did the diary survive from Rywka's arrival in Auschwitz-Birkenau in August 1944 through the harsh Polish winter until the spring of 1945, when it was found by Soviet doctor Zinaida Berezovskaya?

Numerous Holocaust survivor accounts tell us that when deportees arrived at Auschwitz-Birkenau, they faced two possible fates. Rywka could have been selected for the gas chamber and perished immediately, or she could have been spared to become part of the Nazis' vast slave labor force. In either case, all of her possessions would have been taken from her. Once her belongings, including the diary, were gathered together, they were most likely taken to Kanada, Auschwitz-Birkenau's sorting warehouse. There, other concentration camp inmates went through the clothes, packages, and suitcases; their job was to set aside anything that might be useful in the Nazi war effort.

Could someone in Kanada have found Rywka's diary and decided to keep it or hide it? Could it have been deliberately hidden near the crematoria in the hope that someday it would be found? Finding answers to the mystery of Rywka and her diary would eventually involve the efforts of historians and archivists throughout the world from 2008 to 2013.

After Rywka was initially identified by the diary's transcriber, Ewa Wiatr, in 2009, I searched Yad Vashem's Central Database of Shoah Victims' Names for any records relating to Rywka. Names in this database have been compiled from historical records and other documentation and from "Pages of Testimony" submitted by family, friends, and researchers to memorialize individuals who perished in the Holocaust. I found documentation of Rywka Lipszyc in the database from a postwar registry of Lodz ghetto inhabitants, as well as similar documentation about her immediate family members. After the diary had been translated into English in June 2011, I decided to revisit the Yad Vashem database, to see if another search, two years later, might yield more information. A record that I had never seen was revealed, which stated that Rywka had died in Bergen-Belsen at age sixteen! The record was based on two Pages of Testimony submitted by Mina Boier (Boyer), one in 1955 and another in 2000; Mina was identified as Rywka's cousin. She was surely the Minia mentioned frequently in Rywka's diary.

The 2000 Page of Testimony indicated that Mina lived near Tel Aviv, in the religious community of Bnei Brak. I contacted Dr. Anita Friedman, the executive director of Jewish Family and Children's Services, to alert her to the possibility that one of the cousins mentioned in Rywka's diary might still be living. Dr. Friedman was in Israel at the time and immediately contacted the family. Both Mina and Esther, the oldest cousin (Estusia in the diary), were alive. How much could be learned by actually speaking with someone who knew Rywka, let alone the cousins with whom she lived and endured so much! And what an astounding discovery for the cousins to hear, after so many years, about the existence of this diary.

NATIONALITY	SEX	NAME	CHRISTIAN NAME	DATE OF BIRTH	LAST KNOWN ADDRESS
HUNGARIAN	FEMALE	KIHORN	IBOLGA	12-5-1928	Budapest
POLISH	"	KARCZEWSKA	HELENA	8-9-1902	Warsaw
POLISH	"	SZACHOWICZ	JANINA	12-4-1921	Warsaw
POLISH	"	ZYGMUNT	ANTONINA	13-3-1900	Warsaw
POLISH	"	LUDA	SOFIA	15-2-1919	Sosnowic
RUMANIAN	"	GOLDBERGER	IDA	1-3-1918	Bihor-Biosek
POLISH	"	JAKUBOWSKA	ANNA	7-7-1910	Warsaw
POLISH	"	RUSZAK	JANINA	20-3-1916	Warsaw
POLISH	"	RACZYNSKA	MARIA	29-3-1913	Warsaw
POLISH	"	STEPIEN	HALINA	25-9-1908	Warsaw
HUNGARIAN	"	KLEIN	SZARI	26-12-1919	Sasregen
POLISH	"	SITKOWSKA	KAROLINA	1895	Warsaw
HUNGARIAN	"	GERSCH	MAGDA	8-6-1923	Sasregen
POLISH	"	LENARTOWICZ	STANISLAWA	31-10-1914	Warsaw
POLISH	"	NEIMAN	RACHELA	20-9-1925	Lodz
Russian	"	SOKOLEWSKA	AMELIA	28-10-1924	Kamieniec
POLISH	"	KOSMINIEWICZ	STANISLAWA	10-3-1919	Warsaw
POLISH	"	NADROWSKA	JADWIGA	4-3-1903	Warsaw
RUMANIAN	"	ULSCHMAN	HELI	26-4-1928	Marmaros-Siget
CZECH	"	SCHULTZ	MARGIT	11-7-1923	Komarno
RUMANIAN	"	LEBOWICZ	LUIZA	6-11-1923	Sotmar
CZECH	"	LEBOWICZ	SZANA	21-11-1928	Jassina
CZECH	"	KNOULL	HELENA	15-5-1920	Jassina
POLISH	"	MALOYGA	HALINA	29-12-1925	Miszyniec
CZECH	"	HAUER	DOROTHEA	10-10-1912	PRAGUE
CZECH	"	ZYWA	HELENE	16-7-1916	Pafkau
POLISH	"	LISICKA	LUCYNA	7-1-1902	Warsaw
CZECH	"	KAUFMANN	JOHANNA	17-3-1894	Prague
		Kaufmann			

Square 2-Bl. 47

POLISH	"	HABER	ESTERA	15-9-1898	Cracow
POLISH	"	HABER	HALINA	28-5-1923	Cracow
POLISH	"	EISENBERG	LOLA	31-8-1921	Radomysl-Wielki
POLISH	"	EISENBERG	FRIDA	22-2-1926	Radomysl-Wielki
POLISH	"	KUPER	ESTERA	30-11-1926	LODZ
POLISH	"	GUTGLASS	FESEL	22-3-1921	Jawerzno
POLISH	"	GOLDSTEIN	RIZINA	4-3-1920	Lodz
POLISH	"	GRANDOWICZ	MARIA	5-1-1926	Lodz
POLISH	"	SILBER	HALINA	16-6-1926	Lodz
POLISH	"	GRAIMAN	PELA	20-4-1920	Kocin
HUNGARIAN	"	FRIEDMAN	JOLI	10-11-1928	Irsawa
POLISH	"	GRIEN	MARIA	8-9-1918	Lodz
POLISH	"	FRIEDMAN	GELA	1912	
GREEK	"	ANGEL	IDA	4-3-1904	ATHEN
CZECH	"	JAKUBOWICZ	TERESA	19-1-1924	
POLISH	"	KOSMAN	STEFANIA	8-3-1908	Wloctanek
CZECH	"	HERZKOWICZ	ROSA	18-1-1930	Ilenco
POLISH	"	CHISLAW	MARIA	23-12-1921	Czestochom
POLISH	"	WEIS	IDA	30-11-1927	Brzeziny
HUNGARIAN	"	BORSOS	MARGIT	17-1-1917	Esztergye
CZECH	"	FRIEDMAN	MARIA	20-1-1924	Mokario
HUNGARIAN	"	MAJ	HILDE	15-11-1910	Budapest
CZECH	"	KOEFER	MINA	27-7-1926	Berehsen
HUNGARIAN	"	RUTH	RISI	16-5-1923	Moromos-Siget
CZECH	"	STRAUS	ADELA	10-5-1926	Trencin
POLISH	"	JAKODA	DORA	15-1-1924	Sosnowice
POLISH	"	FELD	ESTERA	10-12-1922	Lodz
POLISH	"	LEIBMAN	DORA	16-9-1926	Lodz
HUNGARIAN	"	FELIKAN	OLA	14-7-1910	Budapest
POLISH	"	GOLICKA	DORA	20-3-1924	Lodz
POLISH	"	WYLLESINO	REGINA	24-12-1926	Sosnowice
HUNGARIAN	"	LOB	DORA	13-11-1926	Klosenburg
HUN. ARIAN	"	KLEIMAN	IDA	16-9-1923	Klosenburg
POLISH	"	LIPSZIC	RYWKA	14-9-1924	Lodz

Bergen–Belsen liberation list with Rywka's name (last name on page) *("Nominal Rolls of various nationals liberated in Bergen-Belsen," United States Holocaust Memorial Museum, compilation of Ceges/Soma microfilm RG 65.001M, roll 64, file 4823)*

It was through conversations with Mina's daughter Hadassa that we discovered what happened to Rywka, her sister Cipka, and her three cousins once they arrived at Auschwitz in August 1944. Cipka was immediately selected for the gas chamber, and Rywka was separated from her. Tragically, Rywka Lipszyc was now bereft of every member of her immediate family.

Along with her three cousins, Rywka was sent from Auschwitz to Christianstadt, a women's camp near Gross-Rosen. After months of hard labor, they were marched to Bergen-Belsen. These young women, aged fifteen to twenty-two, had survived the Lodz ghetto, Auschwitz, Christianstadt, and a death march to Bergen-Belsen, and three of them survived to see their liberation by British troops in April 1945. (Chanusia, the middle sister of the cousins, died of typhus in the camp.) According to Mina's testimony, it was at Bergen-Belsen that Rywka died.

In the meantime, requests for documentation on Rywka's fate had been sent to the United States Holocaust Memorial Museum (USHMM) and the International Tracing Service (ITS), as well as numerous other archives, including the Bergen-Belsen Memorial Site. Rywka's name was identified on a list of those liberated at Bergen-Belsen. However, no mention of Rywka Lipszyc was included in the Bergen-Belsen death lists, a fact that Bernd Horstmann, the keeper of the registry, found strange. It was known, more or less, he said, who had died after liberation.

With the assistance of Steven Vitto at the USHMM, a DP (Displaced Person) Registration Record for Rywka was found among the ITS records. The ITS records were compiled after the war by the International Red Cross and the United Nations Relief and Rehabilitation Administration. This vast repository of information contains 50 million records documenting 17.5 million victims of Nazism, including those from displaced persons camps. The DP Registration Record posed many questions and mysteries. First of all, it was dated September 10, 1945, and was filled out at Transit Camp Lübeck. It appeared that Rywka had not died in Bergen-Belsen after all but

Rywka Lipszyc's Displaced Persons Registration Record

("Rywka Lipszyc—Allied Expeditionary Force Displaced Persons Registration Record," September 10, 1945, United States Holocaust Memorial Museum, International Tracing Service collection, Archival Unit Number— 3.1.1.1, document no. 68068248)

Minia Lipszyc's Displaced Persons Registration Record

("Minia Lipszyc—Allied Expeditionary Force Displaced Persons Registration Record," July 7, 1945, United States Holocaust Memorial Museum, International Tracing Service collection, Archival Unit Number - 3.1.1.1, document no. 68068098)

Esther Lipszyc's Displaced Persons Registration Record

("Esther Lipszyc—Allied Expeditionary Force Displaced Persons Registration Record," July 7, 1945, United States Holocaust Memorial Museum, International Tracing Service collection, Archival Unit Number— 3.1.1.1, document no. 68067236)

ITS 067   F 8 - 53

YD.

HOSPITAL PATIENTS SENT 23.7.1945 TO HOSPITAL
NIENDORF (Too ill to be evacuated to Sweden)

No.	NAMES	NATIONALITY	SEX
4421	BUARSTYN Halina	Polish	F.
4823	DEAF Mute	? ?	F.
5268	DRUZBIAK Walenty	Polish	M.
4824	FRENKEL Estera	"	F.
607	GOLDBERG Bella	"	M.
5271	JASIECKI Kazimierz	"	F.
4454	LIPSZYC Rywka	"	F.
6328	MILSTEIN Celina	"	F.
4050	MUSZKATENBLUM Tusia	"	F.
4804	NIEWLADOMSKA Stefania	"	F.
427	ORENBACH Ruth	"	M.
5250	PELINSKI Richard	"	M.
8193	PIECHUCKI Stanislaw		

LANDESKRANKENHAUS NEUSTADT
(Civil Hospital)

Name	Nationality	Diagnose
STREEK Franz	Polish	gunshot-wound
KUBAJAK Stefan	"	furuncle of the lip, Hernia-operation
SCHABINSKI Jan	"	state of exhaustion
PIOTROWSKI Jan	"	enteritis
ZINGER Abraham	"	state of exhaustion
KROSCHAK Ignas	"	typhus
MILEWSKI Wladyslawa	"	Lymphadenitis
KRUPKA Roza	"	inflammation of the thumb
BERKMAN Raja	"	enteritis
EPSTEIN Biba	"	pleuritis
ROTAL Victor	"	ulcer of the throat
STASIAK Jan	"	state after typhus infiltrative T.B.C.

Duplicate names of F8-140/HF
L. Krs. Oldenburg /Holst.

Rywka Lipszyc's name appears on a list of patients transferred to a hospital in Niendorf on July 23, 1945.
The title reads "Hospital Patients Sent 23.7.1945 to Hospital Niendorf (Too ill to be evacuated to Sweden)."
(Digital Archives, ITS Bad Arolsen, document no. 70623435#1)

had survived for months after liberation. A handwritten note on the DP Registration Record indicated that she had been transferred to a hospital in Niendorf, about eighteen miles north of Lübeck on the Baltic Sea, on July 25, 1945.

Copies of the cousins' DP Registration Records show that they, too, had been sent to Lübeck, but their records were dated July 7, 1945, almost three weeks earlier that Rywka's. The cousins went from Bergen-Belsen first to Transit Camp Lübeck and then to Sweden, where thousands of Holocaust survivors were sent for treatment and recuperation after the war. Rywka, apparently, was transferred later, most likely through Lübeck to Niendorf.

Further communication from ITS produced a document with a list of hospital patients transferred to Niendorf's hospital on July 23, 1945, because they were "too ill to be evacuated to Sweden." Rywka Lipszyc's name was on that list.

Why did the cousins think that Rywka had died in Bergen-Belsen? Mina told her daughter that, before she and her sister were sent to Sweden for recuperation, she had visited Rywka in the hospital at Bergen-Belsen, and the doctor told her that Rywka would be dead within days. That was the last Mina and Esther ever heard of her.

Did Rywka die in Hospital Niendorf? If so, we needed to find documentation of her death. (Until her death was definitely proven, there was still hope that she might have survived and lived a full life.) Bernd Horstmann suggested that we contact Timmendorfer Strand, the municipality that includes Niendorf. He was told by archivists there that the Niendorf hospital no longer existed and that there was no mention of Rywka in any of their municipal or cemetery records.

I contacted Lübeck's municipal archives; no mention of Rywka Lipszyc was uncovered, despite intensive searches. Further messages and requests to ITS and USHMM were sent, but no new material was uncovered in either archive. I wrote to the National Archives of Sweden, in case Rywka had returned to Transit Camp Lübeck and then was sent to Sweden. No mention of her name was found there.

Bernd Horstmann suggested that since Hospital Niendorf no longer existed, it must have been a British military hospital, but, upon contacting the National Archives of the United Kingdom, I learned that the British Army did not keep permanent records of individuals in the displaced persons camps that were set up in the British occupation zone after the end of the war. Those records were transferred to the ITS.

A mention of Hospital Niendorf was found in a letter written by British Jewish Relief Unit (JRU) welfare worker Bertha Weingreen and published in the academic database "Post-War Europe: Refugees, Exile and Resettlement, 1945–1950." She wrote that the hospital was run by the "Save the Children fund" and that many Jewish patients who had died there were buried in the Jewish cemetery in Lübeck. Yet archivists at the University of Birmingham, where the institutional records of Save the Children are housed, could find no additional information about the hospital. A member of Lübeck's Jewish community provided us with a list of names of the displaced persons buried there, but Rywka's name was not on the list. Along with staff members at several archives in Germany, we searched for but did not discover any mention of Rywka in displaced persons or compensation claims records.

What could we do next to find out what happened to Rywka? We decided to contact the editor of *Lübecker Nachrichten*, the local newspaper, and ask that it publish an article about Rywka, the diary, and our search. The story was published on February 19, 2012. No new information was immediately forthcoming, but Daniela Teudt, a student of Jewish studies at the University of Potsdam, read the article and stepped forward to offer her help. Daniela was born in Lübeck and had written her bachelor's thesis on the Jews of Lübeck. Full of enthusiasm, familiar with the Lübeck and Niendorf areas, and a student of local German Jewish history, she volunteered to consult archives in the area and to search more deeply to learn about Rywka's fate. It was she who compared the list of those sent to Niendorf hospital with the list of those buried in Lübeck and discovered that of the nine girls on the hospital list, five were buried in the Jewish cemetery in Lübeck, but not Rywka.

In October 2012, I embarked on a fact-finding journey, tracing Rywka's steps from Lodz to Auschwitz to Bergen-Belsen to Lübeck to Niendorf. By doing research in local archives in these locations, viewing records, and visiting cemeteries and memorial sites, I hoped to uncover some answers to the mystery of Rywka's fate.

LODZ

I began where Rywka did, in Lodz. Meeting Ewa Wiatr, my first partner in the search and the diary's transcriber from Polish to English, and her colleague Adam Sitarek, we visited former ghetto sites. Rywka's home in the ghetto, 38 Wolborska Street, was demolished long ago, and in its place stand apartment buildings. I learned that Wolborska Street was very close to the southern boundary of the ghetto, and all of the buildings across the street from where Rywka lived, including one of Lodz's beautiful synagogues, were destroyed by the Nazis in order to protect the rest of the city from the diseases that were rampant in the ghetto.

We visited the location of the concern where Rywka worked—the Wäsche und Kleider Abteilung—on 13/15 Franciszkańska Street. We viewed the building she lived in before the ghetto and the building that the cousins lived in. The ghetto area itself bore very few traces of the terrible years that had been endured by the Jewish community there from 1940 to 1944. We visited Radegast train station, the terminal from which Rywka, Cipka, and her cousins were sent, among thousands of others, in cattle cars to Auschwitz-Birkenau.

We drove to Lodz's Jewish cemetery—the second-largest Jewish cemetery in the world—where 160,000 people are buried. It is a magnificent cemetery, full of history and mystery. The older sections are overgrown with trees and vegetation, and it was hard to imagine the cemetery completely bare of all trees, as Ewa told me it had been. (During the ghetto years, the community had cut down all of the trees to use as fuel.) The Ghetto Field, which held the nearly 43,000 graves of those who died in the ghetto, was in a separate section. Although those who were buried there died under difficult circumstances—of injuries, disease, and malnutrition—each person was honored by a separate grave. In a chilling coda to the visit, near the wall of the cemetery, we viewed four grass pits. These pits were dug by the remaining inhabitants of the Lodz ghetto and were meant to be the site of their mass grave. The arrival of liberating Soviet troops rescued those men from that fate.

The Archiwum Państwowe w Łodzi (State Archives in Lodz) holds one million documents from the years 1940–1944, making Lodz one of the best documented of all Nazi-era ghettos. Microfilm of registries, notices, certificates, identification cards, housing and work documents, sick leave notices, and hundreds of photographs offers insight into the day-to-day lives of those who lived and worked in Lodz's ghetto in all of its variety. Here, I found one new document relating to Rywka—regarding her benefits as an orphaned child.

AUSCHWITZ AND BERGEN-BELSEN

At the beginning of our work on this mystery, Robert Moses Shapiro had mentioned that Rywka's diary could be one of the manuscripts buried by the *Sonderkommando*. Victims of what Primo Levi called "National Socialism's most demonic crime,"[*] the *Sonderkommando* were those prisoners who were made to escort arriving Jews into the gas chambers, remove their bodies to the crematoria, and dispose of their ashes. Isolated from the rest of the camp, the *Sonderkommando* labored under unspeakable psychological, emotional, and spiritual burdens.

---

[*] Primo Levi, *The Drowned and the Saved* (New York: Summit Books, 1988), 53.

Knowing that they, too, were doomed to death, some members of the *Sonderkommando* wrote about their experiences, and in an attempt to leave evidence of Nazi crimes behind after their deaths, placed manuscripts in tin containers and buried them in the soil near Crematorium III. Several of the manuscripts were uncovered after the war. The first, written by Zalmen Gradowski, who perished during the *Sonderkommando* uprising in October 1944, was uncovered by Shlomo Dragon, a former *Sonderkommando*, who pointed the Soviet investigators to it. In total, eight manuscripts were recovered between 1945 and 1981.

Almost all of the manuscripts were those written by the *Sonderkommando*, but one of the members, Zalmen Lewental, also buried a different manuscript—a diary written in the Lodz ghetto by an adult man. Before he buried it, Mr. Lewental wrote a note, dated August 14, 1944, and wrapped it around the diary. Discovered in 1961, the manuscript and note were badly water damaged, but the note refers to other manuscripts buried and ends with the words ". . . search further! You will find still more."*

Could Rywka's diary have been one of the manuscripts he referred to? I visited Dr. Wojciech Płosa, the head of archive at the State Museum Auschwitz-Birkenau in Oświęcim, Poland. After viewing scans of Rywka's diary and the newspaper article that Zinaida Berezovskaya saved with it, he agreed that it was likely that Rywka's diary is the ninth of the *Sonderkommando* manuscripts to be recovered.

Although Rywka's diary remained in Auschwitz-Birkenau, she did not. After months of hard labor at the Christianstadt concentration camp, she and her cousins were sent on a forced march to Bergen-Belsen. It was here that, after years of starvation, suffering, and loss, Rywka was liberated in April 1945. She lived to see her liberation; she lived to be put in a hospital,

---

* "Diaries and Memoirs from the Lodz Ghetto in Yiddish and Hebrew," in *Holocaust Chronicles: Individualizing the Holocaust Through Diaries and Other Contemporaneous Personal Accounts*, ed. Robert Moses Shapiro (Hoboken, NJ: Ktav, 1999), 106.

where she was cared for; and she lived long enough to leave Bergen-Belsen. I met Bernd Horstmann at the memorial; we walked through the site, past the raised platforms of mass graves filled with the bodies of those who perished. They're still here, in the silence of the countryside. Chanusia, Rywka's cousin, is among them.

LÜBECK

It was in Lübeck that I hoped to learn more about Rywka's fate. Visits to the Lübeck archives, however, did not reveal any new information. All records regarding displaced persons were not related to Jewish DPs. I also visited Lübeck's Jewish cemetery in Moisling, on the outskirts of the city. Here it was that those who died in the Niendorf hospital were buried. In the far corner of this hidden cemetery stood the gravestones of eighty-seven Jews who died in the years between 1945 and 1950. We walked through these rows, looking at each name. Most were Polish and young, between sixteen and twenty-four; there were some children. It was in this lonely corner that I located the graves of the five girls who had accompanied Rywka to the hospital in Niendorf but who died there: Tusela Muschkatenblum, Bella Goldberg, Halina Burgztyn, Celina Milstein, and, sadly, the grave of a young woman who was labeled Mute, Deaf on the list, but whose gravestone read Seaf, Mute. Rywka's grave was not among them.

We continued to search in Lübeck's municipal cemetery and the cemeteries in nearby Travemunde, Timmendorfer Strand, Niendorf, and Neustadt. Although we found a single Jewish marker in one cemetery, and the graves of victims of the *Cap Arcona* tragedy,* as well as gravestones for Polish and Dutch prisoners of war, unknown victims of concentration camps, and German soldiers, we did not find one for Rywka Lipszyc.

---

* On May 3, 1945, the German ship *Cap Arcona*, which was transporting concentration camp survivors, was bombed by the British air force and sunk in the Baltic Sea. Nearly 4,000 prisoners died in the attack.

Left: Zinaida Berezovskaya, the Red Army doctor who discovered Rywka's diary in the ruins of the crematorium at Auschwitz-Birkenau in June 1945; photo from 1943 *(Courtesy of her grand-daughter, Anastasia Berezovskaya)*

Below: From the February 9, 1945, edition of *Lenin's Flag*, a Soviet Army newspaper; Zinaida Berezovskaya wrote a note next to the photograph of the ruins of the crematoria at Auschwitz-Birkenau: "This is where I found the diary in June 1945." *(Courtesy of Anastasia Berezovskaya)*

We stopped briefly at the harbor in Travemunde, the place where Holocaust survivors like Rywka's cousins were sent to Sweden, across the Baltic Sea. Finally, we visited the site of a hospital that might have been the one we were seeking. It was built in 1911 and served as a hospital from 1938 to 1948; today it is a facility for mothers and children. Part of the German national health system, it is operated by the Sisters of St. Francis of the Martyr St. George. No one there knew anything about how the hospital was used in July and August 1945, when Rywka might have been there.

LONDON

My search finally took me to London, where I explored records in the Wiener Library and at the National Archives. I was looking for any sliver of information regarding activities in the hospital in Bergen-Belsen in June and July 1945, transfers to Sweden via Lübeck, or of British military hospitals in the German state of Schleswig-Holstein, and in particular in Niendorf. Although I learned much about the heroic efforts of the British military to save the lives of desperately ill survivors, I found nothing to shed light on Rywka's fate.

After years of searching and the collaborative efforts of archivists and historians throughout the world, the answer to this mystery remains elusive. Yet there are always new avenues to explore. We will continue our search for this young survivor and hope that someday we will find the answer to what happened to Rywka Lipszyc.

If any readers have information that could be helpful in the search for Rywka Lipszyc, please contact Jewish Family and Children's Services' Holocaust Center, 2245 Post Street, PO Box 159004, San Francisco, California, 94115 (www.jfcs.org).

Another Mystery

ZINAIDA BEREZOVSKAYA

This note by Zinaida Berezovskaya was found among the items she left with the diary of Rywka Lipszyc. It describes where she found the diary and her attempts to have it translated.

> **Translation of the first page of the note:**
> **Diary**
> **of the [female] prisoner of Osvenzim**
> **found by me**
> **in the Spring of 1945**
> **by the ruins of a crematorium**
> **in Osvenzim**
> **Signed:** *Zinaida Berezovskaya*

> **Translation of the second page of the note:**
> **Many times I tried to obtain translation of this diary!**

1. In June 1945—in Poland (Warsaw) the Poles read it with difficulty, as the author combines modern Jewish language with ancient Jewish.

   In their own words, they related the contents: Author—the Mother—was separated from her daughter in a Jewish ghetto and she became a prisoner of Auschwitz herself, while the daughter was taken away somewhere.

   The main theme of the manuscript—suffering of the Mother as she thinks about her daughter: "G-d! G-d! Last night was worse than the Night of Bethlehem in the numbers of the tortured to death, hanged, and burned here with us. And where are you, my dear daughter!"

2. Here in Moscow the Jews who tried to translate the diary could not do that for the same reasons.

3. M. Klim. Ioffe (Yurasova) also hoped to translate it with the help of older Jews but they could not do it.

Signed, *Zinaida Berezovskaya*

This note, written by Zinaida Berezovskaya, presents yet another mystery in the story of Rywka's diary. In it, Dr. Berezovskaya describes her attempts to have the diary translated. She writes that the Poles had trouble translating the diary because it combined "modern Jewish language with ancient Jewish," possibly a reference to the Hebrew and Yiddish languages. However, Rywka wrote her diary almost entirely in Polish.

The translator indicated that the diary was written in Auschwitz by a mother mourning for her daughter. Yet, as we now know, Rywka Lipszyc was a fourteen-year-old girl who wrote her diary in the Lodz ghetto. We have no explanation for the discrepancy between the actual diary and the one described in Dr. Berezovskaya's note.

Дневник

Узницы Освенцима

найденный мною

весной 1945 года

у разрушенного крематория

в Освенциме

(подпись)

Много крелно пыталась добиться
перевода это дневника!

1.— В июне 1945 года — в Польше (в Варш.)
поляки читали его с трудом, т.к. автор
составлял еврейский современный язык
с древне-еврейским.

Своими словами передавали содержан.
его: — автор — мать разлучилась с дочерью
в еврейском гетто и она стала узницей
освенцимского лагеря, а дочь куда увели
Главное содержание рукописи — страдания
ее при мыслях о дочери... Боже-боже! сколь-
ко мыслей ночи, чтó Вифлеемских по числу
замученных, повешенных и сожженных
здесь у нас! А где же Ты, моя дорогая дочь!!

2. Здесь и в Москве евреи, пытавшиеся
перевести дневник, но тем больше мертвал
не смогли это сделать.

3. М. Клим. Иоффе (Юхесова) тоже надеялась
с помощью старых евреев перевести, но
и они не смогли.

(подпись)

Bibliography

Bentwich, Norman. *They Found Refuge*. London: Cresset Press, 1956.

Bezwińska, Jadwiga, ed. *Amidst a Nightmare of Crime: Notes of Prisoners of Sonderkommando Found at Auschwitz*. Translated by Krystyna Michalik. Publications of State Museum at Oświęcim, 1973.

Cohen, Nathan. "Diaries of the *Sonderkommandos* in Auschwitz: Coping with Fate and Reality." *Yad Vashem Studies 20*. Edited by Aharon Weiss. Jerusalem: Yad Vashem, 1990.

Czech, Danuta. *Auschwitz Chronicle: 1939–1945*. New York: Henry Holt, 1990.

Das Gesicht Des Gettos: Bilder Jüdischer Photographen aus dem Getto Litzmannstadt 1940–1944: The Face of the Ghetto: Pictures Taken by Jewish Photographers in the Litzmannstadt Ghetto 1940–1944. Stiftung Topographie Des Terrors, 2010.

Didi-Huberman, Georges. *Images in Spite of All: Four Photographs from Auschwitz*. Chicago: University of Chicago Press, 2008.

Dobroszycki, Lucjan, ed. *The Chronicle of the Łódź Ghetto, 1941–1944*. Translated by Shane B. Lillis. New Haven, CT: Yale University Press, 1984.

Greif, Gideon. *We Wept Without Tears: Testimonies of the Jewish Sonderkommando from Auschwitz*. New Haven, CT: Yale University Press, 2005.

Grossman, Mendel. *With a Camera in the Ghetto*. Edited by Zvi Szner and Alexander Sened. New York: Schocken Books, 1977.

Gumkowski, Janusz. *Brief aus Litzmannstadt*. Edited by Adam Rutkowski and Arnfrid Anste. Cologne: Friederich Middelhauve Verlag, 1967.

Horwitz, Gordon J. *Ghettostadt: Łódź and the Making of a Nazi City*. Cambridge, MA: Belknap Press of Harvard University Press, 2008.

Langbein, Hermann. *People in Auschwitz*. Translated by Harry Zohn. Chapel Hill: University of North Carolina Press in association with the United States Holocaust Memorial Museum, 2004.

Lavsky, Hagit. *New Beginnings: Holocaust Survivors in Bergen-Belsen and the British Zone in Germany, 1945–1950*. Detroit: Wayne State University Press, 2002.

Levi, Primo. *The Drowned and the Saved*. New York: Summit Books, 1988.

Libitzky, Eva, and Fred Rosenbaum. *Out on a Ledge: Enduring the Lodz Ghetto, Auschwitz, and Beyond*. River Forest, IL: Wicker Park Press, 2010.

Litzmannstadt Ghetto. http://www.lodz-ghetto.com/home.html.0. Accessed 2011–2012.

Mankowitz, Zeev W. *Life Between Memory and Hope: The Survivors of the Holocaust in Occupied Germany*. Cambridge: Cambridge University Press, 2002.

Mark, Ber. *The Scrolls of Auschwitz*. Tel Aviv: Am Oved Publishers, 1985.

Patt, Avinoam J., and Michael Berkowitz, eds. *"We Are Here": New Approaches to Jewish Displaced Persons in Postwar Germany*. Detroit: Wayne State University Press, 2010.

Post-War Europe: Refugees, Exile and Resettlement: 1945–1950. E-book: Gale Cengage Learning, 2007.

Pressac, Jean-Claude. *Auschwitz: Technique and Operation of the Gas Chambers*. New York: Beate Klarsfeld Foundation, 1989.

Prstojevic, Alexandre. "L'indicible et la fiction configuratrice." *Protée* 37, no. 2 (2009): 33–44. http://id.erudit.org/iderudit/038453ar. Accessed April 16, 2012.

Rees, Laurence. *Auschwitz: A New History*. New York: PublicAffairs, 2005.

Rosenfeld, Oskar. *In the Beginning Was the Ghetto*. Edited by Hanno Loewy. Translated by Brigitte Goldstein. Evanston, IL: Northwestern University Press, 2002.

Selver-Urbach, Sara. *Through the Window of My Home: Recollections from the Lodz Ghetto*. Translated by Siona Bodansky. Jerusalem: Yad Vashem, 1986.

Shapiro, Robert Moses, ed. *Holocaust Chronicles: Individualizing the Holocaust Through Diaries and Other Contemporaneous Personal Accounts*. Hoboken, NJ: Ktav Publishing House, 1999.

Shephard, Ben. *After Daybreak: The Liberation of Bergen-Belsen, 1945*. New York: Schocken Books, 2005.

——. *The Long Road Home: The Aftermath of the Second World War*. New York: Alfred A. Knopf, 2010.

Sington, Derrick. *Belsen Uncovered*. London: Duckworth, 1946.

Stone, Dan. "The Sonderkommando Photographs." *Jewish Social Studies*, New Series 7, no. 3 (Spring–Summer 2001): 131–48. http://www.jstor.org/stable/4467613. Accessed May 16, 2012.

Struk, Janina. *Photographing the Holocaust: Interpretations of the Evidence*. London: I. B. Tauris in association with European Jewish Publication Society, 2005.

Strzelecki, Andrezej. *The Deportation of Jews from the Łódź Ghetto to KL Auschwitz and Their Extermination: A Description of the Events and a Presentation of Historical Sources.* Oświęcim: Auschwitz-Birkenau State Museum, 2006.

———. *The Evacuation, Dismantling and Liberation of KL Auschwitz.* Translated by Zbirohowski-Kościa. Auschwitz-Birkenau State Museum, 2001.

Trunk, Isaiah. *Łódź Ghetto: A History.* Translated and edited by Robert Moses Shapiro. Bloomington: Indiana University Press in association with the United States Holocaust Memorial Museum, 2006.

Unger, Michal. *The Last Ghetto: Life in the Lodz Ghetto, 1940–1944.* Jerusalem: Yad Vashem, 2004.

Wyman, Mark. *DPs: Europe's Displaced Persons, 1945–1951.* Ithaca, NY: Cornell University Press, 1989.

Zelkowicz, Josef. *In Those Terrible Days: Notes from the Lodz Ghetto.* Edited by Michal Unger. Jerusalem: Yad Vashem, 2002.

Acknowledgments

A ny acknowledgments must begin at the beginning. Above all, we must thank and acknowledge **Rywka Lipszyc**, the author of the diary; the unknown *Sonderkommando* who buried her diary in the soil near Crematorium III at Birkenau, thus saving it from destruction; and **Zinaida Berezovskaya**, the Soviet doctor who retrieved the diary and kept it safe.

Our heartfelt thanks go to Zinaida's granddaughter, **Anastasia Berezovskaya**, who brought the diary to us in 2008, enabling us to share the words of Rywka with the public. Without Anastasia's dedication and care, the diary could have been lost forever.

Warm thanks to **Leslie Kane**, executive director of the former Holocaust Center of Northern California, for her interest in the publication project; **Zachary Baker**, assistant university librarian for Collection Development–Humanities and Social Sciences and Reinhard Family Curator of Judaica and Hebraica Collections, Stanford University, who provided guidance; **Robert Moses Shapiro**, professor, Judaic studies, Brooklyn College, for sharing his vast knowledge of the Lodz ghetto, for providing connections to scholars and historians in Poland, and for his commitment to Holocaust scholarship; **Marek Web**, former YIVO archivist, for viewing and authenticating the diary; **Tracy Randall** and **Fenwick and West**, for intellectual property consultation; **E. M. Ginger** and **42-line**, digitization experts, for their incredible digital reproductions of Rywka's diary and the accompanying ephemera; and **Karen Zukor**, of Zukor Art Conservation, for her evaluation of the diary and recommendations for its care.

Ewa Wiatr of the Center for Jewish Research at the University of Lodz assisted in this project from the beginning. Ewa transcribed the diary, was the first to identify Rywka and her family, and provided the diary annotations. She continued throughout the project to share her expert knowledge of the history of the Lodz ghetto and the contents of the enormous Lodz State Archives, where the ghetto archives are held. Thanks also to her coworker **Adam Sitarek** for his enthusiastic assistance during research in Poland.

Many assisted with translation: **Ewa Basinska**, translation from Polish; **John Bass**, translation from German; **Alon Altman**, **Shira Atik**, and **Inga Michaeli** for Hebrew-English translations; **Malgorzata Szajbel-Kleck**, initial translation of the diary; and **Malgorzata Markoff**, final translation of the diary.

Ongoing support and encouragement came from so many caring individuals, including **Gunda Trepp**, **Adrian Schrek**, and **Eda and Joseph Pell**. The longtime moral leadership and financial support of **Ingrid Tauber** was also essential to the success of this project and of the JFCS Holocaust Center and Lehrhaus Judaica overall.

We are also appreciative of the staff of the Names Recovery Project at Yad Vashem, with special thanks to **Cynthia Wroclawski** and **Debbie Berman**, whose exceptional work made the connection with Rywka's two surviving cousins possible. Eyewitness knowledge of Rywka in the ghetto and in the camps came from these cousins—**Mina Boyer** and **Esther Burstein**—who rebuilt their lives in Israel after the war. Their resilience and spirit are an inspiration. We are also grateful to **Hadassa Halamish**, the daughter of Mina Boyer, who contributed her family's remembrances and who sets the example for dedication to Holocaust education.

Many archivists, historians, students, and researchers provided essential assistance and valuable information and leads:

Bernd Horstmann, Custodian for the Registry of Names of the Bergen-Belsen concentration camp prisoners, Bergen-Belsen, whose discovery that Rywka's name was not on the death list at Bergen-Belsen began the search for her fate

Steven Vitto, Holocaust Survivors and Victims Resource Center, United States Holocaust Memorial Museum, Washington, DC

Susanne Urban and **Elfi Rudolph**, International Tracing Service, Bad Arolsen, Germany

Daniel Kazez, Czestochowa-Radomsko Area Research Group

Nathan Tallman and **Kevin Profitt**, American Jewish Archives

Dr. Wulf Pingel, Landesarchiv Schleswig-Holstein

Marco Lach and **Meike Kruze**, Hansestadt Lübeck Archives

Franz Siegle and **John Pierce**, for research at University of Heidelberg

Jürgen Sielemann, former archivist at Hamburg State Archives

Heike Hennigsen, Friedhofsverwaltung, Kirchengemeinde Niendorf/Ostsee

Leonid Kogan, Curator of Museum, Lübeck Jewish Congregation

Peter Honigmann, Zentralarchiv zur Erforschung der Geschichte der Juden in Deutschland, Heidelberg, Germany

Anke Hönnig, Staatsarchiv, Hamburg

Marek Jaros and **Howard Falksohn**, Wiener Library, London

Angela Skitt and **Anne George**, Project Archivists, Special Collections, Cadbury Research Library, University of Birmingham

Bruno Derrick, Remote Enquiries Duty Officer, National Archives, United Kingdom

Jan Brunius, Riksarkivet, Sweden

Oliver Vogt, *Lübecker Nachrichte*

Most recently, **Daniela Teudt** joined in the research, lending dedication and creativity to the process of discovery and providing more than one lead. We are also grateful to **Ewa Wiatr**, **Adam Sitarek**, **Bernd Horstmann**, **Dagmar Lieske**, **Leonid Kogan**, and **Christoph Carlson** for their support and assistance during our October 2012 research in Europe.

Thanks also to our production team of **Victoria Cooper**, Publishing Project Manager for Jewish Family and Children's Services, and **Vicki Valentine**.

We are grateful also to those who worked together to bring this diary to light. Thank you to **Fred Rosenbaum**, founding director of Lehrhaus Judaica, for his scholarship, insight, and dedication as well as his contribution of the essay about the Lodz ghetto; to **Alexandra Zapruder** for her sensitivity and understanding of Rywka and her diary, her gentle yet expert editing of the diary, and her beautiful introduction. Thanks especially to **Judy Janec**, former director of Library and Archives at the JFCS Holocaust Center's Tauber Holocaust Library in San Francisco. Since she first saw the diary in 2008, Judy has been the primary coordinator of the effort to publish it. Without her profound commitment, dedication, and resourcefulness, we may never have found Rywka's surviving cousins or traced her survival after liberation from Bergen-Belsen.

Thanks also to the boards of directors of Jewish Family and Children's Services (**Susan Kolb,** president) and Lehrhaus Judaica (**Eve Bernstein,** president) and to the staff of the JFCS Holocaust Center for their ongoing roles in support of Holocaust education.

We are especially grateful for the guidance of the Center's Council of Children of Holocaust Survivors, whose members are **Dennis Albers, Riva Berelson, Robert Blum, Elliott Felson, Anita Friedman, Adean Golub, Davina Isackson, Moses Libitzky, Susan Lowenberg, Joyce Newstat, Paul Orbuch, Dave Pell, Karen Pell, Lydia Shorenstein, Laura Talmus, Ingrid Tauber, Sam Tramiel,** and **Susan Wilner Golden.**

Publication of this book was a labor of love supported by generous and visionary philanthropists. Our gratitude goes to: **the Pell Family Foundation; the Laszlo N. Tauber Family Foundation; the Irving and Gloria Schlossberg Family Fund of the Community Foundations of the Hudson Valley; the Tartakovsky Family Fund; the Taube Foundation for Jewish Life & Culture; Mina Boyer; the Koret Foundation; the Joseph & Rita Friedman Family Fund;** and **the Rozsi & Jeno Zisovich Fund.**

Last, but not least, we are thankful for the leadership of JFCS executive director **Dr. Anita Friedman** and for her commitment to Holocaust education in order to inspire future generations to be more morally courageous. Without her leadership, the publication of Rywka's diary would not have been possible.

About the Contributors

Writer and scholar **Alexandra Zapruder** is the recipient of the National Jewish Book Award in the Holocaust category for her book *Salvaged Pages: Young Writers' Diaries of the Holocaust* (New Haven, CT: Yale University Press, 2002).

Fred Rosenbaum is the founding director of Lehrhaus Judaica, the Bay Area's leading school for adult Jewish education, and the coauthor, with Eva Libitzky, of *Out on a Ledge: Enduring the Lodz Ghetto, Auschwitz, and Beyond* (River Forest, IL: Wicker Park Press, 2010), among six other books.

Judy Janec was the director of the Tauber Holocaust Library and Archives at the JFCS Holocaust Center in San Francisco from 2004 to 2013.